FINN BURNETT, FRONTIERSMAN

FINCELIUS G. BURNETT
From a photograph taken about 1877.

FINN BURNETT, FRONTIERSMAN

>—⋅⟨⋅⟩—○—⟨⋅⟩⋅—⟨

The Life and Adventures of an Indian fighter,
mail coach driver, miner, pioneer cattleman,
participant in the Powder River expedition,
survivor of the Hay Field fight,
associate of Jim Bridger and
Chief Washakie

>—⋅⟨⋅⟩—○—⟨⋅⟩⋅—⟨

ROBERT BEEBE DAVID

With a new introduction by Robert A. Clark

STACKPOLE BOOKS

Published by
STACKPOLE BOOKS
5067 Ritter Road
Mechanicsburg, PA 17055
www.stackpolebooks.com

Cover design by Tracy Patterson
Cover illustration: Fincelius G. Burnett, from a photograph taken about 1877.

Printed in the United States of America

10 9 8 7 6 5 4 3 2 1

FIRST EDITION

Library of Congress Cataloging-in-Publication Data

David, Robert Beebe.
    Finn Burnett, frontiersman / by Robert Beebe David ; with a new introduction by Robert A. Clark.— 1st ed.
        p. cm. — (Frontier classics)
    Originally published: Glendale, Calif. : Arthur H. Clark Co., 1937.
    ISBN 0-8117-2483-2
    1. Burnett, Fincelius G., 1844–1933. 2. Pioneers—Wyoming—Biography.
    3. Frontier and pioneer life—Wyoming. 4. Indians of North America—Wyoming.
    5. Indians of North America—Wars—1866–1895. I. Title. II. Series.

F761.B87 D39 2003
978.7'02'092—dc21
[B]   2002030250

INTRODUCTION

by Robert A. Clark

In October 1935, a manuscript was delivered to the Arthur H. Clark Company in Glendale, California, from Robert B. David of Casper, Wyoming, accompanied by a short note:

> Herewith please find enclosed my new manuscript "Waving War Bonnets," which I should be pleased to have you print at your usual rates.
>
> You will find this to be historically correct in every detail, and most of the incidents and battles have not been previously recorded. You will note that some of the information which Grace Hebard discovered for her book on Washakie came from this source.[1]

The book on Washakie to which David referred had been published by Clark in 1930. The "source" for the book was Finn Burnett.

Robert David was a forty-two-year-old native of Wyoming who was captivated by the history of his state and region, and who eagerly sought out original sources from the frontier and the reminiscences of pioneers. He offered the following short biographical statement to the publisher following submission of the manuscript:

> Robert Beebe David . . . Married, two girls. Education, Ridley College, in Canada, University of Wyoming, Class of 1918 and President of it. An A.T.O. [fraternity]. A cousin of Senator Robert D. Carey, and also of the Dr. Beebe who wrestles with problems in the watery depths of the southern seas. Travel: throughout the United States, was in Paris the day King Edward died, packed, hurried to London, climbed trees in Hyde Park and took pictures of the funeral procession. Has taken forbidden pictures

almost everywhere they are forbidden. Was a logger in the Northwest with the champion prizefighter of the Pacific fleet for his buddy, a bridge ganger when the Burlington was built through Wyoming, and went through the tungsten boom in Colorado in 1916. Went into Denver one day to spend some money, saw some old gentlemen going down the street beating a drum, and followed. Fifteen minutes later was signed up with the regulars to go into Mexico after Villa. After that went into the 148th Field Artillery, went into France as sergeant at a desk in the advance sector. Is a Mason, Episcopalian, V.F.W. Owns his home. Is Credit Manager for the largest automobile agency in Wyoming. Writes for pleasure in his spare time. Owns what is probably the most valuable private historical collection in Wyoming, where he has lived off and on for 42 years. Author of "Malcolm Campbell, Sheriff." Does not depend on his writing for a living. Does not know if this manuscript will be published or not, but believes firmly in the medium of prayer.[2]

In 1931 he had prepared and published the above-mentioned biography of Malcolm Campbell, a prominent pioneer figure in Wyoming who had been an active participant in events surrounding the Johnson County War. The material in the manuscript was based, according to historian Grace Raymond Hebard, on "notes, letters and telegrams that he found in an old trunk of a former Governor of Wyoming, Mr. Barber."[3] David may also have had personal access to Campbell while writing the book, as the former sheriff survived to age 93 in 1932. In a letter to Dr. Hebard in 1931, David explained:

I am sorry to have to admit that every word of the book is my own. Mr. Campbell's original manuscript consisted of about twenty pages written in pencil on school lined paper, and not well done. Please say nothing to anyone about this, however, as so many people have written to him congratulating him on his ability, and he is quite "hopped up" over it. Let him have the glory, he is 92.[4]

Hebard was impressed by the Campbell book and the author's abilities. She wrote to Clark: "I went over the manuscript before he presented it for publication and found he had been more successful in obtaining and securing first class information and data than I had in my research although I had thought I had combed the field very finely. It was a fine piece of work, but there is no question but what it could have been handled in a more historical way."[5]

The book was published in 1932 by Wyomingana, Inc., in Casper. It seems that David was co-principal in this company with Richard V. Copsey, as theirs are the only names appearing on the company letterhead used by David at the time. According to the author they were successful in this publishing venture, as all copies were sold by 1934.[6]

As he was completing the Campbell book, David was gaining access to another significant historical figure—Finn Burnett. Burnett had gone west from Missouri as a youth in 1864. He had participated in the opening of the Bozeman Trail, served at Fort Phil Kearney during the Fetterman Massacre, and participated in the famous Hayfield Fight near Fort C. F. Smith. He worked as a grader on the Union Pacific and was at Promontory, Utah, when the golden spike was driven. He prospected during the South Pass gold rush, and in 1871 he settled in Lander where he directed agriculture on the Shoshone Reservation. He was a wellspring of information on the pioneer era and its figures for a variety of historians, including Dr. Hebard and Robert David.

A one-page contract was executed by Finn Burnett's son, Dr. W. G. Burnett, and Robert David on May 2, 1931. The first paragraph gave background on the original manuscript which was to be given to David as the basis for his biography. It explained that in 1931, Dr. Burnett asked his daughter, Verna, to complete the notes of her grandfather, Finn Burnett. The result was a 177-page manuscript covering Burnett's life between 1862 and 1878, but was acknowledged to be somewhat disjointed. After establishing that Dr. Burnett was the authorized agent of the family, it related that in 1931 he placed the manuscript in the hands of David, and that David "should rewrite and edit those reminiscences of Finn Burnett to become a marketable manuscript if it were possible."[7] The contract then detailed the financial arrangements between the parties:

> It is hereby agreed, on this 2nd day of May 1932, between Dr. W. G. Burnett, as the authorized agent of the Burnett Family, and Robert B. David, as the author, that all profits received from the sale of this manuscript relating the reminscences [sic] of Finn Burnett between the years 1862 to 1878, and at this time titled "Waving War Bonnets" will be divided equally between Dr. W. G. Burnett and Robert B. David.

Over the course of the next three years David reworked the material in the compiled reminiscences and prepared it for publication. For reasons unknown, he chose not to publish the book under his own imprint used on the Campbell book, but instead turned to the Arthur H. Clark Co., an established publisher of Americana which had relocated from Cleveland to Glendale, California, in 1930. The Clark Company had a growing reputation as a scholarly press, and one of their recent publications had been awarded the Pulitzer Prize in history.[8] In addition to its long list of publications specializing in source material on the exploration and development of the American frontier, the company had published several works by Dr. Grace Hebard, one of David's professors at the University of Wyoming in Laramie.

Following the submission of the manuscript, David received a letter from the company's founder, Arthur H. Clark, requesting more background on both the author and his subject. It gave David an opportunity to elaborate on a number of topics relevant to the manuscript:

> You inquire as to my qualifications and training in the writing of historical material. Answering this, and your question No. 3 at the same time, I wrote "Malcolm Campbell, Sheriff," and 2000 volumes were published by Wyomingana, Inc., here in Casper. All were sold in 1932 and 1933, during the worst of the depression. Mr. Rosenstock is, as you know, merely a distributor in Denver.[9] The subject of this book has been a controversial one for more than forty years, and yet I have not had one person point to a single historical inaccuracy in it. Rather, I have had letters from all over the United States which state the book is true in every detail. Write to Mr. Rollins, author of "the Cowboy," I think, who presented the book to Dartmouth University with such high commendation that I prefer you ask him his opinion.
>
> Furthermore, I have lived in Wyoming all my life, although I was educated in the east. My father was an "old-timer," and I have moved in such an atmosphere since childhood. Fifteen years ago, I began to work on my hobby, which was the gathering of the reminiscences of the scouts, trappers, emigrants, and Indian fighters of the Platte valley. Now, I have enough material for many books in my collection, with all the information necessary to prove practically any contention relative to historical

matters in the valley from 1845 to 1895. I have followed closely, as well, the extensive historical criticism and assistance of Alfred Mokler, of whom you know, and who has proved to be accurate in the past.

Questions relating to history of this section have been referred to me many times during the last ten years by the Casper Chamber of Commerce, and other civic organizations. In other words, I am recognized here as one who knows the history of this section accurately. This is all "small town stuff" of course, to you, but we have a valley here which contains more unwritten historical thrills than any other on the continent, I think, and whether you are interested or not it will be recorded in many books some day.

The facts contained in almost the entire book, or manuscript, were told to Mr. Burnett's granddaughter, and she being an excellent stenographer recorded his words at the time, and turned them over to me at the request of her father, for me to round it off. At the time I took it over, Finn Burnett was living, and made several trips to Casper. At these times, I went to his son's home, and took up various parts of his notes with him, and at one time, I had a long session with him downtown. He assisted me gladly and fully, and I checked and rechecked his story in every way, proving everything that was possible. As far as Dr. Hebard's throwing doubt on Burnett's accuracy is concerned, she took pains to conceal it until she had dug everything out of him that he could give her first. And, as far as that is concerned, I can pick quite a lot of her stuff to pieces, myself, if I wanted to. She was my old professor of Political Economy at the University, and I used to love her very much, but she is not by any means correct in everything. So, while I might have painted some scenes up to give them clearer interest, their facts were accurate, and were altered if Finn found them to be wrong.

The first three paragraphs will be changed as you suggest very easily, if you will so notify me on receipt of this letter. I felt the book was ten thousand pages [words?] too long, but others felt that it would not be complete unless all were recorded.

There are authentic pictures of Finn Burnett available, and I will be able to send you a number of other photographs which may be included.

Regarding the Sacajawea interpretation, I am prepared to submit as much proof to the version contained in that manuscript as Dr. Hebard will be able to find, perhaps more. The fact of the fact that her account was published, does not prove it.

We will change the title without trouble when you inform me that you wish it, and I shall be very pleased to assist you in every way. I do not try to hold myself up as great in any way, but I really believe that the backing of such a fund of reminiscence as I have gives my writing and opinions some weight.

You have had this manuscript, now, since early in October, and I will appreciate you letting me know as soon as convenient what you want to do with it. I should be pleased to send a copy of my book if one were available, but I have not been able to get one for some of my closest friends for more than a year.

Yours truly,
Robert B. David

P.S. That last paragraph sounded as if I wanted you to send the manuscript back. I don't, or I wouldn't have sent it to you in the first place. I hope you see your way to getting it out, and I will help you in every way.

I have shown you my qualifications, and I will be able to secure several good illustrations. These are in collections, and will necessitate their removal and rephotographing, so I should like to have definite knowledge that the manuscript will be published before going to the expense, if possible.

Tonight, I shall begin to give some thought to another title. You are entirely right about it, of course, and I will try to arrive at one which will satisfy us both. The first three paragraphs, I will work on next week. To tell the truth, I am getting out two papers now, both historical, one for the yearly industrial edition of the paper, and the other for an organization. But I will have your changes ready next week.

> Please accept my thanks for your interested letter, and
> oblige me further by advising more fully just what you be-
> lieve the title and paragraphs should show.[10]

As David points out, Dr. Hebard had a close familiarity with Finn Burnett. She had first used him as a source in the preparation of her two-volume
work on the Bozeman Trail, co-authored with E. A. Brininstool and published by the Arthur H. Clark Co. in 1922.[11] She utilized his reminiscences
again when writing her biography of Washakie, the Shoshone chief, with
whom Burnett was good friends through their association on the Shoshone
Reservation. Clark was once again the publisher of this book in 1930.

When preparing her biography of Sacagawea, issued by Clark in 1933,
Burnett was a major source for the support of her controversial assertion that
the Indian woman who had accompanied Lewis and Clark had survived to
an old age on the Wind River Reservation. Hebard not only interviewed
Burnett personally, but carried on extensive correspondence with him.[12]

Because of her intimate familiarity with Wyoming history, and with
Burnett and his life, it was logical that her publisher, Arthur Clark, would
turn to her to request an evaluation of the manuscript submitted by David
in 1935. In April 1936, she completed her reading and offered frank com-
ments regarding the material. She began by acknowledging that David had
been her student while attending the University some years earlier. She
then offered this evaluation:

> Now in regard to the new book, which is really an autobi-
> ography of Mr. Finn Burnett. I am considerably surprised
> in the way he has been able to handle the material, and in
> fact, handled it splendidly. All the material that he has in
> his book, Mr. Burnett sometime during the time of our
> acquaintance and during lengthy visitations in my office at
> the University, had told me. I paid very little attention to
> his period as a member of the Civil War period, or at a
> period earlier than that, that appeared in our *Bozeman
> Trail*. I will repeat and say that Mr. Burnett dicatated [*sic*]
> the material to his son's daughter who lives in Casper.
> Whether she reconstructed what Mr. Burnett had dic-
> tated, I am unable to say, or whether the exact wording is
> as it appears in the manuscript. [holographic note: "I am
> told she is bright & might be age in the 30ties"]
>   Sometimes the English is really very beautiful. I
> should say the major criticism would be that the author
> uses no references whatsoever, or no footnotes to show

any research, and at least ninety-five per cent of what he has written was given to me by Mr. Burnett but in very different language. Much of it you will realize comes from my *Bozeman Trail* but since we both had the same fountain-head it is natural that it would be something of a duplication.

I can find no serious historical errors, but will go over the notes which I made as I read the book. For instance, take page 33. I believe there should be a more extended statement as to who Colonel Bretney was, as we know he was located at Fort Caspar. Sublette was mentioned but there were five brothers and it seems he should designate which one it was. There are too few dates. On page 42 he speaks of Captain North. There were two North Brothers who fought on the prairies, one was Luther and one was Frank. I think that one was a Captain and one was a Major, I didn't look it up.

The chapter on the Hay Field Fight, of course, is tremendously interesting. The Hay Field Fight was never written until it appeared in my *Bozeman Trail*. Mr. Burnett told me all those wonderful details as recorded in the manuscript. However, my book was too long without making any further additions. You will find that detailed information about pages 130 and 150. Page 160 is new material to me—I know nothing about it. I knew nothing about his married life, I knew very little about his South Pass life although he had spoken of these incidents. All these episodes are his long experience in the West. The Shoshone Reservation experience was very accurate.

I think I can't say anything more except that I am surprised that this young man has presented the material in an interesting reading way, although it lacks so many times substantiation of what probably are facts but have no facts or references backing them up. At times the language is quite meagre when he speaks about "Finn," four or five times on a page. It sounds like a boy's detective story.

I am glad that Mr. David has preserved this information. It would be a pity to have this story stored away and not printed, but I shall have to leave that without any particular recommendation except that no one else can ever furnish this from first class information now that Mr. Burnett died about a year ago. I enjoyed reading the manuscript and it brought back many pleasant remembrances that I had told to me by Mr. Burnett. I am sending the manuscript by express tomorrow.[13]

Based on his own reading and the recommendation of Dr. Hebard, Arthur Clark agreed to the publication of the Burnett biography with certain conditions. Though standard in most of its clauses, the contract, dated August 5, 1936, did contain the following requirement in Article II:

> That author shall advance to publisher the sum of One Thousand Dollars ($1000.00) payable as follows: Five Hundred Dollars ($500.00) with the signing of this contract, Two Hundred and Fifty Dollars ($250.00) when the galley proofs are submitted to author, and Two Hundred Fifty Dollars ($250.00) when the page proofs are submitted to author.
>
> That this sum of One Thousand Dollars ($1000.00) advanced by author to publisher shall be refunded by publisher to author as follows: When the sale of the work provided for herein has reached five hundred (500) copies publisher shall refund to author the sum of Five Hundred Dollars ($500.00), in like manner when the sale of the work has reached one thousand (1000) copies publisher shall refund to author the further sum of Five Hundred Dollars ($500.00). Said payments shall be made without interest.[14]

This was, of course, no small sum of money in 1936. According to inflation tables, it is roughly equivalent to $12,000 today. Robert David was earning $165 a month as credit manager at the Coliseum Motor Company in Casper, and complained in his reminiscences of his tight financial circumstances. He was able to secure the $1000, though the source is unknown. It may be that the Burnett family was able to be of assistance. He knew before receiving the contract that this financial support was part of the agreement and had written the publisher just prior to the issuance of the contract:

July 25th, 1936

Gentlemen:

The Burnett family has at last agreed to the publishing of the manuscript which I titled "Waving War Bonnets." I am prepared to sign the contract when you send it to me, providing it fulfils what you stated in your letter. I have the thousand dollars in my pocket for you, in return with the contract.

You may proceed with perfect confidence that I will cooperate with you fully, that my word is good, and that I will give you, and expect from you as well, the fullest of fair dealing. This will probably not be the last book which you will publish of mine.

Yours truly,
Robert B. David[15]

The publisher agreed in the contract to print 1000 copies at $6.00 each, and to pay Robert David a royalty of 10% after 250 copies were sold. Additionally, it specified that "the Contract may be cancelled after 10 years, with no further financial obligation to the publisher."

Once the contract was signed, production work began on the manuscript. The publisher then made a special request of David, as he recalled in his reminiscences:

> Arthur Clark, the publisher in Glendale, California, to whom I had sent my manuscript of "Finn Burnett, Frontiersman," wrote me that he was ready to print the book, but that I had to come to California to help with the proof-reading and final details.
>
> I wrote him that I had no money for such a trip. His reply was that I should borrow, and that he would furnish me 90 books free which I could sell and so repay myself.
>
> This I did, and had a miserable time in Los Angeles, commuting back and forth to Glendale.[16]

David's miserable time in Los Angeles was a foretaste of his experience with the book and the publisher over the next few years. After his return to Casper, he completed the index and forwarded it to Glendale. The response he received from Arthur Clark was disappointing: "INDEX. I am afraid I shall have to have this made over. It would never do as it stands. It would be criticized as an amateur index. The reviewers in the historical journals would tear it to pieces. I am sorry to have to do this because it involves considerable time and expense."[17]

David shot back a response in his own defense:

Dear Mr. Clark,

Perhaps I am an amateur, but it was a damned good index, anyway. I thought so, but I hadn't made one before. So I'm leaving it up to you to get the information in your way. I do want to bring to your attention, however, that an index with page numbers, and no explanations is a mess. How many hours I have looked for specific details on a general item, only to paw over the page numbers by the hour until I found what I wanted. If, on the other hand, the detailed information of what could be found on each page had been presented, it would have saved me time.

About the book sale. You have not told me what price you are going to give the book stores, or anything much about anything. Now, I travel around quite a bit, and I probably have about as much money in the old sock as the Wyoming Stationery, and I don't think it would be a bad idea for you to send me a consignment, and let me put them in the bookstores here and there as I go around. I'll take the risks, as I know them all, and it won't be much more work. I am getting orders right along, and there is no doubt but that a great many people will come direct to me for their books. You can send me just as many as you wish, and change what you want to, only let me know all about it.

Yours very truly,
Robert B. David[18]

The last suggestion is puzzling. In his reminiscences, David asserted that the publisher had agreed to defray his expenses for travel to Los Angeles by sending copies for him to sell and recoup his costs. Copies were indeed sent, but according to the publisher's records and later statements, these copies were, indeed, sent on consignment. The author would be required to pay a discounted amount of the list price to the publisher upon sale.

On January 22, 1937, *Finn Burnett, Frontiersman* was received from the bindery. The subtitle contained a summary of the contents: *The Life and Adventures of an Indian fighter, mail coach driver, miner, pioneer cattleman, participant in the Powder River expedition, survivor of the Hay Field fight, associate of Jim Bridger and Chief Washakie.*[19]

Sales began slowly, and both publisher and author were dismayed at the lack of buyer response. David wrote to Clark on March 23:

> In the first place, I believe that apologies are in order for my lack of attention to the sales of my book since Christmas, but, as I told you, I have a job which takes my time pretty well day and night, and as I have been out of town, and out of the state, pretty much since Christmas, doing some reorganization work and checking some dealers out, I have not had the time to pay much attention to any book sales.
>
> However, as this is about the 90 day period when both of us ought to have a report I have taken time out today to check the bookstores, and find that they have not done much. They tell me the price is too great for this country. To date they have sold nine, and I sold thirteen, making 22 sold in all.
>
> Now, it appears that you sent me check for $5.90 for refund of freight charges on the box of books, but the charges I paid here were $8.18, a difference of $2.28.
>
> I am therefore remitting to you by check today payment for 22 books at $4.50, or $99, less $2.28 for freight. If this is not in accordance with your wishes, please inform me.[20]

Clark sent David a copy of a letter he had received from Joseph G. Masters of Omaha, Nebraska, which contained a few specific criticisms of historical facts contained in the book. David was testy in his reply to the criticisms, as shown in the following extract from the same letter cited above:

> The last name of "Big Bat" is not misspelled, and if Mr. Masters would like to bet a thousand dollars cash on it I will be pleased to show the best and final proof possible that any man could have as to how his name is spelled. Figure that out.
>
> You must understand the "Finn Burnett, Frontiersman," was the statement of Finn. It is source material, and is not open to the severe attack which a work copied from a number of other previously published books would allow.

In the end, the book faltered. Whether as a result of its high price, the Great Depression, or the lack of interest by the historical community in Burnett, sales were very slow. In 1938 Clark reported sales of 161 copies, and by 1939 the number had advanced to only 228. Finally, as the end of the ten year period following the signing of the contract passed, Clark wrote to David at the Coliseum Motor Company address:

> Closing Report - Finn Burnett
> Dear Mr. David:—
>
> The sale of your book has not been satisfactory, nor has your account with us, which we have been trying to collect since December 8, 1936. We are cancelling the contract per paragraph 17 of our agreement.
> The accumulated sales at the close of our inventory last month were 395 copies. Your account, due us since December 1936, an original sum of $233.00 which you have continued to ignore, now amounts to $431.12 after compounding interest annually. We have deducted your royalties of $87.00 which leaves a balance due us of $344.12. Your early remittance will be appreciated.[21]

It is doubtful that Robert David ever received this letter. He may well have left Coliseum Motors by this time, and therefore not received the correspondence. Whether or not the cancellation was ever delivered, David and the Clark Company exchanged the following letters just a few years later:

> Casper, Wyoming
> January 11, 1952
> Arthur H. Clark Company
> Glendale, California
>
> Gentlemen:
>
> Following a prolonged illness, the contract entered into between you as publishers and me as the author of a book titled "Finn Burnett, Frontiersman," and dated August 5th, 1936 has now been discovered.
> I wish at this time, before the ten years elapse following the completion of your Agreement, an itemized

accounting of all sales of "Finn Burnett, Frontiersman", from the date of printing to August 5, 1946, said accounting to be made by a recognized and proper firm of Certified [*sic*] Public Accountants, and the report to me shall be made in proper form of legal affidavit. [pencil note on the letter by the publisher: "no"]

Furthermore, I wish a full explanation officially from you as to why such accounting has not previously been made.

I, furthermore, call to your attention certain clauses of the Agreement which require your notification to me of any termination of the contract, "after the said work shall have been published 10 years." No such notification has been received, and I herewith request a further accounting of all sales of my book from August 5, 1946 to the present.

The manuscript was completed, edited by me in Glendale, accepted by you personally, and was printed. Books in sufficient number to repay my expenses for going to to Glendale, editing, and return, were sent to me. Beyond that, you have sent me no accounting, no reports, no royalties.

I shall expect your answer and accounting by February 1st, 1952.

I am well aware that sales of this book have been significant, and I will, after the above date, proceed in any manner that I may feel adequate.

Robert B. David.

The publisher replied:

January 17, 1952

Dear Mr. David:

Your letter of January 11th comes as a distinct surprise. We strongly resent the untruths and the implied threat. You are the one who has ignored us all these years, never replying to any of our correspondence, especially maintaining a prolonged avoidance of your account due us.

We have just reviewed our records and reports. The simple facts are that at the time we cancelled your contract, according to our letter of July 18, 1947 which you also ignored, you owed us a sum of $344.12. The original sum was $233.00 to which interest was added up to the time we cancelled the contract. If you will consult the report we made at the time you will find that the total sales of the book were 395 which entitled you to $87.00 royalty. This left a balance still due us of $344.12.

Time after time we wrote regarding this account, but you never gave us the courtesy of a reply. Why at this late date you should say that we gave you books to pay for your expenses is not understandable. No such agreement was made.

We have always tried to conduct our business on a fair basis and in our fifty years of publishing have enjoyed the friendship and confidence of many authors. There has been no intent to single you out for any different treatment.

Since 1947 we have continued to catalog the book in an effort to make up our loss on the transaction rather than remainder the volume as unsalable.

We regret that you have taken this attitude and believe that you will find that we have here stated the matter correctly.

Sincerely,
P. W. Galleher[22]

At the bottom of this letter is a note indicating that no reply was ever received.

In spite of the disappointing sales and ill feelings between the author and publisher over poor communications and lost income, the book was well received by reviewers and has become a valued source of information on the history of the West. Once out-of-print, the value of the book rose, and today a first edition commands a price of several hundred dollars when available. Some have faulted the book for its sometimes florid style and for its lack of documentation. But as source material based on the recollections of one of the West's true pioneers, it has considerable value.

Robert David passed away in September 1968 at age 74. He had retired in 1960 as local director of the Wyoming State Employment service, and devoted his retirement to writing and historical research. He served as a member of the Fort Caspar Commission in charge of the restored frontier post west of Casper, Wyoming.[23] He was survived by his two daughters.

NOTES

1. Letter of Robert B. David to Arthur H. Clark, October 19, 1935. Correspondence from David to the Arthur H. Clark Co. is located in the archives of the company in Spokane, Washington.
2. Biographical statement accompanying letter from David to Clark, February 22, 1936.
3. Hebard to Clark, April 17, 1936. Archives of the Arthur H. Clark Co.
4. David to Hebard, November 14, 1931. American Heritage Center, University of Wyoming. A special thanks to Melanie M. Francis of the Center for her help in obtaining copies of correspondence concerning both Robert David and Grace Hebard.
5. Hebard to Clark, April 17, 1936.
6. David to Clark, February 22, 1936.
7. "Agreement," copy from the David Collection, Casper College Library. I would like to express my gratitude to Kevin S. Anderson, Western History Specialist at Casper College Library for his kind assistance in accessing material from this collection.
8. Fred Albert Shannon's *The Organization and Administration of the Union Army, 1861-1865* was published by Clark in 1928, and received the Pulitzer and the Justin Winsor Prize from the American Historical Association. Robert A. Clark and Patrick J. Brunet, *The Arthur H. Clark Company: A Bibliography and History, 1902–1992*, Spokane, 1993.
9. Fred Rosenstock was a prominent book dealer and publisher in Denver. He published a number of prominent Western historians under the imprint "Old West Publishing." In the 1930s his career was just beginning.
10. David to Clark, February 22, 1936.
11. Information on the publications of Grace Raymond Hebard can be found in Clark and Brunet, *The Arthur H. Clark Company.*
12. Much of this correspondence is housed at the American Heritage Center, University of Wyoming.
13. Hebard to Clark, April 17, 1936, in the Clark Company archives.
14. Memorandum of Agreement, August 5, 1936, held in the Clark Company archives.
15. Original letter in the Clark Company archives.
16. Manuscript reminiscences of Robert B. David, held in the David Collection, Casper College Library.
17. Clark to David, November 5, 1936, David Collection, Casper College Library.

18. David to Clark, Clark Company archives.
19. The book was later made volume 1 of the publisher's *Western Frontiersmen Series*, and some copies will contain this information on the half title page. Clark and Brunet, *The Arthur H. Clark Company.*
20. David to Clark, David Collection, Casper College Library.
21. Clark to David, July 18, 1947, Clark Company archives.
22. Both letters are in the Clark Company Archives. Paul W. Galleher, who wrote the publisher's response, was co-owner of the Clark Company with Arthur H. Clark, Jr. The founder of the company had passed away in 1951. Clark and Brunet, *The Arthur H. Clark Company.*
23. Obituary supplied by the David Collection, Casper College Library.

Contents

Illustrations

Preface

Preface

Whether the reader be a student of history or merely a seeker after a thrilling pioneer narrative, he is likely to find what he desires in this vivid account of the life and adventures of a western frontiersman.

Finn Burnett was not a soldier who sought encounters with the Indians, yet always he managed to be where the fighting was the fiercest. He rode with Bridger, fought beside Washakie, endured the hardships of the Powder River expedition, graded for the Union Pacific railroad during the turbulent construction days of the first transcontinental line, mined gold at South Pass, blazed the trail for later Wyoming cattle drives, survived the desperate Hay Field fight, assisted in settling the wild Indians peacefully on reservations, and lived to see the passing of the western frontier.

For years Finn Burnett was a fruitful source of information for the historians of the West. His veracity has never been questioned. In his later years, Burnett related at length his pioneer experiences to his granddaughter, who set them down verbatim. It is from these extensive notes that, for the first time, the full story of Burnett's adventurous life and extensive and accurate observations on frontier conditions and events is here made available.

Formal presentation would have destroyed the fundamental spirit of Burnett's account. In those frontier days on the plains, the day or the week or the month meant little. Burnett's greatest contribution to history lies in the minute and picturesque details, the excitement and color, the motives underlying frontier history, and the unrecorded incidents which make days in the pioneer West live again. The author has adhered closely to the running narrative of Burnett's recollections, retaining as far as possible the vivid atmosphere so that the reader actually becomes a spectator behind the scenes, sensing the vague uneasiness of the frontiersman in the presence of the unknown menace which lay in wait on every hand. Burnett gives generously from his rich store of experiences and understanding of the reactions of the frontiersman.

At the time of his death, in 1933, Finn Burnett was president of the Wyoming Pioneers' association. He was universally respected for his honesty and admired for his achievements. Everyone who knew him felt his inner strength and hardiness of character.

ROBERT BEEBE DAVID

Casper, Wyoming
September 8, 1936

Escape to the Frontier

Escape to the Frontier

It was a cold, foggy day. The thick mist from along the Mississippi river swirled across the damp Missouri hills, filling the valleys with a dismal chill.

The little courtyard of Monticello, Missouri, was crowded with the populace from the surrounding country, moving slowly in a surging whirlpool about a platform where stood a line of silent, waiting boys in uniforms of gray. Afar could be heard approaching the steady cadence of marching men. About the yard there hung a fearful spectre of dread expectancy which held the crowd to silence, and made its aimless circling akin to the plodding march of cattle awaiting slaughter in the pens.

It was 1862, when war and pillage and flaming torches laid waste vast areas of the South. Down from Illinois had swarmed a Union rabble composed mostly of Germans, which, having crossed the river at Quincy, had proceeded southward through the fertile, farming country, razing the hard-won homes with flames, and destroying everything of value in its path.

These Union soldiers had dealt harshly with the few ill-prepared and desperate attempts that had been made to halt their march, and had received no blow of retaliation until they had reached the road that led into Monticello. There, like the minute men of an earlier day, had been mustered the determined youth of the district who had banded themselves into an organization called the Monticello Grays.

These local boys had opened up such a withering, blinding fire upon the marauders that the road had become an immediate shambles. The survivors had fled headlong, to leave their dead and dying on the ground, together with their wagons piled high with loot of gold, silverware, and clothing.

Within the week, word seeped through Missouri that the routed soldiers had reached Canton, and had reported there that the country around Monticello was alive with armed rebels. Later came the news that Colonel Palmer with a regiment of Illinois infantry was approaching to punish and destroy the town.

The sheriff of the county had, after the rout of the invaders, ordered that all the loot and teams and wagons be gathered up carefully and placed in the courtyard for their owners to identify and claim.

Now, as the sound of approaching soldiers grew louder, the crowd pressed back to the edges of the courtyard, leaving in the clearing the piles of clothing, sacks of heirlooms, and sheets which bulged with cherished valuables.

The sheriff mounted the platform, his fine, deep-lined face set and stern with the portent of the advancing Union regiment. His steel-gray eyes flickered quickly over the silent crowd about the yard, noting its resemblance to a sullen crouching beast straining at its bonds, and awaiting but an ill-considered word or untoward act to hurl itself upon its enemies.

His chin set a little more squarely as he gazed upon the soiled piles of loot, then his eyes swept to the waiting line of gray-clad boys who had constituted Monticello's recent defenders. On down the row his eyes traveled, past the determined, frowning, youthful faces to where stood his boy, Finn, short and strongly-built, with his face square and brave against whatever the day would bring.

Suddenly there was a bugle call from the road, and the crowd stretched forward to discover the van of Union troops approaching, with their guns at the "ready" across their breasts. A moment later, and the federal soldiers were filing into the yard, suspiciously eying the waiting throng and forming a double line back to back across the grass.

Then, from the huddle of saddled horses by the gate, approached the Union commander, Colonel Palmer, tall, gray, and efficient, to mount the steps and stop before the sheriff, who addressed him.

"I am Sheriff Burnett of this county, colonel," remarked that gentleman quietly. "We are aware of your mission here, and that you anticipate chastising us for the repulse of certain Union soldiers a few days ago. But we can only say in mitigation that we were sorely tried; that those troops had pillaged and burned our homes, as is evidenced by those piles of recovered heirlooms which lie there in the yard."

Pointing to the line of Monticello Grays he continued.

"There, colonel, are the myriads of rebels of whom you have been hearing. In reality they are the men who fired on an undisciplined rabble in defense of their homes. We attempted to tear up the bridge which you just crossed to prevent their escape, and had we been successful not a Dutchman would ever have reached you with his story."

Colonel Palmer nodded shortly, and standing squarely in the center of the platform he gazed around at the heaps of plunder, and at the quiet, expectant line of boys who undoubtedly feared the worst, but who were putting up a brave attempt at manly indifference. His eyes narrowed in thought as though he were picturing again the wasted countryside through which his troops had marched that morning.

Abruptly, he swung around to Sheriff Burnett with his hand outstretched, and a grim smile flickered for a moment across his lips.

"Sheriff," he declared, "I am pleased to meet you, sir, and your heroic defenders. My only regret in the entire business is that those boys didn't get that bridge torn up in time."

With that dramatic moment began the swift march to adventure of young Finn Burnett. Born in 1844, he had lived his first eighteen years among a slave-owning people, learning to handle horses and oxen on the farms of Missouri, shooting turkeys along the wooded fringes of the fields, and assisting engineers on the steamboats along the Mississippi river.

In October of 1864, two years after Colonel Palmer's march to Monticello, all the boys of Missouri were notified that they were conscripted, and that they would be compelled to enlist in the Union army. Every one of them who had no dependents promptly deserted and fled westward to the frontier. This emigration had been anticipated, and a cordon of guards had been placed across the state boundaries, which allowed no one to pass through unless he was supplied with farming equipment and professed a desire to take up a homestead.

Sheriff Burnett, therefore, procured a plow, rake, and harrow, which he loaded into a wagon, and told his neighbors that his son, Finn, was driving to Iowa to take up land with another boy, Joe Kidwell. After a lengthy family conference, where careful plans were made and helpful suggestions given, there were hasty farewells, and the two boys hitched up their wagonload of implements, and started out on the road to adventure.

Had the two boys been aware of what lay before them, they would have turned back, for the entire middle west was in a turmoil, with civil war, guerrilla fighting, looting, and savagery a daily occurence on every side.

Quantrill had led his band of guerrillas on Lawrence, Kansas, two years before in the most famous border raid of Civil war history. Groups of undisciplined "border ruffians" were fighting confused skirmishes against the settlements of Kansas. Everywhere was suspicion, ambush, murder, and robbery.

But the two youths drove northward from Monticello with their wagonload of farming implements, passing between the armed groups of guerrillas by sheer audacity, or ignorance, until they arrived in Davis county, Iowa.

There the elements brought to the boys the misfortune which had been withheld in the districts where difficulties had been anticipated. Rain descended in torrents upon the Iowa countryside until every hollow became a pool, and each roadway became a slippery morass into which horses and wagon floundered and stopped. Hundreds of other refugees already had fled over these roads, and their wagon wheels had dug the soft ground into pudding. The two boys soon perceived that their escape was being retarded, and that their only hope for reaching the frontier was to abandon their clumsy wagon.

Everything excepting the two fine thoroughbred horses and their saddles was therefore sold in the first Iowa town. The farm implements, wagon, harness, and food were bartered for whatever they would bring, which was not a great sum, in view of the disorderly times and the doubtful condition of business.

Then, after the two boys had started out from Davis county, Iowa, making westward for Omaha, they were harassed and chased from cover to cover by everyone who saw their excellent riding stock. Had the young men been riding ordinary plow horses they would probably have reached their destination unnoticed, but, mounted as they were, they became the objects of extended pursuit whenever they met Iowa citizens.

They found Iowa then to be a great, grassy waste, flat and untenanted except for infrequent sod-houses and dug-outs with their small vegetable and grain tracts.

Towns were avoided by the pair, for the appearance of the two in any community was the signal for a group to eye the horses with envy and then to berate the boys for being "bush-whackers" and deserters. These discussions always ended in flight on the part of the youths, and a long race across the country until their poorly-mounted pursuers had been left far in the rear.

Night after night they slept out on the prairie, hungry and dispirited. Finn had a .22 calibre Smith and Wesson pistol with which he had been very proficient back in Missouri, but now it perversely refused to hit the rabbits and game birds along the way.

Doggedly they continued westward, dropping to the hard ground at night to sleep hungry and fearful under the stars. Then, at daybreak, they effected a quick saddling-up, and an early start, to skirt any chance clusters of unpainted, sod-roofed shacks which squatted on the wastes, and which always held the menace of more questioners and more pursuers.

Finally, when they had reached the point of starvation, Finn decided that he was going to eat if he died for it. Joe Kidwell agreed with him, and as they rode onward, they sighted a little group of buildings which proved to be a community named Corydon. Into town they rode, bravely returning the stares of suspicion which met them on every side. The two hollow-cheeked boys, well-mounted, immediately became objects of anticipation to several rascals of the place.

Leaving the horses at the livery stable, with the precaution that the mounts must be kept ready for a quick get-away, the youths made for a nearby restaurant, where they ate the first square meal that they had enjoyed for days.

For several minutes, both were busy gulping down potatoes, beefsteaks, turnips, bread, and coffee, eating against time with their eyes watching the door for the entrance of their enemies.

Suddenly, there appeared a huge, bullying type of man who strode belligerently to their table. He was fat and greasy, with black hair straggling from beneath his flat-topped hat. With his arms akimbo he stopped before the boys.

"Where you goin'?" he demanded loudly.

"Oh, we're lookin' over the country," Finn answered. "We expect to homestead somewhere when we find a good place."

"I don't believe it," the bully snarled. "You're a pair of rebels or deserters, and you're under arrest."

"Have you got a warrant?" asked Joe.

"No, but I'll get one pretty quick," returned the citizen of Corydon as, turning, he plunged back out the doorway, and up the street.

It took but a moment to stuff the remainder of the meal into their pockets, hurry out the rear door and up an alley to the livery barn. There they tightened cinches, paid the bill, mounted, and galloped out of the town and across the prairie followed by several horsemen who soon turned back in disgust.

It proved to be a fortunate experience for Finn Burnett and Joe Kidwell, however, that they had braved the town of Corydon that day for a hurried meal, for they rode westward for two days and nights thereafter without seeing a town, house, or farm upon the wastes of western Iowa.

Again they were reduced to the point of starvation, and their weakness was rendering them reckless when, on the afternoon of the third day, they discerned a lone house far out on the prairie. By that time, neither cared who lived in the shack. They must have food.

They rode up to the house and dismounted. Finn strode to the door and knocked. Everything was quiet. The eyes of the boys swept around the level horizon dispiritedly. There was no other opportunity for finding food, and both were trembling with weakness.

Presently there was a movement inside the door, and it was unlocked and opened by a little, white-haired, old lady who stood eying the two youths with wise and kindly eyes.

"Ma'am," Finn said, taking off his hat reverently at the sight of this oasis of comfort and homeliness in the waste, "we are two boys who are very hungry and we wondered if you could give us something to eat. We would be glad to pay you for it."

"Why, bless my soul, of course I kin," she answered, motioning them in like some motherly old hen sweeping her chicks to safety within the coop. "I'm just startin' some supper. You boys look like you might be soldiers. Be ye?"

They told her that they had been in the army, and

she during her chattering said that her husband had been killed and that her two sons had "fought for the North."

Heaped against the wall she had a pile of weeds which looked like dried sunflower stalks, and these she split and used for starting the fire in her stove, putting large, hard ears of dried corn on top as one would use coal. Then she commenced to cook an enormous meal for the two wanderers, keeping up a continual string of questions as they sat watching. Where were they from? Where were they going?

Finally, as the room filled with the odors of delicious home-cooking, and as the lamp light threw the walls of the home into comforting shadows, the morale of the boys became softened, and before they knew it they were pouring out to the kindly little woman the story of their hardships and of their rude treatment at the hands of the people of Iowa.

As a result, Finn and Joe were "mothered" unceasingly. Both were fed until they could scarcely walk and then they were shown to a great, deep, feather bed in another room where the two sons had always slept before they went away to war. So, that night, secure, well-fed, and care-free, the two boys slept in that lone house far out on the Iowa prairies.

Next morning they awakened late, to find the horses already fed, and a breakfast table piled high with steaming, fragrant corn bread and meat. Both of them were reluctant to start out again, but after being told the proper trail to Council Bluffs, and having received a store of food to be taken along, they bade farewell to the little old lady, and proceeded on, being destined never to see or hear of their benefactress again.

The food lasted until they reached Council Bluffs.

Here they found that the ferry which crossed to Omaha was docked down the river a little distance. As they rode on toward it a big, burly man on a white horse suddenly rode out to stop his mount across the road in front of the boys. They paused and watched him carefully.

He looked the two over from heels to head, noted their youth, and evidently decided that they would put up very little struggle against him.

"I'll tell you what I'll do," he said suddenly. "You just give me those horses, and I'll let you go."

"What do you mean, 'let us go?'" Finn returned. "Do you think we are horse thieves?"

"That's all right about that, son," he growled. "You just turn those horses over to me, and I won't make any fuss about it. You can go on about your business, and get the ferry, and everything will be all right."

"Well, we aren't horse thieves," Burnett answered. "And as these are ours, we certainly won't give them up."

With this, Finn started forward, and on glancing back he saw that Joe was pale from fright. Joe was the younger, and had been through much trouble the last few days, so Finn did not blame him.

The man, however, seeing Joe's indecision, reached out and grasped the halter strap from the boy's hands. With that action, Finn lost his temper and jerked the halter free with one hand while he slashed the man across the eyes with the other.

Both of the boys then wheeled their horses, and fled for the ferry, but they had little need for speed, as the man sat in the road behind them, with his hands over his eyes, roaring with rage and pain.

The Hanging of the Chiefs

The Hanging of the Chiefs

Omaha presented an interesting sight to the eyes of the two adventure-seeking youths that evening when they trotted up the slope from the river and slowed down at the edge of the town. Its population totaled approximately ten thousand people, with a floating group of itinerants which numbered five thousand more. The latter were young men who had come west for adventure, and most of them were waiting for an opportunity to hire out to the new Union Pacific railroad which had already built a five mile spur westward from Omaha toward the Rockies.

After finding a livery stable, the two boys secured a ready purchaser for their riding horses in a Mr. Wilbur, who paid them $700, a sum which they believed sufficient to support them through several months, if spent frugally.

Later in the evening Joe Kidwell met four other boys at this same livery stable, and with Finn Burnett they put their heads together to plan their future actions. One of the boys, Kemp Caldwell, was an unusually fine young man, and Finn began a life-long friendship with him at their meeting.

The other three had been staying at the Farnum House, and that evening they took the two newcomers with them and introduced them to the proprietor and his wife. Mrs. Farnum was truly an angel of the frontier. During those rough, unruly days of early Omaha she mothered all the homesick, stray boys for whom she could provide, giving them board and room for $21 a week, a ridiculously small sum in those boom days of high costs and expenses.

Finn immediately told Mrs. Farnum of his desire to see the West, and she lost little time in impressing her husband with the need for watching a chance to get the boy into a job with a wagon-train.

During the long days of waiting, the boy made his preparations for the future. First, he cleaned up his pistol. He had been a crack shot in Missouri, having earned many a dollar from his uncle for shooting the wild geese that flew in white swarms to the fields and threatened to ruin them.

Now, on pushing a rod through the barrel, Finn found his gun to be plugged with lead to such a degree that accurate firing of the weapon was impossible.

Finn was exceedingly fortunate, for on the sixth day after his arrival in Omaha, Mrs. Farnum sent word to him to go immediately to the hotel lobby. As the boy entered the crowded room he saw the proprietor standing with a tall frontiersman at the desk, and made his way to them.

"Well, Finn, I believe I have found a place for you," Mr. Farnum said. "Meet Mr. Leighton. I think both of you need each other."

In this manner, Finn Burnett clasped hands with the man who was destined to play a great part in the building of his future life.

A. C. Leighton was the name of his new friend, a resident of Ottumwa, Iowa, a well-to-do storekeeper who had observed the possibilities for profits to be made in the handling of sutlers' supplies at the various posts on the frontier.

The sutlers' stores were the civilian canteens of the army posts which were strung along the western trails. They catered to those soldiers and frontiersmen who were the more fastidious and who were willing to pay for luxuries which were not included in the army issues. Most of these stores contained a barroom with a large assortment of liquors, but their main trade was in tobaccos, cigars, candies, better provisions than were provided in the army mess, warm and comfortable clothing, and articles which could be used for trading with the Indians.

At this time, Mr. Leighton had received the appointment of sutler for an expedition under General Patrick Edward Connor which was to be known as the first Powder River expedition. His plan was to proceed with several wagons loaded with sutlers' goods, to provide a moving canteen for the soldiers on the road, and to leave supplies at new stores which would be opened at various army posts on the way.

"Do you know anything about the handling of mules, son?" Mr. Leighton asked quietly.

"Well, sir, I'm a Missourian, and I've had my heels kicked raw many a time trying to break them," Finn answered.

"All right," Mr. Leighton smiled. "You are hired. Your wages will be $65 a month with bed and board furnished. You will have to go back into Iowa with me tomorrow and help me buy and bring back thirteen four-mule teams for the trip."

Mr. Leighton also hired Kemp Caldwell for the expedition, and put him to work at loading up the wagons while Finn went to assist in finding mules in Iowa. The farther east they journeyed the fewer became the animals which they could purchase, as the government had bought them for use in the Civil war. So the entire number of fifty-two mules was bought within fifty miles of Omaha, none of them being more than three years old, and costing $500 a span.

Finn and Mr. Leighton drove them back to Omaha, and on their arrival the mules were driven into the corrals of the Checkered Stable, so named because its entire front was painted with red, white, and blue diamonds. It was situated across the street from the Farnum House. There Mr. Leighton soon had a blacksmith at work, shoeing them all at a cost of five dollars a team.

It was about the first of March, 1865, when Kemp and Finn helped to hitch the mules to the high-piled wagons, and departed on the most thrilling trip of their lives.

The two young men found everything to be of wondrous interest. There were fifteen teams of mules in the outfit, including two belonging to old Charlie Vampros who had joined the train for convenience and safety in crossing the plains. Mr. Leighton's portion of the caravan had been ordered to unite with the expedition near Fort Laramie on the Platte river.

Finn felt very brave that morning when the outfit started out in a long line stretching westward from Omaha. He had bought a new Ballard rifle with fifty rounds of ammunition, a Navy revolver for which he carried a powder flask, and a pocket full of bullets, all of which he believed he would need for protection against Indians. His expectations were to be fully verified.

The first stop of the wagon-train was at Fremont, the second at Columbus. At that time each of those places was a settlement consisting of a store, blacksmith shop, and barn. The third rest was at Loup Fork of

BULL OUTFITS

the Platte river, where there was a trader's store and a grain-and-feed stable. Here they ferried across the river. The next settlement west of Loup Fork was on Wood river in Nebraska, and there Finn found all the people to be Hollanders who were making a brave effort to raise grain and vegetables. Theirs were the last farms to be found on the trail until those of Utah were reached.

Throughout the trip so far, the road traveled was well packed by the passing of myriads of "forty-niners" and others bound for Oregon. The country was one of endless horizons, flat, grassy, and monotonous. Finn's eyes fairly ached for the sight of the blue, calm Rocky mountains he knew would appear before they reached Fort Laramie.

They had been nine days on the road when the train reached the crossing of the South Platte river near old Fort Kearny, Nebraska. There they had to ford the stream at daybreak, and it was a difficult undertaking. The river was more than a mile wide at that place, filled with slush ice and with islands dotted here and there above a bed of quicksand.

The fifteen teams of mules were concentrated on two wagons. Then, with fifteen men whipping them, they were urged into the river and out toward the bits of land in midstream. One after another of the islands was safely reached and finally each outfit splashed up the far bank, there to unhitch and return for the others.

The mules and wagons were kept moving continuously, for a moment's halt caused them to sink deep into the quicksand. When an animal balked, he would soon be belly deep, and would have to be unhitched. Then one of the men would sit in the ice-cold water and hold the mule's head up until the outfit came back and pulled the obstinate beast out.

There was one bright spot in the proceedings, however. Mr. Leighton had gone ahead and had set a case of whiskey on each island, and the teamsters drank the liquor like water.

It was nine o'clock when the last wagon was safely across, and by that time few of the men could sit in their seats. Their beds were unrolled on top of the loads, and each driver lay down on his stomach facing his mules with his hands out in front holding the reins. In this manner the caravan drove in to Dobe Town, and when it arrived, every teamster was fast asleep. The people of the settlement turned out to unhitch the mules and to put the travelers to bed.

On awaking next morning, Finn found that the outfit had joined the McCormick train for the remainder of the trip to Fort Laramie. The two McCormick brothers, Dick and John, were well known to everyone west of the Missouri as honest hard-working freighters, and their wagon-master was William Paxton, who later was the founder of the famous wholesale house of Paxton and Gallagher.

Before leaving Dobe Town, Mr. Leighton bought another wagon, with four mules and harness, for which he paid $1000 cash, and added them to his caravan. The combined outfits started out for Fort Laramie, and experienced little difficulty on the trip. They were at Fort Sedgwick, Cottonwood Springs, Nebraska, when the Civil war ended, and at Julesburg when President Lincoln was assassinated on April 14, 1865.

A few Indians attempted to steal the mules in the nighttimes, but they were never successful. There were thirty-six teams, and thirty men in the train, which was too large a number for redskins to attack openly.

All of the men had signed on for wages of $65 a

month, with bed and board furnished. Each bed consisted of a buffalo robe and two pairs of blankets, but most of the drivers doubled up and so had two robes and four pairs of blankets, which made them comfortable.

Fast time was made from Omaha to Fort Laramie, as only thirty days were consumed on the trip. It was at this famous old fort that Finn spent his twenty-first birthday.

It was an important post in those days, with a semicircular row of buildings set in the center of the flat river bottom, close to the trees which lined the Platte, and with mountains looming blue above the western horizon. A part of the 11th Ohio Volunteers was garrisoned there, together with the 1st Colorado and the 2nd California Volunteers. All were seasoned Indian fighters, of great bravery and little discipline.

At the time of Finn's arrival, the soldiers at Fort Laramie were incensed to a high pitch which bordered upon mutiny. During the early fall of the year before, a wagon-train had been ambushed and burned by Indians east of Fort Kearny. Every man had been massacred, but two women of the train, a Mrs. Larimer and a Mrs. Joseph Eubanks, together with a little fifteen-year-old girl, had been carried off by the redskins to a terrible existence.

The child was soon killed. Her little body was shot full of arrows as she tried to run away, but the fate of the women had been far more brutal, as they had been obliged to live as the slaves and playthings of two chiefs, Mrs. Larimer being allotted to Little Thunder, and Mrs. Eubanks to Walks-under-the-Ground.

General Robert Mitchell was in charge of the department, and on hearing that the two women were still alive, he began negotiations with the chiefs for their return, finally agreeing to pay a large sum of money for their safe delivery.

Before they arrived at Fort Laramie, General Connor relieved General Mitchell as the department commander, and he was on one of his business trips to Fort Leavenworth when the three chiefs, Little Thunder, Walks-under-the-Ground, and Two Face, the latter also having participated in the transaction, came in with their two women prisoners on May 20, 1865.

At first, the three Indian warriors were inclined to swagger before the scowling soldiers, but, as Mrs. Larimer told her story of outrage and brutality suffered at their hands, the savages began to feel uneasy at the rising tide of animosity which greeted them everywhere. Finally, as all the details became known, the unbounded anger of the white men became so threatening that the three chiefs were locked in the post guardhouse for their own protection.

The 2nd Californians and 1st Coloradoans, however, could not be restrained. They were veteran Indian fighters, brave and resolute at all times, but with a decided disrespect for army discipline and regulations. They, on this occasion, became hourly more infuriated.

Young Finn Burnett was standing with Kemp Caldwell in the sutler's store when the indignation of the garrison reached the breaking point. One by one, various spokesmen had mounted barrels to curse the Indians and all their actions, to call upon the innate manhood of the frontiersmen to revenge this savage violation of all decency.

Finally, with a roar, the crowd of mixed soldiery burst forth from the store, carrying Finn and Kemp along with it to the guardhouse doors. There, already, were four soldiers working quickly with steel bars to open the way to the prisoners. The guards and sentries had been wise enough not to attempt to interfere.

After a moment of hacking work, the grating fell outward with a crash, and the crowd burst in to emerge a few seconds later with the three terrified chiefs. They had little opportunity for affecting a dignified stride as they were pushed, mauled, and kicked from all sides by the hoarse and red-eyed soldiers.

Arriving at the parade grounds, a large circle was made about the flag pole, and Mrs. Larimer was called for. After a minute's wait, she was brought forward supported by two husky sergeants of the 2nd California to a position facing her late captor, Little Thunder. There she suddenly became hysterically infuriated as memory flooded in upon her of the indignities which she had suffered at his hands.

"Tie him," she shrieked. "Tie his big, red hands to the flag pole there, and let me scalp him. Let me have my reward by cutting the dirty scalp from him."

Her words were greeted with a ringing cheer, and a few minutes later the Indian stood bound to the designated pole, and Mrs. Larimer was handed a long, keen, skinning-knife.

She walked up to the stolid captive with weapon in hand and with her face blazing with resolution and triumph. But, as she stood before him, gazing at his pleading eyes, she suddenly swerved aside, threw the knife from her in disgust, and covering her eyes with her hands, she cried out, "I can't. I can't take the life of anyone."

Little Thunder's reprieve was short-lived, however, for as two men hurried Mrs. Larimer away, his bonds were cut, a long rope was tied about his neck, and the brutal crowd began to drag him in the dust of the fort. Whenever he gained his feet, there were a dozen of his tormentors ready to trip him, until at last he began to weaken, and he was pulled along like a bundle of rags behind the infuriated soldiers.

Suddenly, as the crowd passed the sutler's store, the figure of the post commander, Colonel Baumer, was seen upon the porch of the building. A moment later, his voice could be heard demanding silence. The mob hesitated more from curiosity than respect for discipline, then waited to hear what he had to say.

"Men," he called, "listen to me. I understand your hatred for the actions of these savages, and I respect your manhood in desiring to make an example of them which other Indians will remember.

"But there is something beyond our present feelings to consider. The same end that we desire tonight can be accomplished properly and officially if we proceed through military channels.

"If we continue as we have started, none of you will be allowed to proceed with General Connor's expedition; all will be confined to quarters; some of you most assuredly will be severely dealt with.

"Let me urge you to put that Indian back into the guardhouse while I telegraph to the general for instructions. I know him to be fair and as much of a man as any one of us, and I am sure he will tell us to proceed immediately with what we all desire."

There was a milling indecision throughout the crowd. Several men near Finn and Kemp began to argue.

"But what if the general says to let them go?" called someone from the rear of the mob.

"In that case I will wash my hands of all responsibility," answered Colonel Baumer. "You can do as you wish, if that happens."

There was a short period of argument after that, but, as Colonel Baumer had the reputation for being a man of his word, ten minutes had not gone by before Little Thunder had been returned to his cell in the guard-house, and the crowd had begun to straggle toward the little telegraph office.

The commanding officer already had sent his prom-ised telegram to General Connor, and the soldiers wandered aimlessly about the fort, occasionally meeting in groups to conjecture of what would happen on the morrow. Would the killing be an orderly affair or a frenzied lynching?

Finn and Kemp pushed forward curiously through the door of the telegraph office until they were able to look over the operator's shoulder and read the mes-sages that unreeled on the long tape of the telegraph machine.

The room was crowded with an impatient press. The air was blue with tobacco smoke. Outside the door, the lantern light shone upon a host of white, staring faces. Everywhere was tension, a crouching alertness.

Suddenly, there came a scraping of the operator's chair as he leaned forward. There was silence in the room as the telegraph instrument ticked its fateful mes-sage. A moment later a loud voice began to read General Connor's answer.

"Tomorrow morning at nine o'clock, hang Little Thunder, Walks-under-the-Ground, and Two Face with fifth chains. After hanging twenty minutes, fire a volley of twenty pieces at them, and leave them hanging until further order."

Immediately there was a cheer from everyone within the room, and, as the word was passed to those outside, there was an answering roar from the remainder of the garrison. Impatient with the wasting of a minute, all set about immediately in the darkness to erect a gallows.

Two posts were set in the ground on one side of the parade ground, with room enough between them for a wagon to pass. A beam was then placed across the top and securely fastened.

The following morning dawned warm and clear. To the westward, beyond the winding trail to Oregon, the mountains loomed blue and calm, with sharp-tipped Laramie Peak squatting among them, its rugged crown piercing a flat and biscuit-shaped cloud.

In the surrounding sage, the meadowlarks warbled their welcome to the sunrise. Larks' wings twinkled in the air where they hunted for early flies still chilled from the cold of night.

The bugle of reveille awoke the garrison to a quick activity, and at "Assembly," the lines of blue-shirted men answered to their names and marched to the stables, to water the army horses at the river, and to pile cured native timothy hay before them for their breakfasts.

But, after the morning mess, no policing details straggled off to do their labors. A mounting excitement seemed to grip the fort; the air was surcharged with tragedy.

Drill call blew at nine o'clock, and as each company was formed it marched to the parade ground from the barracks to add its portion to a huge, hollow square. Finn Burnett and Kemp Caldwell found themselves in a group of civilians, mule-drivers, emigrants, traders, and frontiersmen of the garrison who crowded together directly facing the towering gallows.

Then, from behind the guardhouse, marched a file of twenty soldiers. Their guns glistened as they wheeled into line before the place of execution. A lieutenant officer of the day halted them, and all stood at ease, waiting.

There was little conversation in the ranks of soldiers and groups of civilians. All eyes seemed drawn repeatedly to the scaffold with a fascination born of dread and horror. The fury of the night before had chilled with the cold, calm dawn.

Now there came a rattle from the distant barns, and all faces turned to see an empty, cumbersome garrison wagon with a soldier on the seat driving his six-mule team to the guardhouse. As he halted, the barred door opened to emit the three chieftains, walking with their arms bound securely behind their backs, and four guards beside them. Quickly, they marched to the wagon, and a moment later Chiefs Little Thunder, Walks-under-the-Ground, and Two Face sat tied and helpless in the wagon-box.

As the driver cracked his whip above the mules, there came loud orders of "Attention" from the officers to their waiting companies, and a moment later, the wagon drove across the parade ground between the silent ranks, the rattling of the wheels sounding loudly in the ominous air. The doomed chieftains began to chant their hideous native death-songs to add to the horror of the scene.

Halting between the gallows posts, the driver sprang to assist two non-commissioned officers who climbed into the wagon-box, there to throw the three chains which hung from the cross-beam overhead about the necks of the stolid prisoners.

"Sergeant, are you ready?" called the officer of the guard.

"Yes, sir," came the reply, as the driver leaped to his seat, and the sergeants jumped from the wagon to take their places beside the upright posts.

"Go ahead," rang out the order, and with a snap of the driver's whip, the mules plunged forward to drag the footing from beneath the captives, to leave them plunging and twisting in the air.

The lines of waiting soldiers stood tense and white. To kill a man in battle was to every one of them a duty, but to put to death a bound and helpless human being in a precise, cold-blooded execution was an act which chilled most of them with horror, and made them turn their eyes away from the desperate, diminishing struggles of the dying Indians to where the officer of the day stood, watch in hand, awaiting the passing of the necessary twenty minutes.

The time seemed ages in its passing. Muscles seemed to ache, so tense were they held awaiting the final act of execution which would liberate the soldiers from the scene of retribution.

Finally, the lieutenant closed his watch with a snap, and wheeled upon his squad.

"Attention." The soldiers stiffened more.

"Load." There came the rattle of twenty breeches.

"Aim." A line of guns sprang to shoulders.

"Fire." There came a roar, as relieved bullets tore their way into the dangling, strangled bodies of the savages to complete the final humiliation.

An hour later, all the soldiers of the garrison were going about their duties stoically, but all were quiet from the shock. Many a day would pass before Finn and Kemp could efface from their minds the swaying forms that hung upon the gallows at Fort Laramie.

In fact, it was impossible for Finn to forget the hanging chieftains whenever he passed through the fort during the remainder of the summer. The three bodies hung in their chains, swaying slowly in the hot prairie winds. As the months passed, the long, thin forms became mummified and dry until their bones rattled in the fall blizzards, disturbing many a lonesome sentry at his post.

Had Finn been older and wiser he would have agreed with Jim Bridger, the famous old scout, who prophesied that this hanging would lead to dreadful consequences later on the trails.

Fighting on the Platte

Fighting on the Platte

The situation on the western plains at this time was one of continual warfare between the advancing white men and the Indians. Until the rush of gold hunters to California in 1849, the red men of the frontier had been at peace with the whites because they were undisturbed, but with the thrusting of the Oregon trail through their finest hunting land, sniping commenced and gradually merged into general engagements at every opportunity.

The southern Cheyenne, Arapaho, and Sioux under George Bent and Chief Roman Nose, harassed the trails east and south of Fort Laramie, while Chief Sitting Bull became the guiding genius of those Sioux along the Missouri, and Chief Crazy Horse led the forces of northern Cheyenne and Sioux on Powder river.

Chief Red Cloud, a leading Ogalalla chieftain, was in supreme command of the combined tribes during most of the greater battles and conferences with the white men. When the fact is considered that the Ogalalla tribe numbered but 1500 warriors, it speaks obviously of the wisdom and ability of this great chieftain that he became the undisputed leader of the 70,000 Sioux as well as of the Cheyenne and Arapaho.

The Oregon trail up the Platte valley was in an almost continual state of siege. Small army posts had been placed at intervals along its route, but the Indians were in such numbers that determined attacks on wagon-

trains even when within rifle shot of these forts resulted
in annihilation for the travelers that the garrisons were
powerless to resist.

To the north of the Platte, the country swarmed with
armed war-parties of the Sioux, who had raided the
Oregon trail with such deadly regularity that it had
become dotted with burned wreckage and with graves
within nearly every mile of the distance from Fort
Laramie to South Pass.

To attempt to cope with this situation, it was decided
to proceed with what was to be known as the Powder
River expedition which would move northward deep
into the heart of the Indian country, and there establish
forts which would provide a measure of protection and
refuge for those travelers who left the Platte valley to
journey to the gold country in Montana. Inasmuch as
Powder river and the Big Horn mountains were the
sites of the largest Indian villages, and were, as well,
swarming with hostiles, the expedition was fore-or-
dained to be a fighting organization, and the forts which
it would establish were assured of a terrible existence.

It was about the first of May, 1865, when the order
was issued which directed Mr. Leighton's wagon-train
to proceed to the Platte bridge, west of Deer creek
crossing, there to unite with the Powder River expedition. Finn and Kemp set out with the caravan for that
point escorted by the 11th Kansas Cavalry and a twelve-
pound howitzer under the command of Colonel Thomas
Moonlight.

This officer had a most unenviable reputation among
his men for discipline which was unnecessarily severe.
An illustration of his methods was displayed during the
first day of the trip. The wagon-train was late in starting
from Fort Laramie for Horseshoe Station, twenty-five

long, hard miles away, and when dark set in Colonel
Moonlight refused to camp and ordered the men to
march through the night. It was impossible to see the
road, or to avoid obstacles, and on coming down a steep
and rocky hill several soldiers were hurled from the
wagons to be painfully injured.

The wagon-train continued on the Oregon trail up
the south side of the Platte river, with the Black Hills
of Wyoming to the south. On their arrival at the fort
beside the Platte bridge, they were directed to make
their camp on upper Garden creek, about four miles
southeast of the post. This place was known as Camp
Dodge, and was situated on the east side of the stream
and close to the trees which fringed the foot of the hills.[1]

It was a beautiful spot. Northward, was a broad vista
of prairies rolling and dipping in grassy rises to where
the Big Horn mountains peeked above the horizon. But
Indians were hidden in every gulch, and the soldiers
were obliged to keep a continued vigilance.

The teamsters were camped below the troops on the
creek, and as the water was fouled and dirty by the time
it passed the soldiers' camp, Finn and Kemp decided
to dig a well for fresh water. The ground was found to
be very hard, and after digging for more than an hour
they gave up their task, but filtered some of the creek
water into it through the sand. Later, this well was to
become a spring which provided a settler with fresh
water for over thirty years.

The first day after their arrival, all were busy making
camp, mending harness, and overhauling equipment.
Sentries were posted at strategic positions, and everyone
kept his guns in readiness for a surprise attack.

---

[1] Camp Dodge was located five miles south of the present city of Casper,
Wyoming.

At dusk that evening, everyone went to his blankets tired. Finn shared his bed under his wagon with Kemp, and the troopers rested in little tents.

Suddenly, a sentry saw a black shape at the edge of the woods, and fired at it. Instantly, everything was in an uproar as a huge animal hurled itself into camp, blundered through a tent, putting one paw squarely in the stomach of a sleeping soldier, and then fled on through the picket line, throwing the horses into a tumult. Finn, sitting up in his blankets, saw the shape of the large, black bear disappearing over the sky-line a moment later with the desperate speed born of dire necessity.

Nor was this the only incident in which wild animals played a part while the soldiers were camped on Garden creek. Two mounted troopers saw a mountain lion slink into a short, deep canyon. One rode to the upper end while the other remained watching below. The former fired upon the lion which bounded sideways to safety and dashed down and out the lower end, colliding with the soldier stationed there, knocking him from his saddle and tearing the flesh from his jaw and from one side of his head. This is one of the few instances where mountain lions have been known to attack a man.

The days idled along one after another, and the men living in Camp Dodge began to exercise themselves with climbing up the steep face of the hills to explore the more distant canyons. Many of them found keen delight in rolling boulders from the top of the higher ledges, and in watching them rush through the bushes until hurtled far out over a cliff, to shatter into fragments on the grassy slopes below.

Finn Burnett and Kemp Caldwell, being apart from military routine, had many a day of idleness to fill, and so they often climbed among the trees. Once as they made their way above and east of the Garden Creek Falls, they discovered a peculiar sheet of metal. A huge tree had been thrown down by a hurricane, and the deep roots had brought to the surface some inorganic body which had later been struck by a lightning bolt. This had melted the mineral and it had spread over the ledge before it cooled and hardened into a mass.

Believing this to be silver, the two young men broke off pieces from the edges of the lump, tied them in their handkerchiefs and coats, and returned to the camp.

The 2nd California regiment had been quartered in Utah for some time during preceding years and most of the soldiers were familiar with the appearance of the various ores. These veterans examined the specimens and announced that they were composed of galena, which was worth from fifty cents to a dollar a pound at that time. Galena is a lead sulphide, and is generally found close to silver deposits.

Years later, Finn was to return to search for this treasure-bearing spot, only to discover that a forest fire had burned the trees from the face of the mountainside until it was impossible to find the rich location.

Had Finn and Kemp been able to return to that place immediately, they might have become more familiar with its position, but, on the following day, orders were given that no one was to leave camp. Large groups of Cheyenne and Sioux were concentrating along the Platte, and especially in the proximity of the fort at the bridge. Evidently, the arrival of the soldiers at Camp Dodge had suggested to the redskins that military activities of some sort were to be undertaken.

From the day that the restricting orders were issued, Indians made regular demonstrations around Camp

Dodge, and harassed the fort at the Platte bridge. Lieutenant-colonel Preston B. Plumb arrived during these
threats, to take over the command from Colonel Moonlight. One of the first actions of Colonel Plumb was
to ride to the fort where he informed Lieutenant
Bretney,[2] the commanding officer, that the next time
Indians bothered the post he should notify Camp
Dodge, and a company of the Californians would come
to his assistance.

From along a high ridge which ranged on the west
side of Garden creek, Indians now appeared daily to
harass the camp. They would suddenly dart over the
top in force and pretend to attack. The twelve-pound
howitzer would be trained on them, and, when fired,
all of the jeering redskins would drop behind the crest
until the shot had gone over them. These demonstrations
continued until the soldiers began to demand an opportunity for attack.

Their requests were answered on June 3, 1865, two
weeks after Colonel Plumb's arrival, when a mounted
rider dashed into camp one morning with the information that Indians were approaching from the north and
west in force, and Lieutenant Bretney would appreciate
the assistance of some soldiers from Camp Dodge.

Colonel Plumb immediately ordered a company of
the 11th Kansas into their saddles, and gave Finn permission to accompany them. On the arrival of the reinforcements at the fort, Lieutenant Bretney spied the
boy, and, taking an instant liking to him, he ordered
him off his sorrel pony, and gave him his own thoroughbred black horse for the fight ahead.

Colonel Plumb and Finn Burnett led about forty

---

[2] Lt. Henry Clay Bretney, Company G, 11th Ohio Volunteer Cavalry (later captain).

troopers of the 11th Kansas and twenty from the 11th
Ohio Cavalry of the post that morning, to attack the
Indians across the river. The colonel had the mistaken
idea that many of the frontier officers had in those days.
He believed that any detail of white soldiers could out-
fight an overwhelming number of ignorant savages. It
took many tragic lessons in massacres to convince this
type of leader that the Indians had a powerful fighting
organization, and that some of their chiefs showed
evidence of possessing excellent generalship. Camouflage, as a military measure, had already been highly
developed by the Sioux and Nez Perce.

As the little band of white soldiers proceeded across
the Platte bridge, they approached a high bank on the
far side, and saw beyond it a sandy, hilly country extend-
ing to a ridge about eight miles to the west and north.

Scattered bands of Indians mounted on their little
ponies watched the approach of the troopers. Their
feathers flapped in the air as they threw up their hands
and yipped with defiance, only to retreat at a gallop
as the whites drew nearer. Finn felt in his heart that
they were withdrawing far too quickly. It appeared to
be a ruse even to his unknowing eyes.

Farther back into the hills the redskins retreated,
and after them trotted the soldiers unconcernedly, with
Colonel Plumb at their head. For five, then for eight
miles, the movement proceeded under the bright, clear
morning sun, until the fort became a distant refuge in
the trees along the river, and the detail was deep into
the heart of the sandhills with half-guessed ambushes
on every side.

Arriving at the foot of the ridge, Colonel Plumb gave
a quick command to gallop, and all raced to the top.
The sudden increase in speed was their salvation. Be-

yond the crest were massed hundreds of Sioux and Cheyenne preparing to mount their ponies and attack the leisurely advance of the detail. At the sight of the soldiers, all of them gave a loud whoop of surprise, and rushed for their horses.

Colonel Plumb halted his command.

"How much ammunition have we?" he roared.

Some men reported forty rounds, some twenty, some as few as ten, depending on their foresight.

"Well, we haven't enough to fight all those Indians," growled the colonel as he eyed the preparations down the far side of the hill.

"No, and we haven't enough ammunition to run from them, either," reminded a grizzled veteran of the Ohio Cavalry. For it was a well-known fact to the frontiersmen that, at the first move to retire, Indians always attacked with redoubled intensity.

Retreat in an attempt to regain the refuge of the fort at the Platte bridge, was now the only course, however, and Colonel Plumb ordered his detail to withdraw. As the troopers turned their horses' heads about and fled, Finn took a last glance at the mounting redskins behind the hill, and at others who were bringing up saddled horses from a sandy draw. There seemed to be at least a thousand of them.

During two miles of fast galloping, the command experienced no trouble, and then, in a moment, every sagebrush, gulch, and hill around them seemed to be alive with a horde of savages, all dressed in their paraphernalia of war, painted hideously, firing and screeching and hacking at the soldiers in terrible pandemonium. Every trooper, every man and boy, fought for himself, shooting, clubbing, killing, until a hole was blasted ahead. Then each would dash forward, fighting foot by foot toward safety.

Had Finn not been mounted on Lieutenant Bretney's thoroughbred, he would have been lost immediately. As it was, he fired into the mass before him with all the coolness of his worthy ancestry, shooting accurately and well, until the horde drew back. Then he put spurs to his magnificent mount and raced forward with the others until another solid wall of fighting Indians blocked the way.

Leaving the reins free, the better to load and shoot and reload his gun and revolver, Finn found the horse to be thoroughly familiar with what was going on about him, and as mile after mile was successfully passed toward the fort, his heart was filled with admiration for the animal.

Time and again, Finn had no time to reload, and was obliged to swing his gun as a club to crack the multitude of heads before him. Several times when he found himself on the fringe of the fighting, the black sprang ahead, pawing a swath with his hooves which enabled his young rider to gain another yard toward safety.

Suddenly, after the troopers had lost account of time or distance covered, the Indians thinned from before them, and the white men beheld themselves at the north end of the Platte bridge, across which they clattered wearily and thankfully.

In the safety of the fort, all dismounted and slipped sobbing for breath to the ground. Out there among the sandhills, seven blue-shirted troopers lay surrounded by the redskins who were hacking them to bits with hunting-knives and war-clubs. Seven of the survivors were sorely wounded, and had regained the garrison only by weakly hanging to their horses' manes.

All were in a state of extreme exhaustion, and their clothing was torn and ragged from hundreds of tearing knives and clutching hands. Finn was breathless an

hour later when he exchanged horses again with Lieutenant Bretney, and told him of his thankfulness. The
fort's commander merely smiled knowingly and laid
his hand tenderly on the neck of his thoroughbred which
nickered softly and began to nudge his pockets for sugar.

For several days after that, the soldiers had a period
of rest and recuperation, but none of them found prolonged inactivity to be desirable. All looked forward
with keen impatience to the advance of the expedition,
and growled as the days passed without receiving orders
to proceed.

But the truth of the entire matter was that the war
department was in a state of considerable indecision.
As was always the case, politics, internal dissentions,
and jealousies were playing their parts behind the scenes
in Washington. General Connor, fretting to be away
with his expedition, was ordered to Fort Leavenworth
repeatedly to confer on various phases of the venture,
reflecting alternate moods of hope and disappointment
when he returned to Fort Laramie.

It was whispered up and down the Platte that spring,
that strong influences had been brought to bear against
the expedition. The regular army believed that it would
have a stiff political fight before it could continue in
existence after the Civil war was ended. It was foreseen that its numbers would be cut to practically nothing, and its generals in Washington feared that the
success of volunteer western troops on an expedition
against Indians would greatly imperil the prestige of
the regular army. With this attitude eating at the very
heart of the army headquarters in Washington, it was
not surprising that military activities on the plains
proved to be somewhat half-hearted and desultory
affairs.

As a consequence of this attitude of indecision, the command at Camp Dodge was obliged to march and counter-march repeatedly in a manner which was most disheartening and detrimental to the morale of the detachments.

Finn Burnett was kept busy, however, by Mr. Leighton, for he drove daily up and down the trail under the military escort of the 2nd Californians, carrying supplies to all of the stage stations which were situated between Fort Laramie and Burnt Ranch on the Sweetwater river, and which were under the jurisdiction of the 11th Ohio Cavalry. These stations were strung out along the valley, one on Horseshoe creek, one on Deer creek, and others at Poison Spider creek, Independence Rock, Split Rock, Three Crossings, and St. Mary's. Each was guarded by a non-commissioned officer and six privates of the 11th Ohio, a number wholly inadequate to the duty imposed.

Finn was especially interested on one of these trips to observe at Independence Rock the names of his two uncles, George and William, painted upon the face of the rock with pine tar, the frontier axle grease, and bearing the date 1852.

At Three Crossings on the Sweetwater several soldiers were found to be spending their leisure hours at placer mining, filling lemon extract bottles with gold dust.

From 1829, when William Lewis Sublette [3] had trailed from St. Louis with ten wagons and two "dearborns," the Oregon trail had become deep-rutted from the passing hundreds of thousands of wagon wheels. Most of the trail was made up of from two to six parallel

[3] William Lewis Sublette, a partner in the fur-trade with Robert Campbell. He was credited with having led the first wagons over the plains to the Rocky mountains.

roads throughout its 2000 miles of highway, and showed the wisdom of its earliest pioneers by its use of the driest and safest ridges, flats, and valleys.

Now, Finn found it to be dotted from the Platte bridge to Burnt Ranch with the graves of soldiers of the 11th Ohio who had lost their lives in an effort to keep the trail safe for travel. Tragic mounds marked the last resting-places of those emigrants who had been killed in surprise raids, or who had died from accident or sickness. Later, the soldiers' graves would be removed to government cemeteries, but in 1865 one was never out of sight of some lonely mound along the road.

Frequently, on these trips, hostile Indians were sighted on the surrounding hills, and the 2nd Californians under Captain George Conrad relieved the monotony of the days in every instance by refusing to wait for them to attack. The troopers would give a ringing challenge and charge toward the redskins, to chase them for miles until every savage was killed or driven far from the trail.

Finally, about the 15th of June, the entire command at Camp Dodge was ordered to return to Fort Laramie, there to outfit for the Powder River expedition. Everyone greeted the news with enthusiasm, for the inaction of the last few weeks had been terribly wearing on the nerves of everyone.

Safely back in Fort Laramie, where the three Indian chiefs still swung in the wind, Finn and Kemp were kept busy loading the wagons with canteen supplies that the soldiers would need on the march; shaving equipment, brushes, fancy ornaments, arms, and ammunition were loaded in large quantities. Mr. Leighton had made an arrangement with the military authorities so that soldiers could make· purchases without money

CROSSING ON THE SOUTH PLATTE RIVER
From a contemporary sketch by C. Hall.

by signing orders which would be redeemed on pay-days, or honored by the pay-masters at the fort.

It now appeared that the teamsters and men working for Leighton were beginning to grumble about their wages. All had signed up in Omaha to go on the expedition for $65 a month and board. Now, they had discovered that there was a universal demand for men on the plains at much higher wages, and they were dissatisfied with the terms of their contracts. Mr. Leighton stood firm, however, and his men were obliged to continue on his terms.

There were three divisions of the Powder River expedition which were to set out that summer, known as the western, central, and eastern divisions. The portion to which Mr. Leighton was to be attached was known as the western division, and was under the command of Brigadier-general Patrick Edward Connor of the Third Infantry, California Volunteers, who had been promoted for his heroic conduct on Bear river, and who was of decided character, discreet, and much beloved by his men. Subsequently, due to army jealousies and politics, his name was more or less submerged by other frontier leaders who were far less worthy of acclaim.

This western division presented a formidable array of hardened, experienced Indian fighters. Major Nicholas J. O'Brien commanded his 7th Iowa Cavalry and 180 Winnebago, Iowa Indians under Chief Little Priest, all of whom had fought with distinction in the Minnesota Indian war. There were one company of the 7th Iowa Cavalry, two companies of the 2nd California men, three companies from the 11th Ohio with their quartermaster corps, a number of United States army signal corps men, and several companies of the Sixth

Michigan Cavalry who were to garrison the fort that was to be constructed.

The most interesting group of the entire expedition consisted, of course, of the scouts, the finest of these being the 90 Pawnee under Major Frank Joseph North.[4] These were the only Indians with the possible exception of the Shoshoni, who would stand and fight in a battle like white men.

Both of these tribes, peculiarly, traced their ancestry back to the Comanche. Originally, the Shoshoni were the strongest of any tribe anywhere in the United States, and the Comanche were a branch of this tribe, as were the Pawnee, Ute, Navajo, and Piute.

James Bridger was the chief of all the scouts, having as his lieutenants Jack Stead, and Nick and Antoin Lajeunesse, who were half French and half Sioux.

Bridger had been with the 2nd Californians and 1st Coloradoans for some time and had gained their unanimous regard, which was unusual among such a hardy lot of veterans. He was then about 65 years of age, five feet ten inches in height, slightly stoop-shouldered, and small of face.

He was always neat in appearance, and during all the time that Finn knew him, he never drank to excess. He was a blood brother and a chief of the Crow tribe, his Indian name being "Kash-sha-peece," meaning "Fine Cloth." On one occasion when Finn asked him how it had come about that the Indians had given him that name, he answered, "I was one of the boys when I was a young man among them."

To explain this, he went on to state that the redskins

---

[4] Frank Joseph North was commissioned a captain of a regular Pawnee scout company on October 24, 1864. Three years later he was advanced to the rank of colonel of a battalion of four Pawnee companies as a result of his outstanding success with these famous scouts.

bought broadcloth in quantities, some of it being red and some blue. They would take a width of red cloth and one of blue, as it always was sold in quantities a yard wide, and would sew the two pieces together. The squaws would then bead a fancy strip down the seam with porcupine quills. This made a dress blanket for the braves, and Bridger's, having been unusually brilliant and well beaded, had brought him his name of "Fine Cloth."

To supply this expedition, 200 wagons were loaded with provisions and material, forty of them belonging to Edward Creighton, thirty to Thomas Pollock, and the remainder being A. C. Leighton's.

Altogether, it was a remarkably fine fighting organization. The veteran fighters were mounted on excellent western ponies. They were well equipped, with the best of scouts to guide them, and with ample provisions. The venture was foreordained to be one of distinction.

Here again, the fine hand of army jealousies showed its work. When the orders were finally issued, it was found that transportation wagons were not furnished for the troops of the expedition, and it was necessary for General Connor to press into service the privately-owned wagons of the civilians at the fort. These were the trains of Creighton, who was building a telegraph line, Pollock, Leighton, and others.

Furthermore, sufficient forage and other essentials were not furnished, and it appeared that withal the fine array of soldiery, the expedition would experience great difficulty on the march, due to the detrimental actions of its own war department.

War in the Sage

War in the Sage

The morning finally arrived when the expedition started on the march which was expected to have such far-reaching results that the future peace of the white emigrants would be assured. The grass around the fort had been thoroughly eaten away by the hundreds of emigrant horses which grazed there daily, and when the cavalcade moved out on that bright and sunny morning, it was with orders to proceed to the mouth of Chugwater creek, twenty miles up the Laramie river, and remain there until the mules and mounts of the soldiers had been strengthened on the luxuriant grass.

Crossing the Laramie river below the fort on the old Oregon trail, they proceeded up on the east side, and, after arriving at the designated depot camp, all rested until July 5th, 1865.

It was here that the first trouble was experienced among the personnel of the transportation convoy. Creighton's men had mingled with the other teamsters and had given out the report that their boss had secured the contract to build a telegraph line to Alaska, and that his men were working for higher wages than Leighton had been paying. They told Finn Burnett and Kemp Caldwell that they were fools to work for a pittance when men were in such demand.

Pay-day at the Chugwater camp finally brought the crisis to a head. Everyone was paid off at that time, and then Mr. Leighton's men proceeded to their employer's tent in a body and there demanded more pay in the future. Finn and Kemp did not participate in the movement.

Mr. Leighton refused to grant their request, telling them that their work would not be as arduous nor as dangerous as would that of the workers on the telegraph line, and that his type of business would not produce him a profit on his investment if he paid them more.

His teamsters quit on the spot, and began to pack their belongings for the return trip to Fort Laramie. General Connor, hearing of the trouble, strode over and informed Mr. Leighton that soldiers would take the places of all the deserting men. In this manner, the first threat against the progress of the expedition was dissipated.

Everyone in camp watched the preparations of Leighton's teamsters. The tents of all the men had been pitched close to the east bank of the Laramie river which was running flood high at that time. The foothills around them were rough and thickly timbered.

Some leader hit upon the idea of making a large raft on which all of the deserters could float down the river to the fort. Cottonwood logs were cut and hauled to the river bank where they were lashed together expertly with long, pliable willow branches. This labor took an entire day and was tremendous work for every man of them.

Early next morning, the raft was pushed into the river by all the teamsters, and their bags of clothing and bundles of equipment were piled upon it. They then bade their late comrades farewell, and got aboard.

As Finn and Kemp leaned idly against a tree watching the departure, Mr. Leighton strolled up to them.

"Aren't you boys going along?" he asked quietly.

"No," answered Finn. "We're satisfied to stay. We made an agreement, and we are willing to go through with it."

Mr. Leighton looked at the two boys for a moment thoughtfully, then his eyes strayed to the busy men on the raft. He nodded.

"All right, boys, you won't regret this," he declared, and strode away.

All was excitement on the river. The last boarders of the raft were pushing the heavy affair away from the bank with poles, and upflung hands of farewell could be seen here and there among the cheering passengers. Several derisive and defiant taunts were hurled shoreward. Then the swift current of the river swept them from the eddy, and on out upon the swooping bosom of the stream.

The raft logs were heavy, and the combined weight of the men and bundles was not sufficient to sink the craft more than a few inches as they floated away and were swept out of sight around a curve between the banks of thickets.

Finn and Kemp returned to their wagons, and began to look after their equipment. They knew that soldiers would soon be among them, and various gear had to placed for them to find readily. The camp seemed strangely quiet and deserted.

Suddenly, from down the river came the sound of shots. Everyone in the camp stopped his work and listened. The detonation of a volley floated to them on the clear morning air, followed by a confused distant clamor. Undoubtedly, the raft-full of men had gotten into difficulties with Indians.

The soldiers ran for their guns, and all began to prepare the camp for an attack. The forage was piled in strategic positions, a thousand sacks of corn were heaped to form an emplacement facing the clear space toward the river, and wagons were pushed closer together to make a corral.

During these preparations, the first of the deserters began to arrive in twos and threes from down the river, all running, some carrying a portion of their belongings, most of them arriving with nothing but their clothes and a terrible fear of the pursuing Indians. All were breathless and shaking with fright. Indians had suddenly fired at them from the trees, after the raft had carried them but a scant five miles. Everyone had immediately jumped into the river, waded to shore and fled back toward camp.

Now they begged Mr. Leighton to reinstate them at any wages. Evidently during their five-mile run a safe job had seemed a desirable security to every man of them, and that night found them working willingly and thankfully at the same wages.

The fourth of July was celebrated by everyone with artillery and rifle practice directed at a stone ledge across the river from the camp. This shelf was part of the badlands of the district, whose hacked, torn gulches running from the high levels of the tablelands resembled gaping carcasses lined side by side in ugly disarray.

On this occasion, Major O'Brien demonstrated his brilliant marksmanship. After several had fired at a high point on the ledge, and had failed to register a single hit, the major proceeded to knock it over with his first shot.

On July 30, 1865, the expedition started out on its historical march northward. First, the scouts went ahead and wide of each side of the cavalcade, watching for "sign" of Indian skulkers. Then came the mounted soldiers with their howitzer, and, following them, the rumbling, bumping transportation wagons of Creighton, Pollock, and Leighton. More than a thousand sacks of corn forage had been left at the camp for lack of the necessary equipment for carrying them.

The route traveled was known as the Cottonwood route, which followed northward along the foothills of the Laramie range of the Rocky mountains before the expedition turned westward along the Platte. The first halt was on Cottonwood creek, and then on to cross the Overland trail at Horseshoe Station on Horseshoe creek, twenty-five miles west of Fort Laramie. The North Platte river was crossed at Bridger's crossing, which was approximately at the spot where the Colorado & Southern railroad bridge was later to be built below Orin. That night the expedition camped on the river bank several miles above this ford.

From there they toiled on up the north side of the Platte to a point near the mouth of Sage creek, and across the river from where Fort Fetterman was later established. From there, Bridger led the cavalcade northward on the virgin prairie, a day's march up Sage creek, with no road of any kind to guide them. Bridger remarked then that ten years had elapsed since he had been through that portion of the country, yet he proved that he remembered accurately the region before them, and the best watering and camping places.

The prairies were rolling and sandy, covered with dense, gray sage. There was little need for scouts close to the column, for a mounted man could be discerned miles distant on those level plains, and the gulches and draws were infrequent and shallow, offering little shelter for any large group of Indians in ambush.

The day's march from Sage creek to the Dry Cheyenne river was over rougher country. Laramie Peak faded below the southern horizon, and the expedition then became a plodding, tramping, moving thing engulfed in a cloud of hovering dust amid sweltering heat waves.

Companies of the 2nd California regiment under Captain George Conrad and Captain Albert Brown, being the best mounted, were kept continually on the alert, doing scout duty under the guidance of Jim Bridger, while the Pawnee scouts of Major Frank North brought in scalps every day from their maneuvers beyond the horizon of the column.

The third day after leaving the Platte, they reached Brown's or Antelope Springs, and then Bridger headed the cavalcade down what is known as the Dry Fork canyon of Powder river to where Powder river itself offered an excellent camping place. Here was to be established a new fort which would be named Fort Connor, situated on a level bench on the west side of the river, and about five hundred yards below where the camp was made. It was 169 miles northwest of Fort Laramie.

On the 14th of August, 1865, George Sinclair and Finn Burnett took their mules and drove them to the foothills to the west. The timber along Powder river had been found to be short and scrubby, so the two men made their way into the timber of the mountains, and from there dragged down the first logs for the new fort. Shortly afterwards, others joined in the work, and soon a large pile of straight, clean logs was ready for the builders. The guardhouse, powder magazine, and quarters for the men were built in the open outside the protection of the stockade, while the stables and warehouses were within.

The country around Fort Connor presented frequent locations which afforded cover for Indian surprise attacks. Along the river, 140 feet below the fort, the cottonwoods grew gnarled and closely thicketed, which fact enabled redskins to ambush many a careless soldier in later years. Among the thickets were the debris of hundreds of Indian tepees, as that point was a favorite Sioux camping place.

Scarcely had the soldiers begun to build the fort when small hunting parties and war groups of the Sioux tribe began to appear on the surrounding hills, there to stand motionless in all their beaded buckskins, war-paint and flapping feathers, watching the work. Some became bolder as the days passed, and rode closer in an attempt to estimate the strength of the whites. None of these ever returned to their villages with any information, for the Pawnee scouts hated the Sioux with traditional hostility.

These Pawnee were camped below the stockade on the river, and on several occasions the Sioux mistook them for members of their own tribe and rode down. Their mistake was tragic in every instance. They would jog into the Pawnee camp on their ponies, and before they could turn to escape, dozens of leaping Pawnee would fling themselves upon them, knives and tomahawks would flash and swing, and all would be over.

Major "Nick" O'Brien and Mr. Leighton had by this time become intimate friends, and Finn Burnett had found himself more closely associated with his employer. As a consequence, the young man was permitted unusual freedom, being allowed to leave camp with Kemp Caldwell on several excursions.

On August 16th, about 3 o'clock in the afternoon, a number of Pawnee came running into the half-com-

pleted fort shouting "Sioux, Sioux," at the top of their
voices. Captain North questioned them and learned
that a large party of that hated tribe had been seen
coming from the east.

Immediately, all was in confusion in the camp as the
Pawnee ran for their horses, then mounted and galloped
away, stringing out along the river. Major North, Mr.
Leighton, and Finn happened to be the only white men
who were on horseback at the time, and they followed
with the racing scouts.

Major North called to some Pawnee chieftains that
they could pursue the Sioux and capture them if it
were possible, which statement was met with redoubled
whoops from the scouts. The three whites galloped
swiftly in the midst of the madly racing Pawnee who
whipped their ponies desperately, and who kept their
black eyes straining forward fiercely in anticipation of
the coming fight.

As they followed the trail down the river, Finn
noticed what he thought was a wagon track, and thought
that possibly the Pawnee had made a mistake and that
they were following some white people, as Indians did
not use wagons.

However, they followed along the trail until dark
set in, and still the Pawnee kept on, the keen eyes of
the foremost scouts picking their way unerringly until
about midnight the leaders halted and pointed ahead
through the dark.

All stopped on a hillside, and discerned along a river-
bottom a number of campfires flickering beside shadowy
tepees in the trees. Softly, the Pawnee slipped away
into the dark, stealing in twos and threes through the
thickets until, when daybreak came, they had the camp
entirely surrounded.

As the first light filtered across the eastern hills, the white men on the hill heard a quick volley, and then the air was rent with the shrill war-whoops of leaping Pawnee. For several minutes all was a terrible melee, and savage clamor hid the screams of the dying and the sorely wounded. Hand to hand the Sioux and Pawnee fought, and as the sound of conflict diminished and died, the whites rode down to learn that the camp had contained forty-two Sioux braves and two squaws, all of whom had been killed and scalped.

It was discovered then, that the tracks which had been seen on the trail had been made by a travois drawn by one of Ben Holladay's stage horses. The Sioux had been using this means to transport an Indian with a badly-crushed leg. There were a number of Holladay's horses in the camp, all branded "B.H.," and a quantity of women's and children's clothing, all of which indicated that the band had recently surprised, captured, and plundered an emigrant train.

Furthermore, a considerable amount of equipment and fresh scalps were found which were later believed to have been taken from soldiers in the battle at the Platte bridge on July 26th, which had taken place far to the south several days previously. In this battle Lieutenant Caspar Wever Collins had been killed, and the fort later was named for him, as was the city which grew up there.

Finn learned at that time the Indian method for preserving scalps. The skin that was cut from the top of a victim's head was thick and about five inches in diameter, and some scalps also had the ears attached. After fleshing the scalps down until they were thin and pliable, a hoop was made with a willow branch, and the scalp fastened to the circlet. The inside, or flesh side, of the scalp was then painted red, and all was then tied to what the Indians called a "coup" stick, which staff they always carried in war-dances and ceremonials.

Not content with riding away from camp to kill the Sioux, the Pawnee, in their idle time, contrived the most devilish means for luring their enemies into camp. One of their favorite sports was the picketing of a white horse a little distance from their tepees. In the darkness he could be seen clearly.

Knowing the Sioux aptitude for stealing horses, the Pawnees would then scatter in the sagebrush and wait for their decoy to bring in a victim. Time after time the scheme worked, and as skulking redskins came creeping through the dark to that lone, white horse, they were pounced upon and gleefully finished by the waiting Pawnee. That horse cost the Sioux many a warrior.

The day finally arrived when two companies of the 11th Ohio regiment on detached duty trotted in from the south to take over the completion and garrison work of Fort Connor. Everyone in General Connor's force began his hurried preparations for a campaign against the Indians to the northward.

Mr. Leighton moved all of his canteen supplies into the new sutler's store, and put Kemp Caldwell in charge. Finn was to continue as wagon-boss, to accompany the expedition with supplies, running a moving store which would open every evening wherever they camped, to sell the soldiers their tobacco and other necessities.

Up to this time, considerable money had been taken in by Mr. Leighton in orders on the pay-master, and in cash. He found that he had now accumulated more than $15,000 in orders redeemable at the pay-table in

Omaha, and he felt obliged to send his younger brother, Jim, east to collect the amounts due.

The cash which had been received was becoming daily more bulky. The idea had been conceived early on the trip of saving the empty cigar-boxes. Every evening, after the day's business, the greenbacks were straightened out and packed in one of these containers. When a box became heaping full, the cover was closed, Mr. Leighton stood on top to mash the bills together, and Finn nailed it tight. The filled boxes were then tied together until they became a large square bulk which eventually contained nearly $40,000. None but Mr. Leighton, Kemp Caldwell, and Finn Burnett knew what those cigar-boxes contained.

The Tongue River Battle

The Tongue River Battle

The expedition strung out westward on another typical Wyoming morning, one that was bright and crystal clear. The soldiers were eager and enthusiastic as they were bound for the Crazy Woman's fork of Powder river, twenty-five miles away, where the Sioux camps were to be found.

The long line of mounted men had barely started before they beheld seven Indians a short distance away. They had ridden too close to the fort, not knowing of its existence, and now, perceiving their mistake, they turned and fled westward.

The men were eager for a chase, and, as it would take them in the direction which the expedition was following, General Connor gave permission to the company of 2nd Californians under Captain Brown to pursue them. Immediately, the favored troopers put spurs to their horses, and dashed away grinning like schoolboys, while the remainder of the column trotted along the trail behind them.

The seven Sioux were evidently making for Crazy Woman creek, where they knew they would find heavy reinforcements, but the horses of the troopers were far superior to the Indian ponies. Ten miles from Fort Connor, the slower-moving cavalcade came to the first casualty, a dead Indian lying beside the trail dressed in a sergeant's uniform. He was a heavy-set, fat fellow, and his pony had been unable to carry him far. All the remaining six Sioux were knocked from their horses within the next few miles. Captain Brown, however, did not rejoin the expedition until later, on the Tongue river. He decided to take his soldiers for a scouting trip along the Big Horn and Little Big Horn rivers before he returned.

There proved to be no Indians on Crazy Woman's fork when General Connor arrived, so the column continued on to Clear creek, Lodge Pole creek, then to Rock creek, and on to the Big Piney creek where Fort Phil Kearny was to be established the following year. Here camp was made and everyone rested for two days, as the feed for the stock was excellent at that place.

Leaving Big Piney creek, they crossed the divide to Peno creek, where one man was drowned at the ford. Following this stream to its juncture with the Tongue river, the expedition traveled on. During the first day's march down the Tongue river, Bridger told the officers that they would cross a small stream ahead which contained poisoned water. His knowledge undoubtedly saved them from watering their stock at that place.

At noon on the day following the crossing of this poisoned stream, Bridger and Major North rode in from far ahead of the column with the report than an emigrant train was surrounded by Arapaho about thirteen miles south of them, and that the defenders had been continuously attacked for three days. This outfit later proved to be that of Colonel James A. Sawyer which had been sent out from the east, seeking a direct route to Montana, a cut-off which was later to be known as the Bozeman trail.

General Connor immediately made camp. During the unhitching of the wagons, Mr. Leighton rode over to Finn Burnett with the interesting news that the general proposed to surround the village of the attacking

Arapaho during the night and that he and Burnett could go along.

That night of August 29th was black and moonless. The stars in the sky seemed close above the camp in the cool, rarified air, and gave a faint illumination to all the bustle and methodical procedure which marked the departure of the troops for the battle. Horses were saddled, light equipment was tied in place, and, at the command to mount, the soldiers swung upward in unison and were ready to move out.

Bridger, Major North, and the Pawnee scouts started first, followed by the 2nd California Volunteers and a part of the 11th Ohio. Then came the 7th Iowa Cavalry under Major O'Brien, with the howitzer and the supply train. The Winnebago remained behind to guard the camp.

Slowly and carefully the column traveled up the valley, and young Burnett frequently in his excitement believed that he could see the forms of creeping Indians flitting among the shadows in the sage beside the trail. Finally, all were halted. Officers and non-commissioned men gathered around the dark form of General Connor and received their instructions. Then, in groups, the soldiers melted away into the night to take their places around the Arapaho village.

The Pawnee were given the post of honor. They were ordered to proceed around the village to the far end of the valley, and to hold it against any escaping Indians.

General Connor walked forward quietly with Mr. Leighton and Finn Burnett, until the ridge was reached which sheltered the sleeping camp. Lodges loomed gray and brown from beside the flickering, dying embers of their campfires, and only occasionally could the movement of some horse-tender be seen adding an additional bit of wood to the sparks.

Then, above the starlit horizon to the east, there appeared a slight grayness which broadened and reached with ever-widening fingers until the black distances resolved themselves into shadows and then brightened to become surrounding hills. Dark, half-guessed spots revealed thickets, and the Indian camp awoke to life as the first red rays of the sun splashed the tips of the distant peaks with hazy tints of crimson and emerald.

Suddenly, in response to an order, the seventeen-year-old bugler, "Little Dick," brought his trumpet to his lips, sounded the charge, and spurred his horse to his place beside the general.

Immediately all was pandemonium. Down from the ridge dashed General Connor on his horse, followed by his men, to find that his impetuous charge had placed him between the fire of his own troopers and the volleys which now began to spit at them from among the lodges.

"Lie low on your horses," roared the general, and all of his troopers buried their faces in the manes of their mounts. Finn, riding beside "Little Dick," threw himself forward, and as he did so the bugler was struck by a bullet which entered below his cartridge belt, the ball later being removed from under the skin between his shoulder blades. Dick refused to stop for first aid, and throughout the day continued riding over the battlefield carrying dispatches.

The Arapaho village was now a seething mass of fighting savages. Evidently they had learned that a large number of white soldiers were close to them, for they had already driven their ponies into camp, and were busy packing when the attack began. Now, while the Indians flung themselves into the thickets around the camp from whence they blazed away with their rifles at the encircling troops, the ponies loaded with buffalo robes, beaver skins, camp equipment and paraphernalia broke loose and plunged everywhere in their frenzied fear, to add to the general disorder.

At first, the soldiers fired into the camp from the surrounding hills, but, as the thickets of the valley became filled with Indians, the battle became a hand-to-hand affair. The troopers slipped forward slowly, tightening their circle, and gradually silencing the belching volleys in their paths.

The twelve-pound brass howitzer had been brought close to the top of the ridge to be ready for use, but as yet the fighting lines had been so close together that it could not be used.

Suddenly, a large group of Arapaho ran from a clump of willows, threw themselves upon ponies and dashed away down the creek. Perceiving that they would reach the open, Major O'Brien gave the quick order to bring the howitzer into action. Finn helped the willing soldiers who pushed at the wheels, and the gun was reaching a position on the crest of the ridge when, with a crash, the left axle of the carriage broke and slumped sideways. Notwithstanding this difficulty, the artillerymen unlimbered and fired at the galloping savages.

Behind the main group of escaping Arapaho was one buck who was riding a black horse. The first shell fired from the howitzer apparently exploded directly over his head, for his mount galloped on unharmed with but a small portion of the rider remaining in the saddle.

Quickly, the artillerymen rigged up a pole and fastened it under the broken axle to enable them to drag the gun to a better place. The battle, however, continued so closely engaged that not another shell was fired from that howitzer during the rest of the day. It is probable this gun might have been used again to halt the escaping Indians, but as soon as it was brought into position, a rabble of shrieking Arapaho suddenly flung themselves from the brush upon the artillerymen and all were sorely beset for several minutes in a hand-to-hand fight, before the redskins retreated.

The intensity of the battle down the valley was increasing with every minute. Shrieks of rage and savage whoops mingled in each group of trees and willows where blue-clad troopers threw themselves forward to meet the hurtling, clubbing Arapaho in single combat. Knives flashed in the sun, sodden, chopping noises bespoke the wielding of war-clubs. On every side was death and the feeble moans of wounded men.

Finn, having received his baptism of frontier fighting at the howitzer, and having found that his confidence was mounting as he accounted for two of his immediate assailants, now proceeded with a group of artillerymen who followed Mr. Leighton and Major O'Brien down into the valley to assist the troopers. This group went to the creek bottom, and immediately found itself to be the target for a number of Arapaho snipers in the willows ahead. Carefully the white men pushed forward through the tangle with rifles ready, firing at the flashes ahead, or at the sound of twanging bow-strings. Crashing in the thickets testified to the accuracy of the troopers' fire.

Suddenly, two squaws, one old and gnarled like an aged oak, and a young miss, appeared from one side to approach smiling and calling "How! How!"

It was a miracle that both were not shot down immediately, for everyone was keyed to a high pitch, and any movement was the signal for a snap shot.

As it was, they advanced safely, and the old woman put out her right hand to Major O'Brien in greeting. He stepped forward grinning, with his hot pistol in one fist, and was grasping her outstretched hand with the other, when a soldier yelled a sudden warning. One of the old squaw's hands had been held behind her back, and as the major reached her, she suddenly whipped out a war-club and threw it at him.

Instinctively, as he twisted his head aside, O'Brien's fingers tightened with sheer reflex action about his gun, and it exploded. The shot almost tore her head from her shoulders.

The face of the big genial officer was suffused with horror as he gazed down at the slumped body of the native woman. His mouth worked soundlessly with evident repulsion as he looked helplessly from his gun to its victim. Then he reeled around to the waiting men and cried, with his voice trembling with anguish, "For heaven's sake, boys, never tell this on me."

The young squaw had begun to scream and to beg for her life with gestures, believing that she, too, would meet the same fate. Major O'Brien, with an exclamation of disgust for the entire gruesome business, took her by the arm and hustled her back to place her under guard.

Finn and a California soldier then paired themselves and began to search the thickets. Beyond the trees the battle raged. On the outskirts of the village, groups of soldiers were working through the willows along the creek bottoms, ridding them of snipers. Finn and his comrade accounted for two more Arapaho within a short distance, when they found themselves halted by the accurate aim of an Indian who shot his arrows so swiftly and surely that they could not hope to continue until he had been put out of action.

"Let's charge him and get him," the soldier called.

"No," Finn answered. "He'll get one of us if we do."

So they continued for some time attempting to out-flank the warrior. In and out, and all around the thicket they dodged, firing and twisting aside from the whirling arrows until the soldier suddenly lost his temper en-tirely and forgot his caution. He observed a movement and plunged headlong through the bushes toward the brave.

The Arapaho raised up at the first sound, and fired an arrow straight at the soldier, hitting him in the mouth. At the same moment, the Californian fired his gun, and his enemy fell, shot through the heart.

Finn was but a few yards away, and on hearing the shot he rushed to his friend to find him on the ground groaning with agony, and holding his hands to his mouth. The shaft of the arrow stood out between his fingers, and the blood which was gushing down his chin was a terrifying sight.

Laying the wounded man on his back, and drawing his hands aside, Finn saw that the arrow had pierced the tongue and the point had lodged in the jaw-bone.

It was this experience which taught the young man the habit of those arrowheads which had been made of iron. When they struck a bone they almost always bent over and clinched, making it a very painful and difficult task to extract them.

In this instance, the blood loosened the sinew about the shaft, which was withdrawn, leaving the point im-bedded, where it remained until the man could be removed to the medical tents thirteen miles away. Subsequently, Finn was to learn that when an arrow was imbedded in flesh beyond the point, it was dangerous to attempt to withdraw it. The arrowhead was always pushed on through to the nearest place on the surface, care being exercised to pass around the vital spots.

The firing had died down when young Burnett returned from assisting his comrade to the medical officer. Occasional bursts of firing could be heard here and there in the thickets where snipers lurked, but the fighting in the Indian village had ended. The lodges had been riddled by bullets, and the ground was littered with blankets, skins, and pots of every description. Thirty squaws and children shrank back into huddled groups at the stalking approach of watchful troopers, but no Indian warrior was alive. More than sixty braves had been killed.

It was soon apparent that the Pawnee up the valley had disregarded General Connor's orders. They had been told to hold their position there to prevent the escape of any Arapaho, but when the ponies had stampeded in their direction loaded with a rich wealth of furs and robes, the avarice of the Pawnee had triumphed over their training, and they had begun a mad scramble for the spoils, absolutely disregarding the escaping enemy.

That afternoon, the command returned to their camp after burning the village with all its lodges. The women and children were taken along, with the big herd of captured Indian ponies and horses.

Next morning, General Connor assembled the entire command and ordered that the Pawnee scouts be brought before him. His red hair seemed to blaze when they arrived and he began to rail at them for their cu-

pidity of the day before. For more than twenty minutes
he raged at the abashed warriors, then he ordered them
to bring to him all of the loot which they had taken.
One by one they went to their tepees, to return with
arms heaped with robes and choice hides. These they
threw together on the ground until a huge pile had been
collected. At the general's order, fire was set to the pile,
and all was burned to ashes as a punishment for the
Pawnee's disregard for his orders.

The thirty squaws and children were under guard
apart from the soldiers' camp. They were sullen and
defiant, refusing to answer any questions. All sat in their
blankets of buckskin and mountain sheep, there being
not a shred of cloth among them. The Pawnee wanted
to slaughter the lot of them, saying that if they were
spared they would make more Arapaho to fight them in
later years.

Finding that they would not volunteer any information to the interpreters, Antoin and Nick Lajeunesse,
General Connor ordered them to go to the herd where
they could select what ponies they needed, and go their
way to their own people. Evidently the captives had
believed that they were to be killed, for on learning of
this order they immediately began to talk and laugh
with relief, telling all the news of their tribe and of the
attack on the emigrant train.

General Connor then proceeded to the relief of Sawyer's caravan, and found that with the destruction of the
Indian village the attack on the train had ended. An
escort was then provided for the emigrants whose outfit
consisted of forty wagons and 150 persons. They were
moved with safety to Pryor creek, from whence they
were able to cross the Big Horn mountains by way of

Pryor's Gap, and then to continue on into the country of the friendly Crows.

Of the Indian ponies captured, several hundred head were taken along to be used as remounts for the Ohio cavalry whose horses were rapidly becoming useless. The supply of grain had long since been exhausted, and the mounts would not take on weight when grazing on dry prairie grass alone. Many a time, General Connor longed for those sacks of grain which he had been obliged to abandon on the Chugwater.

The expedition now proceeded down the east side of the Tongue river, making short marches each day to enable the stock to graze. Nevertheless, the horses and mules continued to become thinner and weaker each day. Scouts were sent afar on each side of the line of march in an attempt to contact other divisions of the expedition which were supposed to be moving in the vicinity.

These scouts finally located the eastern and central portions. They were in an even worse condition. Most of their horses and mules had been lost, the soldiers had abandoned many of their wagons, had thrown their artillery into a river, and were now making their way, ragged and afoot, to Fort Connor. The general sent word to them to return to Fort Laramie while he continued on.

When the column had reached a point sixty-five miles from the mouth of the Tongue river, Bridger, Major North, and the Pawnee rode in with the news that a large Sioux village containing several hundred lodges was situated on a small tributary ahead. General Connor decided to go into camp for a day, believing the horses would be in better condition for a battle after the rest.

The scouts in the meantime kept close watch on the Sioux village to determine if the Indians had become aware of the presence of the expedition.

After camp had been made, the soldiers busied themselves getting everything in readiness. Night was falling when mounted soldiers were discerned coming down the valley, and General Connor went to meet them. They proved to be two companies of the 6th Michigan regiment, whose commanding officer carried an order from headquarters in Washington which directed General Connor to cease all hostilities immediately, and to return to Fort Laramie without delay.

General Connor was tremendously offended at the news. He stormed and raged at the ill fortune which had caused him to delay an entire day before attacking the Sioux, which period of time had enabled the Michigan soldiers to stop him with the orders. He declared that a decided victory against the hostiles at that time would serve as a far-reaching example to all the Indians on the plains.

His words were prophetic when he roared to his officers that with the men available he could rub out this nest of the fighting Sioux who would otherwise cause endless trouble and destruction later. In view of the fact that it was this same host of Sioux who later accomplished the Fetterman massacre at Fort Phil Kearny, who participated in the Custer disaster, and who laid waste countless wagon-trains and isolated cabins, the termination of General Connor's expedition on that particular day was a plains-wide tragedy.

He swore that he would disregard the orders and attack anyway. It took the combined efforts of his entire staff to dissuade him from this course, but in view of later events and the fact that his enemies in the war department obliterated his name from prominence, and kept his memory from the honor due him, it is regretted that he did not pursue his inclination. He would not have served himself worse, and assuredly future generations would have reverenced his accomplishments the more.

As it was, however, he yielded, and ordered his command to start back on the morrow, September 6th. With this action he placed the responsibility for eleven more years of Indian atrocities and the killing of hundreds of white people squarely upon those swivel-chair officers in Washington who, envious of the man in the field, as ever, accomplished more for the fighting Sioux than did their own chieftains.

Thus, with his return to Fort Laramie, passed from the West one of the finest groups of veteran Indian fighters ever organized to march across the plains. There departed, as well, one of the bravest officers of our military history, beloved by his men, and defeated only by those who had not the attributes to stand beside him.

Fighting Homeward

Fighting Homeward

The journey southward to Fort Laramie was uneventful. When the column reached Fort Connor, Mr. Leighton unloaded all of the supplies and left them with Kemp Caldwell, and took Finn along with him as wagon-boss.

The wagons were emptied except for the two large cases which contained the $40,000 in greenbacks packed in cigar-boxes, and these Mr. Leighton marked with painted letters a foot high, "Silver Fox Skins," to appease any chance curiosity which might be entertained by the soldiers.

On arriving at Horseshoe Station again, Mr. Leighton received bad news. John McCormick had telegraphed from Omaha, "If you want any of that money that your brother Jim has collected, you had better hurry to Omaha." For Jim Leighton, when he had drawn from the pay-master the $15,000 which the soldiers owed, had started out to have a riotous time with the money, drinking and gambling.

Mr. Leighton hurriedly placed Finn in charge of his wagon-train, ordered him to proceed to Leavenworth, and galloped away, leaving a somewhat bewildered young wagon-boss blinking his eyes at his sudden responsibilities.

On Burnett's arrival in Fort Laramie, he found his pay and that of his men awaiting him at the pay-master's office. To his surprise, the wages for Kemp Caldwell and himself had been doubled since the day of the teamsters' strike on the Chugwater.

Then, when Finn made ready to start out on the trail to Fort Leavenworth, he found himself faced with new difficulties. The government again had proved itself to be negligent in providing transportation for the troops of that area. Wounded soldiers had been sent in to Fort Laramie from the outlying posts. Many of them were serious cases of scurvy who needed hospitalization at Fort Leavenworth, but there being no means for transporting them, they had accumulated at Fort Laramie until the post hospital had become filled to overflowing.

Almost all of these patients with scurvy were men from the 11th Ohio who, in their performance of duties of garrisoning and guarding the trail from Julesburg to Burnt Ranch, had contracted the disease through lack of proper food.

The Indians had methodically herded all game away from the Platte valley, in order that the troops could get as little fresh meat as possible. As the frontier army rations consisted solely of bacon, beans, and coffee, the soldiers were obliged to subsist on a poor quality of stale food and soon contracted scurvy. Now they were lying in the Fort Laramie hospital in a terrible condition.

Colonel Baumer, the commanding officer of the fort, was desperate. Hearing of the contemplated departure of the empty wagons of the Leighton train for Fort Leavenworth, he decided to press them into service as a military necessity.

Ninety patients, under the command of Sergeant Stewart, an old veteran Indian fighter of the 11th Ohio, were loaded into Finn's wagons. Spencer rifles were issued to all with ample ammunition in case of attack from Indians on the road. This was a very fortunate move, for if any wagon-train was to need soldiers, guns, and plenty of ammunition, this was the one.

No trouble was experienced on the trail until the train crossed the South Platte river at Julesburg. The days had been those of steady plodding on down the road across the monotonous, rolling prairie with the teamsters blinded and sweating amid the swirling heat waves.

The provisions which had been loaded at Fort Laramie for the soldiers had been found to be ruined. The hard-tack was old, and impossible to masticate, and the bacon was spoiled.

Having nothing else to eat, the travelers were obliged to do their best with what they had. The hard-tack was found to be filled with bugs and worms, and every night sufficient of these hard biscuits for the morrow's breakfasts were placed in buckets which were then filled with water.

In the morning, the inhabitants of the hard-tack would be found floating on top of the water, and would be drained off. The resulting mush would then be fried with the musty bacon, which, when eaten with beans and coffee, composed the entire menu for the caravan.

Each evening after camp had been made, and when the wagons had been drawn up to form a large, circular corral which was protected outside by vigilant guards, and with the stock safely within the limits of the enclosure, everyone played cards.

Many a time old Sergeant Stewart and other soldiers played their games in the wagon with Finn Burnett, using for a table the boxes marked "Silver Fox Skins." Twice after the evenings' entertainments were over, and the lighted candles on the boxes began to flicker at the base of their wicks, the troopers asked Finn to open up the boxes and show them the skins. His excuse that Mr.

Leighton had packed them carefully and had given strict orders not to open them under any consideration served his purpose and averted suspicion from the contents.

Many a night, Finn awoke in his blankets beside the treasure boxes, believing that he heard suspicious noises around the wagon. His fears caused him to believe on many occasions that someone knew of the money with which he was entrusted.

On arriving at Julesburg, it was found that a large emigrant train was due in shortly from the west, and the superintendent of the stage station asked Finn to wait until it arrived. Indian raids had been frequent on the trail east of Julesburg during the last few days. The war-party was of such numbers that it had overwhelmed all opposition. It was decided that the emigrant train should accompany Finn Burnett, to gain the added protection of his scurvy-ridden soldiers.

Proceeding on, then, this double train reached the first stage depot west of Alkali Station. As they pulled in, the very atmosphere of the settlement seemed surcharged with excitement. The division agent for the Overland stage ran out to greet them with the news that the regular stage was being attacked at that very minute by Indians down the road, and that he feared the station also would be overcome.

Finn quickly corralled his outfit and was soon galloping down the road with a number of soldiers and armed freighters, to assist the stage. About a mile beyond them, the coach could be seen down the trail, rolling and bumping in a cloud of dust, with its three teams of racing horses straining toward safety. On the seat above the stage, the driver, with reins tightly looped about his hands, could be seen jerking up and down frantically as he plied his whip to his teams and harangued them for greater speed.

On either flank could be seen Indians darting in and out on their swift ponies in pursuit of the lumbering stage. Arrows were sticking in the woodwork of the vehicle, and a veritable bombardment of thrown lances and tomahawks beat about the ears of the terrified passengers within.

Old Sergeant Stewart, with his wealth of knowledge gained from years of frontier fighting, took command of the relief. He quickly chose a draw which ran across the trail and through which the stage would pass, as a logical place for an ambush. Everyone concealed himself behind the banks and waited. The yells of the driver could now be plainly heard, together with the whoops of the Indians, and the racing feet of horses.

Closer they came, and then the stage lurched down into the draw and across the sand to the bottom. As it appeared to the waiting men, the horses were lathered and mad with fear, the coach wheels were whirling sand high into the air as they churned across the draw, and the driver was leaning far forward as though his earnest spirit was attempting to carry his passengers ahead of his teams.

Immediately behind them came a solid mass of charging, screeching redskins, naked to their waists, spattered with paint, and waving their knives and clubs aloft as they darted after the coach.

"Fire," roared Sergeant Stewart, and at the first crashing volley from the draw, more than half of the band of pursuers seemed to buckle at the waist to go plunging down to the sand beneath the feet of their pitching horses. It was but a second before another volley from the reserve guns bellowed, and few of the Indians remained in their seats.

To every side, the remnant of the band fled like rabbits, howling with fear, to make for the back trail where their main camp evidently was situated.

Sergeant Stewart, Finn, and the others were laughing uproariously as they mounted and jogged back to the station. The driver of the stage had apparently been unaware of his deliverance, for he had whipped his horses all the way in without once looking back.

On arriving at the little cluster of buildings, the soldiers and teamsters stopped beside the coach to note the heaving, wheezing horses, and the passengers who had lived through such a desperate incident. One man only had been wounded. The seats on the inside of the vehicle had been filled, and he had been obliged to sit outside with the driver. He was not seriously hurt, but his coat, as was that of the driver, had been literally filled with spent arrows which hung and flapped from the cloth.

The horses had been such magnificent animals that the Indians had not attempted to harm them, believing that their capture was assured. For, had Finn Burnett's train not arrived with its quota of soldiers, such a large band of Indians would undoubtedly have pursued the stage on into the station and there would have destroyed the settlement, as well.

An hour later, after hearty good wishes had been expressed on all sides, the wagon-train lined up and started on its way. For ten miles it plodded along, noting evidences on all sides of the attack on the stage. Arrows were strewn on the ground as were many broken war-clubs and shattered lances.

Four miles west of Alkali Station, the foremost riders of the train halted as they reached the top of a ridge, to throw up their hands as a signal for all to stop. Finn spurred forward and beheld before him a broad valley, and in the distance could be discerned two wagon-trains which were desperately fighting off the attack of another large group of Indians.

Those two trains, consisting of ten wagons each, had been camping about a half mile apart when the red-skins attacked. Each train had been corralled. The Indians had directed their concentrated efforts on the foremost circle of wagons first, and their onslaughts had been so overwhelming that the defenders had been obliged to leave their corral with all its stock and goods, to fight back to the protection of their comrades in the second group.

As Finn's column came in sight, the redskins were setting fire to the first wagon-train, and a black pillar of smoke was mounting high into the blue sky.

Sergeant Stewart took charge of the situation again. His train proceeded in a double line down across the grassy valley toward the burning wagons, and at the sight of this new promise of easy plunder, a mass of Indians sped forward to do battle. When they arrived, the wagon-train had been corralled, and a withering fire from the soldiers knocked thirty savages from their ponies before they could retreat out of range.

Immediately, the train strung out again, proceeding slowly and surely across the valley. Again the Indians charged, and at their first sign of attack, the train corralled quickly, and met them with another volley which riddled their ranks.

The derisive yells of the savages had now changed to ferocious war-whoops. The easy prey which they had anticipated had become a silent, deadly menace to their hopes for slaughtering the combined emigrants in the valley.

Once more they charged, determined at any cost to halt the steady march of the newcomers, and again they fled with diminished numbers. The soldiers with their Spencer rifles were all crack shots, and the losses among the Indians were terrific.

The prairie across the valley behind the train was now black with the bodies of the redskins, and the prostrate forms of horses lay on every side. A clear swath from the top of the ridge marked the trail of Finn's fighting column of soldiers and emigrants.

Finally, as the Indians had become weaker in numbers and correspondingly lacking in decision, Sergeant Stewart gave the order to charge, and the white men launched themselves straight into the midst of the savages. Without waiting to receive the thrust, the Indians turned and fled, to stop on the surrounding hills to await developments.

Finn's train then moved unmolested to the burning corral and found that nothing could be salvaged. Wagons and goods were ablaze and only the strenuous efforts of a number of teamsters extinguished the flames in the grass, and so ended the menace of a prairie fire.

This burning wagon-train had been loaded with groceries and provisions for the little town of Denver. Much of the stuff had been strewn over the ground. The flour sacks had been ripped open, as was evidenced by numerous cone-shaped hills of flour in the grass, but the empty sacks had been carried away, as Indians considered them to be of great value. Flour at that time was worth fifty dollars a sack, and freight to Denver was thirty cents a pound that year, so the loss of the train had amounted to a very considerable figure.

The combined wagon-trains set to work with the survivors at the corral which remained intact, to entrench against further trouble. Their oxen and cattle had all been driven away by the Indians, and the young boy who had herded them had been captured. There were therefore no draft animals left with which to continue their way, as they had used oxen exclusively in the hauling of their wagons.

Defenses were thrown up around the corral which would enable them to withstand any further Indian attacks. Their teamsters could return to Alkali Station to buy some more draft animals. The train which remained unharmed was found to be loaded with hundred-pound gunny sacks filled with corn which were to be used at the government posts along the trail. These were now piled around the wagons to form a most effective breastworks, and trenches were dug in strategic positions.

The men in Finn's column then decided it would be safe to leave them, so they hitched up and started on toward Alkali Station. They had gone scarcely half a mile when more than five hundred Indians swooped down upon them like a host of hornets.

There was barely time to wheel the wagons into a circle before the savages were upon them. Quickly diving beneath the wheels, the soldiers poured out a murderous fire at the darting, whooping figures beyond until they withdrew momentarily, to renew the attack before the defenders had had an opportunity for a breathing space.

Their onslaughts were so determined and were so nearly successful that it was doubtful at various times whether the train could turn back the tide or not. Finally, Sergeant Stewart gave the command which slowly moved the corral backward toward the safety of the breastworks of the other wagon-train. All heaved a sigh of sincere relief when they joined their late friends.

All morning long the fight continued. The Indians surrounded the combined corrals and breastworks with hundreds of shooting, galloping braves who rode around and around the defenses, lying low on their horses' backs and whooping like fiends. Showers of arrows landed in the enclosure. Several white men were killed.

The accurate fire of the soldiers caused losses which mounted into an impressive figure, but dozens of savages seemed to spring from the earth to take the place of every fallen brave. They appeared to be determined to wipe out the men who already had exterminated such a host of them. The outcome presented dubious possibilities for the white men.

Three miles away down the valley, the buildings of Alkali Station could be plainly seen, and late in the morning when the fighting was becoming hourly more desperate, several of the soldiers volunteered to attempt to ride through the Indians in an effort to reach the station and there obtain relief for the beleaguered corral.

Sergeant Stewart reluctantly gave his consent, and just after noon, seven men saddled their horses and prepared to make their sacrifice. Each realized the desperate chances that he took, and shook hands in farewell with his comrades. A moment later, and they dashed out from between two wagons and spurred away.

It was a hopeless waste of life from the start. Everyone in the enclosure watched their attempt with a prayer for their safety, as they swooped across the grass, lying low on their mounts, and shooting savagely at the Indians who galloped from all sides to intercept them.

One by one, the brave men fell to the ground where they were immediately surrounded by a throng of jeering redskins. After each killing, the savages dashed toward the enclosure led by a chieftain who held aloft in triumph a fresh, bloody scalp for the white men to see.

One messenger escaped, however. Flat along the neck of his thoroughbred mount, the defenders saw him emerge beyond the Indians, to race away toward Alkali Station, followed by a crestfallen, straggling line of redskins who soon gave up the chase. Every white man gave a cheer at the sight, and hope began to lighten every heart.

Perceiving that relief would undoubtedly soon arrive at the request of the lone rider, the Indians stopped fighting and retired to a hill-top out of rifle range, a mile and a half away. Here they began a pow-wow, or conference, and while this was going on, seventeen Pawnee scouts, dressed in army uniforms, broke from a place of concealment on the ridge and galloped to the corral. They had been hiding in the distance awaiting an opportunity to get into the battle, and they stated on their arrival that they knew where the oxen and cattle were, and that they could be recovered if the owners would give their assistance.

The Pawnee were well mounted, but there was scarcely a mule in the entire combined enclosure which was not wounded or completely worn out. It was therefore decided that forty men would accompany the scouts on foot, and the remainder would stay within the breastworks to cover, if it were necessary, the return of those men with heavy firing.

Finn went along, and as the Pawnee and white men left the enclosure, the Sioux herders, who were with the stolen stock in the distance, drove the herd farther north. When the group reached the Overland trail, where the oxen had been, it was discovered that all had disappeared over the hill.

The Pawnee then declared that if the white men would lie along the trough of the trail and wait, they would ride after the herd and drive it back to them. The men in the road would then be in an excellent defensive position if the Pawnee were pursued.

All lay down in the trail, and the Pawnee rode on over the hill and out of sight. Finn lay there looking about him. Overhead, the sun shone hotly down upon the waiting men; behind them stretched the valley with the main group of Indians at their pow-wow on a distant hill. In the middle distance was the enclosure with its breastwork, and its huge circle of canvas-topped wagons, silent and awaiting the outcome of this attempt. To the left, three miles away, were the unpainted garrison buildings of Alkali Station. No firing was going on. It was a calm scene surcharged with deadly possibilities.

Suddenly, over the hill there came the sound of firing and the thunder of galloping animals approaching. Finn shouted an order to the men in the road to divide into two groups to leave a lane through which the stock could stampede. This had scarcely been accomplished when the first of the oxen appeared, followed by the rest of the herd, all of which raced down the lane and on toward the enclosure.

Behind the cattle came the Pawnee scouts, but they were being sorely beset, and were fighting a hand-to-hand battle with an overwhelming number of Sioux. So mixed up were they with their enemies that none of the men in the road dared to fire, fearing to hit a Pawnee. All came clashing down the hill in a ferocious, hacking, rough-and-tumble fight, to ride through the line of waiting men.

There followed a terrible mix-up. The Pawnee sprang from their saddles, and dropped beside their white friends to assist in pouring a withering volley from the ground into their enemies. The fight was ended in a minute. All of the Sioux were killed, or fled back to the hills.

Then came another commotion from up the hill. All turned to see a little, black mule with a Sioux warrior on his back pulling and tugging at the reins frantically in an effort to stop. The redskin had tied himself to his mount in the Indian fashion, with a rawhide thong over each shoulder and around the mule's belly. The animal was inconsiderate of the warrior's anxiety and refused to turn, running and jumping straight at the waiting whites until he nearly ran over Finn, himself. The young man rolled over on his back, aimed his gun at the Sioux, and fired as he went by.

At this, the obstinate mule wheeled, and ran straight along the line of white men, each of whom emptied his gun at the Indian as he passed. Finally, the Sioux sank forward with his arms dragging, and the mule fell dead on top of him. There was scarcely a spot on either mule or Indian which did not show a bullet hole.

The emigrants in the enclosure were now jubilant. With the recovery of their oxen they began to believe that they had not come out second best in the battle in view of the tremendous slaughter to which the Indians had been subjected.

One man stood guard, however, with a field-glass, watching the pow-wow on the hill, ready to give warning if the Indians showed signs of continuing the attack again. At the sound of an exclamation of horror from him all ran to his side. He explained that the Sioux had brought forward the boy who had herded the stock, and while two of the savages were holding him erect with his arms outstretched, another was cutting him with a knife from his shoulders to his heels. They were literally cutting him to ribbons.

The boy was a seventeen-year-old lad with light, curly hair, and had been a general favorite in his wagon-train. Hearing of his torture, everyone took his gun and started out toward the pow-wow, creeping along a dry protecting gulch that led toward the hill.

Arriving within range, all fired a volley into the cluster of braves, and several of them were seen to fall before the rest mounted and fled. Finn accompanied several men up the hill, and the boy was found to be dead and terribly mutilated.

Sergeant Stewart ordered that the body be carried back to the enclosure. Throughout the fighting this old veteran had been the mainstay of the defenders. With his bravery, coolness under fire, and level-headed decisions in every emergency, he had undoubtedly been the greatest factor in saving the lives of all in that great corral. During the attack which had as its object the rescue of the boy, the old soldier had calmly looked over the ground, ordered the men to adjust their sights at the proper ranges, and had directed the fire so accurately that another large number of Sioux had been added to the killed.

The body of the boy was brought to the corral, and there he was buried. The earth above his grave was carefully leveled and a campfire was burned above it to obliterate all traces, lest the Indians dig up the body later. Then a long trench was dug, and the seventeen others who had been killed during the day were also buried.

On the following morning, about nine o'clock, two companies of cavalry from Alkali Station rode in to relieve the beleaguered band, and Finn left them at the breastworks when he proceeded on eastward with his train.

Orders had been given by Mr. Leighton that Finn was to purchase what provisions he needed when he reached Dobe Town from William Thomas and Mr. Michell, who kept a general outfitting store at that place for freighters and emigrants.

The train arrived in Dobe Town without further trouble, and Finn went immediately to the store.

"I want to speak to Mr. Thomas," he stated to a big, black-haired man behind the counter.

"I'm Thomas. What do you want?" was the reply.

"I'd like you to provide feed for our teams and lodging for my men for the night," Finn answered.

"What outfit is yours?" asked Thomas.

"A. C. Leighton's," returned the young man.

Thomas started, and leaned forward excitedly across the counter.

"Why, that's impossible," he exclaimed. "Leighton's train was captured by Indians three miles west of Alkali Station. All the wagons were burned and the men killed."

"Just the same, I'm Finn Burnett, Mr. Leighton's wagon-boss, and that's his train standing out there in the road," answered Finn.

Thomas leaped the counter, and ran from his store to telegraph the good news to Mr. Leighton, who was in Omaha in the depths of despair, believing that his outfit had been destroyed, together with his $40,000 in greenbacks.

Later in the day came his excited telegram to Thomas, ordering him to hold the train there until he could reach Dobe Town by stage.

"Give them everything they want," he wired; and then, as an afterthought, "are the boxes of fox skins safe?"

After the mules had been led away and fed that night, Thomas sat with Finn beside the stove in his store.

"Well, young man," the storekeeper said, "I guess you had better turn over those boxes to me that Leighton marked 'Silver Fox Skins,' hadn't you?"

"No," smiled Finn. "When my boss gets here he can turn them over to you, if he wants to."

Mr. Leighton arrived in Dobe Town a few days later, and after a joyful reunion he accompanied his train to Leavenworth. On the trail they encountered frequent evidences of Indian depredations, especially on the Little Blue river east of old Fort Kearny. Evidently a large war-party had been through the country recently, because all buildings had been burned, and the fences torn down, and crops trampled and ruined. The corn had just ripened before it had been destroyed.

From that point on, it was a beautiful country that they drove through. Settlers had begun to take up holdings, and neat little farms were beginning to dot the eastern prairies.

Then, about forty miles west of Marysville, Kansas, they were overtaken by a prairie fire. The country was level, with grass growing fully knee high. The road was a hundred yards wide, as wagon-trains traveled in two lines through hostile country to enable them to corral quickly in the event of Indian attacks. There were three streams nearby, the Blue, the Walnut, and the Vermillion, all of them being little creeks bordered by a narrow belt of timber in which the wild turkeys roosted when they came in from the prairies at night.

Seeing the fire on the horizon, with flames spitting up into swirling, black and white billows of smoke, the wagons were lined in the middle of the road, the mules were unhitched and tied securely to the wheels, and the men quickly set about to blaze a backfire on either side of the road for a distance of a hundred yards.

The wind was blowing from the west, driving the flames and smoke before it faster than a horse could run. In some instances, tufts of burning grass flew ahead on the breeze, jumping a hundred yards at a time, and igniting a new blaze at each place of landing. The heat was blistering, and the dense smoke which rolled in great surges ahead of the fire almost strangled everything in its path.

The road was soon filled with game which sought refuge from the fire, coming in from the great spaces around which had provided such luxuriant feeding grounds. Antelope, deer, wild turkeys, wolves, coyotes, everything that lived above ground in the vicinity, raced to this sanctuary, and mingled in temporary armistice until the common menace had passed. Prairie chickens and grouse, having flown as far as their strength could carry them, lit on the road in swarms, to run to the shade of the wagons and crouch there trembling with fear.

For fifteen or twenty minutes it was a fiery inferno all around the train, and then, almost as suddenly as it had come, the smoke and heat cleared, and the travelers were safe again.

The men hitched up and drove on, finding that they were to have no more trouble on their way in to Leavenworth. After leaving the soldiers there, the Leighton train turned up the Missouri river, ferried the Platte, took the stock and wagons across at Plattsmouth near Omaha, and rented a pasture for the animals from a man who fed stock during the winter months with hay and corn.

Finn helped this man erect a temporary shed with poles which they cut along the edge of the farm, and then he returned with Mr. Leighton to Omaha.

The morning after their arrival, Finn received his salary in full to date, and Mr. Leighton asked him to take a walk downtown with him. They went into Henry Elling's Clothing Store, and there Leighton told Elling to fit Finn out with the best suit of clothes in the place, together with hat, boots, and two suits of underwear. He made Finn a present of the outfit.

The young man then informed his boss that he had had enough of the West, and that he was going home. Mr. Leighton tried to dissuade him, telling him that he would not be satisfied to settle down on a farm after the experiences which he had already gone through. But Finn was determined. He stated that he never wanted to cross the Missouri river again, and finally Mr. Leighton let him go, stating, however, that the job of wagon-boss was waiting for him when he returned.

Finn took the coach from Council Bluffs to Des Moines, Iowa, and from there to Keokuk. When he arrived in his home town, everyone believed him to be dead. A cousin of his mother's had read the dispatch which told of the destruction of Mr. Leighton's train.

Finn was walking up the street dressed in a soldier's overcoat, blue with a cape on it, when he saw his father strolling with his Uncle George, and coming toward him. The young man pulled the cape up around his face and started to pass them, when the father wheeled around and threw his arms about his son.

The Burnett homestead was sixteen miles out in the country, and in a few minutes the three of them were whipping horses joyfully toward home, and planning how best to surprise Finn's mother. They walked into the house unconcernedly, while Finn kept his face hidden. Mr. Burnett and Finn's Uncle George kept up a chatter, standing in front of the mother, but suddenly she gasped, and looked past them.

With a little, choking noise, she pushed the men aside and stumbled dazedly to Finn, and without a word gathered him close to the dearest breast in all the world.

Red Massacre

Red Massacre

The first few weeks proved to be a delightful rest for Finn. Many a day he spent in tramping the fields and woods with his gun, meeting old comrades on the neighboring farms, and exploring again the old haunts where he played at Indian fighting as a boy.

In the evenings he sat in the Burnett family circle listening to the tales of his Uncle George of far-off lands and of the vast, unconquered valleys of Oregon. Then, sometimes they called on Finn to add the story of his experiences and listened proudly as he thrilled their ears.

But restlessness set in. There was a sameness to the farming life, a calm, plodding security that guaranteed an ultimate reward which required neither courage nor excitement.

The winter passed, and in the spring of 1866, true to the predictions of Mr. Leighton, Finn's eyes turned longingly toward the west again. He dreamed of the wagon-train at Omaha starting out without him, of Kemp Caldwell, of the rugged beauty of the mountains, and of the subtle fragrance of the sage.

Finally, unable to restrain his restlessness, Finn Burnett packed and bade his family good-bye. Forty years were to pass before he returned to Missouri again; forty years of Indian experiences, of railroad building, and of gold mining on the frontier.

True to his word, Mr. Leighton was waiting for Finn

with the job of wagon-boss still open, and within a week
from the day of his arrival the young man was on the
road again, bound for the Platte valley.

The Union Pacific railroad tracks had by this time
stretched westward to Columbus, Nebraska. There was
great activity all along the trail between Omaha and
Columbus. Hundreds of wagons, bunched in trains and
piled high with provisions and lumber, moved westward, while others, empty, flowed' back to Omaha to
reload.

There were fourteen wagons in the Leighton train
that spring, and after crossing the South Platte at Fort
Kearny, they joined the Wells Fargo mule-train of forty
wagons which were loaded with government supplies
for Fort Laramie, Fort Connor, and two new posts
which were then being established, named Fort Phil
Kearny and Fort C. F. Smith.

Fort Connor, as has been stated, had been erected by
General Connor during the previous year, and was situated 169 miles northwest of Fort Laramie on the Bozeman trail, the "cut-off" route to the gold fields of Montana. This post was to be moved during this year to a
point forty miles west of its present position, there to be
rebuilt into a four-company garrison by the second battalion of the 18th United States Infantry under Colonel
Henry B. Carrington. Furthermore, its name was to be
changed to Fort Reno, another effort of the war department to eliminate the name of General Connor from
honor, the reason being publicly given that no fort could
be named for a living officer. This post garrisoned 260
men, including the clerks and band, and was the first
fort to be reached on the trail from Fort Laramie to
Montana.

Because the fact is of interest in later events, it should

be noted at this point that Fort Reno had one vulnerable point. Powder river ran close to the buildings on the east side, and the thick cottonwood timber grew from the banks of the stream to a spot so close to the post that barely enough room remained for a man to ride horseback between the trees and the edge of the enclosure. Below the post, the valley widened out into a beautiful timbered basin.

This new Fort Reno became an open post, except that the warehouses and stables had a rough stockade. Officers' and men's quarters, guardhouse and magazine, were built on a flat tableland, 140 feet above Powder river. Drinking water had to be hauled in wagons.

From Fort Reno, the Bozeman trail continued slightly west of north for about 150 miles to where Fort Phil Kearny was situated at the forks of Piney creek, and at an altitude of 6000 feet above sea level. In those days the Big Piney creek was a rather large stream.

Fort Phil Kearny was erected in July, 1866, by Colonel Carrington from specifications which had been drawn up by army officers earlier in the spring at Fort Kearny. Its location was a beautiful one, being close to the foothills of the Big Horn mountains, and set so prominently that the eye could travel for miles in almost every direction to discern huge, rocky cliffs, timbered with thick pines and cedars. Below the fort, along the river bottoms, the thickets were dense, and it was there that many soldiers were to lose their lives while escorting wood-trains to and from the fort.

Several hundred feet above this post on a nearby ridge were discovered the remains of an old Indian fort which was thirty feet square and built of stones. This aged and forgotten spot was known as Fort Ridge by the soldiers of the frontier, and though its defenses were remodeled by building a stockade of logs around it, there is no record of its use at any time.

Fort C. F. Smith was another post, situated 91 miles northwest of Fort Phil Kearny and close to the Big Horn river at the spot where the Bozeman trail turned due west to enter Pryor's Gap, from whence it proceeded on past Clarke's fork to the Yellowstone river.

This post was built in August on a tableland or bench, about 150 yards east of the Big Horn river and a little more than two miles north of the Big Horn canyon.

The fort was about 200 feet square, with solid buildings forming most of the stockade, having no doors or windows on the outside. The south and west ends were composed of soldiers' quarters exclusively, while in the center of the stockade, running east and west, and leaving only sufficient room for wagons to pass between the buildings, were the quartermaster's storehouses and commissary.

The north wall was built of adobe and boulders, and contained the only entrance to the enclosure. West of this gate was the adjutant's quarters, and the sutler's store was erected outside, about 100 feet north of the wall and slightly west of the gate.

It has been said that from the spring of 1866 to 1868 there were more Indian fights around these three isolated little forts on the Bozeman trail than there were days in each year. Seldom did twenty-four hours pass but one or two or all of them were obliged to repel attacks on their wood-trains.

These forts were reached, one by one, by Leighton's train. At each post was one of Mr. Leighton's sutler's stores, and at every one was unloaded a large stock of canteen goods to be sold to the soldiers.

Fort Reno was in the process of construction when the

train reached that point, and Finn put his men to work for a month there hauling logs for the buildings. The young wagon-boss herded the mules. He grazed the animals close to the fort, fearing Indian raids, never letting them roam beyond a deep, dry wash on the west side of the river. Daily he watched that gulch, riding up and down its lip, lest the Sioux sneak down along the high banks and take him unawares.

Yet, one day, an Indian surprised him, and slipped from behind a bank to race toward the mules. The Sioux had but one pistol while the wagon-boss had two, with the result that after each had emptied his gun at the other, Finn still had a shot in reserve, and the redskin lay dead in the sage when the young man ran the herd back to the safety of the post.

When all the garrisons had been supplied, Finn Burnett found considerable spare time on his hands. He moved from fort to fort as it was necessary to transfer stores, but frequently he was able to hire out the train to post quartermasters for army work, and so reaped profits from his idle time.

His first government trip was from Fort Phil Kearny to Fort Laramie. A wagon loaded only with grain was requisitioned, so Finn took but one four-mule team and a wagon for the haul, leaving the remainder of the wagons at Fort Phil Kearny, and putting the mules under the supervision of a herder named John Dale. Mr. Leighton was going east at the time, and accompanied Finn on the trip down to Fort Laramie.

The day after Finn left, John Dale took his mule herd out to graze close to Fort Phil Kearny, and they had scarcely begun to feed when Indians swooped down out of the hills and ran off forty-two of them. Dale barely escaped with his life.

As the mules were worth $500 a span, and as they were then in the government service, Mr. Leighton put in a bill for them that summer to the war department. It was twenty-four years later, in 1890, when he received his check from the government for their loss.

When Finn returned from Fort Laramie to Fort Phil Kearny, he found a job waiting for him with General George P. Dandy, the quartermaster. The government cattle at the fort were losing weight, and Finn was ordered to fatten and slaughter them. The forage around the post was becoming scarce, and the killing of the beef had been decided as a military necessity. There was a small, cast-iron mill at the fort in which he crushed the coarse meal for their feeding, and when they had taken on sufficient weight he slaughtered and dressed them.

Indians attacked the soldiers daily. Wood-trains going to the timber in the valley for logs were set upon repeatedly. Emigrant and supply-trains on the Bozeman trail were continually harassed and ambushed. Mail-men and dispatch-riders whose duties demanded that they cross the country singly in the performance of their duties, frequently dropped from sight and were never heard from again.

"Mich" Pourier, a half-breed Sioux, carried the mail once a month between Fort C. F. Smith and Fort Laramie. Before each trip, he was always given his choice of any government horse in the post to carry him through his dangerous undertaking, and frequently he killed two horses on the round trip.

Pourier never failed to get through with the mail. Indians always chased him, and on many occasions he was obliged to kill his horse and make his way afoot. He had orders never to leave a horse alive for the Sioux to use. When hard pressed he frequently shot his tired mount and retreated into the thickets of the hills, to hide there until he could slip through the night to the safety of the forts. Always, he arrived with a grin and the words, "Well, they can't seem to get old Mich."

Finally, on December 21, 1866, the massacre of Captain and brevet Lieutenant-colonel William J. Fetterman and eighty-five men near Fort Phil Kearny climaxed the year of fighting.

The morning dawned chill and full of promise for a stern blizzard. The hills surrounding the fort were cold and dismal with their mantles of snow. The landscape itself, as though intent on becoming a fit scene for a stupendous tragedy, was harsh and forbidding.

The wood-train started out from the fort as usual after the morning inspection. Logs for firewood and additional buildings were brought to the post every day, providing work for the garrison which eliminated leisure time with its attendant worries.

On this morning, the train, deep in the timber, was suddenly attacked from all sides by the Sioux. The detail corralled at the first sign of ambush, and the escort of troopers poured an annihilating fire upon the Indians.

The sentinel at the fort saw the plight of the wood-train and gave the alarm. Colonel Carrington, the post commander, immediately had the entire personnel of the garrison assembled, and ordered brevet Lieutenant-colonel Fetterman to take a strong force to the relief of the ambushed men.

A few minutes later, the gates of the stockade were opened and Colonel Fetterman galloped through with his detail. As he passed, Colonel Carrington called to him, repeating the orders which had been given to him previously, not on any condition to go beyond the ridge.

After the relief had gone, the post commander discovered that in the hurry of departure no medical man had been assigned to Fetterman's command, so he ordered Dr. Harris to follow them. He started out, but returned a few minutes later to report that the wood-train was out of danger, but that Colonel Fetterman had gone on beyond the place of ambush and such a force of Indians were hidden in the thickets that he could not get through alone to join the relief.

Colonel Fetterman was, unfortunately, another officer who believed that a handful of white troopers could successfully engage with an overwhelming number of Indians warriors. At this time, being somewhat disgruntled with Colonel Carrington over a previous trouble, and desiring to deal the Sioux a lasting punishment, he had disregarded his orders and had charged with his men over the ridge to oblivion.

Chief Red Cloud had hoped that the command would pursue, and had left his main body of braves hidden behind the crest of the ridge, allowing a few warriors to attack the wagon-train and then to lure the relief detachment to pursuit and disaster. This was the usual Indian mode of warfare, and had Colonel Fetterman been more experienced he would have perceived it.

Immediately, as the relief charged over the ridge, the Sioux fell upon them like an avalanche of fighting fiends who tore and hacked and shot down the troopers from every side. Dismounting, and gaining every cover which could be found, the soldiers fought back, successfully withstanding the attacks for half an hour.

Then the supply of ammunition began to run low, and panic broke out when this fact became known. As one man, the detail finally rose from its place and started a somewhat frenzied retreat to the top of the ridge, and, as was always the case in such instances, at the first sign of withdrawal, the Sioux redoubled their attack.

Two experienced fighters, James S. Wheatley, who was a quartermaster clerk, and a man named Isaac Fisher, had joined the party when it left the fort. Wheatley had just received a new Henry rifle, and now, as the soldiers fled, he together with Fisher and the bugler, Metzker, proceeded to write their names on the rolls of those entitled to undying fame. Remaining in their places, and tearing holes in the ranks of the Sioux who sought to pass them, they repelled again and again the frenzied efforts of the redskins to dislodge them, and attempted with every ounce of heroism that they possessed to stem the tide and so permit their comrades to reach a place of safety.

But the Indians were not to be denied. The soldiers were in a perfect trap and beyond all help. The 1500 Sioux hurled themselves first upon the valiant three within their path and then upon the defenseless troopers, flashing their red knives and tomahawks, shrieking in triumph as they pulled down the bloody, desperate men who feebly fought them off with empty guns.

It was all over in a few minutes. The last soldier was cut down, and Colonel Fetterman with Captain Frederick H. Brown had committed suicide together. All that was left was a scene of brutal scalping, bloody mutilation, and frenzied trampling of the bodies into the dust.

Only the dead body of the bugler, Metzker, was left untouched. His heroism had aroused the admiration of even those blood-crazed savages, for they covered his corpse with a buffalo robe as a symbol of extreme respect. There were those who recalled at the time the fact that some years earlier, when Red Cloud was a wandering and unknown buck, he had gotten into trouble with white men, and had been championed by this same bugler, Metzker. Some were of the opinion that, by covering the dead body with a robe, Red Cloud was proclaiming his regret at the death of his friend.

Meanwhile, in the fort, everyone was waiting for news with fearful expectancy. The firing could be heard plainly beyond the ridge, and, as it grew in intensity, Colonel Carrington ordered Captain Tenedore Ten Eyck with 76 men and two wagons full of ammunition to hurry to Colonel Fetterman's relief.

As Captain Ten Eyck proceeded with his command toward the ridge, the sound of firing lessened, and when he reached the summit at 12:45 p.m., the fight was over.

Looking down the far side, he beheld the valley literally filled with dancing, gleeful Indians who beckoned to him to come down to them, and who greeted the appearance of his soldiers with loud whoops of derision. Hundreds of them were grouped about the spot where later were found the bodies of Fetterman's command.

Finn, in the fort, watched Captain Ten Eyck's soldiers, and saw the orderly, Sample, leave them to gallop down from the ridge. On his arrival, he informed the horror-stricken garrison that nothing could be seen of Fetterman and his men; that the valley was swarming with Indians who were challenging Captain Ten Eyck's command to come down, and that it appeared that all who had previously gone over the ridge had been massacred.

A sudden, dumb silence met his words. Isolated far from help, in the dead of winter, the loss of such a number of defenders meant dread possibilities for all the garrison. Every face went white, every movement halted, and then a woman choked and groped her way, to cling to another who was bereaved. Everywhere was sobbing and gasping and dull despair.

Darkness had fallen when Captain Ten Eyck returned, his soldiers bringing with them forty-nine bodies in the ammunition wagons, and verifying the worst of fears.

Next morning, Finn set out with his wagons to recover the remainder of the bodies from beyond the ridge. Everyone worked in grim silence on that day. Scarcely a word was spoken, so tragic was the grief on every side. The women of the garrison were overcome with sorrow, and the men found themselves confronted with the extreme possibility of complete massacre for the entire crippled post.

It was a terrible work to load the frozen corpses into the wagons. The ground was fairly sodden with blood, the smell of which frightened the mules until they were well-nigh unmanageable. A man was obliged to hold the head of every animal while other teamsters loaded the naked, mutilated remains like cordwood into the wagon-boxes.

When the first wagon had been half loaded, the mules began to lurch and kick, until they succeeded in throwing the men aside. Turning the wagon around, they overturned it in their frenzy, and the bodies were dumped out before the animals could be recaptured and subdued. It was a terrible sight and a horrible job. Finally, all the dead were removed to the fort, and there they were dressed in new uniforms and placed in boxes for burial.

Wheatley and Brown had been members of a party of emigrants who were waiting at the fort to join a stronger wagon-train before proceeding to Montana through the Indian-infested country. Both of them had been captains in the volunteer service during the Civil war, and had come west in an effort to gain commissions in the army on the frontier. Brown had applied for his, and it had been granted. In fact, it was on the way when he was massacred, and was brought to the post by the first relief detachment which was sent from Fort Laramie. Camp Brown, which was established later on the Popo Agie river where the city of Lander was to grow, was named in his honor.

Wheatley was married and his nineteen-year-old wife had accompanied him to the West. She was a beautiful girl, and a fine woman, and she remained at the fort until the following spring, when Webb Wood arrived with her brother, John Morrison. They left for their home in Ohio with the first wagon-train that started for the South, and the garrison at Fort Phil Kearny always remembered her as a brave, splendid little soldier.

Red Cloud in later years admitted that the Sioux lost 180 warriors who were killed in that fateful day of the massacre, as well as an almost unbelievable number of wounded, many of whom died later of their wounds. And, while this battle was terrible in its brutality and needlessness, yet the Sioux loss had been so great that plans for the total destruction of Forts Phil Kearny, Reno, and C. F. Smith were halted by Chief Red Cloud for the time being.

Colonel Carrington, immediately after the massacre, felt the imperative need for help, and requested volunteers to come forward for the task of taking word to Fort Laramie of the sorry situation at Fort Phil Kearny.

None would risk the desperate venture. A ride through more than 190 miles of drifted, bleak country in zero weather, surrounded on every side by savage

JOHN PHILLIPS'S RIDE
From a contemporary sketch.

Sioux, was in the opinion of everyone little less than suicide.

Finally, a man named "Portuguese" Phillips, a black-haired little plainsman who had come to this country from the Azore Islands, and who was thoroughly familiar with the country and with Indian fighting, came forward. Of all the men in the garrison, he knew the risks far better, which fact made his courage the more pronounced. He asked for the best horse in the post, and was given Colonel Carrington's own blooded thorough-bred, the pet that was closest to the officer's heart.

Then, with some crackers for himself, and a quarter of a sack of grain for the horse, Phillips set out through a blizzard on his terrible journey. The sentry at the gate of the fort watched him as he rode away, expecting at any moment to hear the cracking of guns, but he slowly went ahead until the swirling snow-blasts hid him from sight.

The vicissitudes of his heroic journey have never been recorded. Buffeted by icy winds, turned aside by piled snowdrifts, chased for miles by vengeful Indians, he forged onward hour after hour, a lonely, mighty little man against the combined ferocity of nature and of foe.

It was Christmas eve in old Fort Laramie when he arrived. The season was being celebrated, and a great dance was being held in "Old Bedlam," the barn-like entertainment building of the post. Outside, the blizzard roared down from the west, obscuring everything.

A hunched figure on a swaying, stumbling horse rode across the parade ground, pushed forward seemingly by the driven snow. Before half of the open space had been traversed, the horse faltered and then, with a groan, sank dead upon the snow. The man shook himself loose, and plodded onward toward the lighted windows from behind which the strains of "Oh, Suzanna" came fitfully to his ears. His legs were bound with sacks, and a great coat of buffalo skin was tied closely about him.

He stumbled upon the porch, lurched against the door, burst it in, and stood there swaying as the music stopped, and quick, understanding hands were all around him.

So came the message to Fort Laramie of the massacre at Fort Phil Kearny. Fainting, he managed to control his lips until he had made his report, and then he passed into a coma from his exposure and fatigue.

The message which he had carried was found in a pouch which was belted about him. It had been written by Colonel Carrington, and read as follows:

I have had today a fight unexampled in Indian warfare. My loss is ninety-four killed. I have recovered forty-nine bodies. Among the killed are brevet Lieutenant-colonel Fetterman, Captain F. H. Brown, and Lieutenant Grummond. The Indians engaged were nearly three thousand. I have every teamster on duty, and at best 119 men left at the post. Give me two companies of cavalry or four companies of infantry. Promptness is the vital thing. The Indians are desperate, and they spare none.

The scene of action told its own story. The road on the little ridge where the final stand took place was strewn with arrows, arrow-heads and scalp-poles. The battlefield shows that the command was suddenly overwhelmed, surrounded, and cut off. Not an officer or man survived. Nearly all the bodies were heaped near four rocks, inclosing a space about six feet square, this having been the last refuge for defense.

Fetterman and Brown had each a pistol shot in the left temple. I am convinced that they fell by each other's hand rather than undergo the slow torture inflicted upon others.

The mutilations were terrible; some of them were as follows: eyes torn out and laid on the rocks, ears cut off, entrails taken out and exposed, hands cut off, eyes, ears, mouth, and arms penetrated with spearheads, sticks and arrows; punctures on every sensitive part of the body, even to the soles of the feet and the palms of the hands. In the body of one of the civilians were 105 arrows. In the opinion of our post surgeon, a large number of the men were wounded and slowly tortured to death by mutilation. . .

For this remarkable act of heroism, John Phillips was not rewarded by the general government until many years later. Then, in 1872, marauding Indians destroyed Phillips's wagon-train near Fort Fetterman, and although he was given a judgment in the court of claims for $2,210, on account of this loss, the amount was never paid because of a technical error in the proceedings.

Finally, a bill introduced in the senate by Senator Francis E. Warren, secured an appropriation of $5,000 for his widow, Hattie A. Phillips, as a "compensation for services rendered."

Back at Fort Phil Kearny, no one believed Phillips had lived to traverse ten miles of his ride. Daily, the Sioux kept up their raids to the very gates of the fort. Huge snowdrifts heaped outside, and eventually entirely covered the stockade, providing ready means for an attacking horde to enter the post had they dared or had sufficient numbers.

The garrison gave up all hope for relief before the following spring. All were put on half-rations. Seldom did anyone have fresh meat. Every man, woman, and child lived on bacon, hard-tack, and a half portion of flour each day.

The mules were supplied with an abundance of corn, however, and Finn remembered his boyhood days in Missouri, and the method with which the negro women had prepared lye hominy. So, Finn stole some of the mules' corn and burned some ashes with which to make lye.

This was made strong, then the corn was soaked in it

until the hulls became loosened and could be removed after a slight rubbing between the hands. The husked corn was then soaked with six changes of fresh water to remove all traces of the lye, after which it was fried in bacon grease.

Finn soon had made a great reputation in the post for his lye hominy, and others learned the trick, so that many in the garrison that winter lived well by stealing the mules' corn.

Skirmishes on the Trail

Skirmishes on the Trail

When spring came in 1867, Finn Burnett took his wagon-train to Omaha to load with sutlers' supplies for the forts. By that time, the Union Pacific railroad was running a regular freight service as far west as North Platte, and Mr. Leighton decided to speed up the return trip by using this new means of transportation.

The wagons were, therefore, loaded with their supplies in Omaha, and were run up onto cars where they were blocked and tied securely. The mules were herded into stock-cars.

When they unloaded at North Platte, Mr. Leighton left the outfit to rest while he took Finn and set out on horse-back to visit Jack Morrow's ranch on the south side of the South Platte river. This ranch had been a famous trading point during the days when the trail was clogged with emigrants, but now the new railroad was providing quicker transportation and his business had dwindled to nothing. He had made a fortune, however, in past years, and was ready to move on.

During the second day of their visit, Jack Morrow was sitting with Mr. Leighton and Finn on the porch of his ranch-house. Suddenly, he turned to the young man.

"How do you like this lay-out?" he asked, sweeping his arm around at the house and barns.

"Fine," returned Burnett. "It's as pretty a place as I've seen out here."

"Well, if you want it, you can have it for a gift," was

the startling reply. "I'm quitting business here. I'm moving to a place on Bitter creek, and this ranch might as well go to someone who will look after it."

Mr. Leighton began to joke Morrow about the offer, however, pointing out that there was no water available for the grass, that there were no meadows or fields, and that Finn had no money with which to stock the ranch.

At first thought, Finn had been pleased with the idea of owning such a large outfit, but finally Mr. Leighton's amused but practical suggestions relative to expense and Indian depredations convinced the young man that the job of wagon-boss offered more tangible profits.

Returning to North Platte, Mr. Leighton found Webb Wood with his fourteen teams returning eastward empty. The sutler thereupon decided to hire Wood's train, and loaded him with several carloads of supplies which he had had shipped to that point for future haulings.

The combined trains started for the forts, and on the third night out encountered their first Indian trouble.

Wood had a young negro whom he had employed to herd his stock. On this particular evening, as camp was being made, the herder started with two pails for the spring which was about a hundred yards from the wagons.

There were fifteen Indians lying in the thicket around the spring waiting for someone to come for water, and when he approached they fired on him. They evidently saw that he was not a white man, so they tried to scare him to death.

Over and around him they shot, laughing and yelling behind him as he dropped his pails to run into camp with his eyes bulging with fright and his mouth hanging open.

Later that evening, the negro was still shaking with fright, and vowing that he would go no farther into such a terrible country. All efforts to dissuade him were useless, and next morning when the east-bound stage came by, Wood paid him off and let him climb aboard. Wood, as a result, offered Finn double wages to herd the stock in the negro's place, and the young man accepted.

Five miles east of Julesburg, the train crossed the Platte, and corralled for the night. Finn took the mules out to graze south of the road on the side of a ridge.

Suddenly, in the darkness, all of the animals stampeded down the hill, for no discernable reason. Finn followed them, and heard them stamping and grazing a short distance down the road and close to the old Overland telegraph line. He began to scout around carefully, leading his little Spanish saddle mule, in an effort to see if it had been Indians who had frightened the herd, and if any skulkers still lay in the grass.

It was a quiet, starlit night, and he could see the telegraph poles plainly where they reached upward into the air. As he came to one point where a pole was lined against the white wagon-tops of the corral, he saw the huddled shape of an Indian by the foot of a post.

Finn crawled stealthily forward with his gun in front of him until he could see the movement of what he thought was the Indian's blanket. Although it was too dark to see the sights, he "got a bead" on the mule-thief and fired. A tremendous thrashing in the grass showed that his aim had resulted in execution, and Finn ran forward only to find that he had killed by mistake the best mule in the herd.

The men in the corral had been aroused at the sound of the shot, and soon a number of them approached, calling to Finn and asking what was the trouble.

Wood was with them when they arrived, and on learning that the young herder had killed a mule instead of an Indian there was great hilarity on all sides. There had never been a redskin in the vicinity that night, and the mule had been shot cleanly through the head. The men went to the position from which Finn had fired, discerned the clump of brush by the telegraph pole which the young man had thought was an Indian, and then pointed to the dead mule which lay twenty feet out of line to one side, exclaiming at his peculiar marksmanship, and at how safe an Indian would have been that night.

Wood laughed at the entire proceeding, and remarked, "Well, Finn, your double wages won't amount to much by the time you have that mule paid for."

They proceeded on their way next morning, and at Fort Laramie, "Portuguese" Phillips joined the train with an ambulance loaded with mail for the forts, escorted by a detail of soldiers commanded by Captain David Gordon. When they camped on Horseshoe creek, west of Fort Laramie, Indians attacked the train in an effort to drive off the mules, but after a lively skirmish which lasted for more than an hour, the Sioux withdrew and the stock was safe.

Next morning, the train started on, and after having traveled for five miles it was discovered that Phillips had returned to the camp. Subsequent inquiry revealed that one of the government mules belonging to his outfit had been sick during the night and the soldiers had abandoned it that morning. As it was against all the unwritten laws of the frontier to let a horse or mule fall into the hands of the Sioux, Phillips had evidently gone back to recover the animal.

The Indians had hidden themselves in the brush

around the place where the soldiers had camped, and Phillips rode unknowingly into the midst of them. When he started to drive the mule out ahead of him, however, the redskins charged on him from all sides. Several tried to pull him from his saddle with lariats, but he had a fine, brown horse, and putting spurs to the mount he dashed away from his enemies and returned to the train unharmed.

Phillips was employed by the government from the time of the Fetterman massacre to carry mail from Fort Phil Kearny to Fort Laramie. Many such mailmen were being killed at that work, for never more than a dozen soldiers were ever detailed at any one time to escort the mail through the country which was more overrun with countless bands of fighting warriors than was any other portion of the West.

Crossing the Platte at Bridger's crossing, the train continued up the river on the north bank, for a day's drive. There, the soldiers who had been scouting in advance, came back with the report that an ox-train was being attacked by Indians a few miles ahead of their column.

Wood corralled the trains while Finn and his teamsters accompanied the soldiers to look over the ground. There was a large area of open, grassy land at that point, with high hills to the east. It was the spot where the town of Douglas, Wyoming, was later established.

An outfit of seventy-five teams was corralled close to the river, with men prone beneath the wagon-boxes firing between the spokes of the wheels at the encircling redskins. A large contingent of Sioux were massed at the moment in a draw to the north of the corral, and, as Finn's group looked over a hill, these Indians were slipping quietly down upon their victims. They were so intent on reaching their objective that the approach of assistance for the white men was unnoticed.

It seemed but a matter of seconds before Finn and his outfit reached the edge of the draw where they delivered a devastating fire into the surprised Sioux. Several of the warriors fell dead or wounded at the first volley, and the rest turned and sped eastward toward the hills, yipping with chagrin, and pursued by the vengeful whites.

Lieutenant Belden, Finn, and another soldier became separated from the others in their common pursuit of one Sioux chieftain who had lagged behind his band. Together they raced after him until the soldier shot down his pony. The Indian then leaped free and raced into a gulch which was choked with sagebrush, and where he continued to jump from place to place as the three men flanked him out.

Finally, he was surprised at one spot, and was so nearly brought down that he dropped his gun and escaped with only his bow and arrows for protection. On examining his weapon later, it was found to be a Winchester, eleven shot, .44 calibre carbine, the first of its kind that any of the frontiersmen had ever seen.

By this time the officer and the soldier were becoming very impatient at their delay in finishing the Indian. They decided to charge in and get him, although Finn did all he could to dissuade them. Together they dashed into the brush on horseback, and the soldier's mount immediately fell with an arrow in his heart, while the lieutenant received another in his knee.

Finn had held back, waiting, and when the Sioux saw the two men fall, he left his cover and began to run afoot toward the hills. He proved to be a perfect target for Burnett, and he was brought down with the first shot.

The fighting had all died away by this time. Soldiers and teamsters were trotting slowly down from the hills in twos and threes toward the train, and soon Finn's group joined them.

The beleaguered corral proved to be one of Majors' outfits, and its defenders had been fighting continuously for three days and nights. There had been apparently no Indians in the little grassy basin when they drove in the first evening. Two men had left the corral up on the bank to go down to the river for water and had not returned. A search had been made for them, and their dead bodies had been found unscalped under the high bank at the river's edge. They were buried where they had fallen.

Later that evening, the Indians had attacked. The following day, the corral had been advanced a short distance up the river, moving one side of the corral around the other, so that their cattle could graze inside the enclosure, and leaving the side facing the river open, so that the stock could drink from the Platte.

On each succeeding day, the corral had progressed in the same manner, carefully enclosing the best grass, so the cattle had been kept in good condition.

Finn and the others strolled over to the place where the two men had been buried by the river. There they found that the Indians had dug up the bodies and had scalped both of them twice, taking two scalps from each one, and leaving the corpses on the ground. Again their comrades buried them.

There were no further signs of Indians, and next morning the train hitched up and went on to Fort Fetterman,[5] a new post which was being established close to the south side of the Platte. Mr. Leighton unloaded a part of the supplies for his new sutler's store there, and allowed the work animals to rest.

---

[5] Fort Fetterman was established on July 19, 1867.

Ambushes

Ambushes

The escort of cavalry remained at Fort Fetterman when Leighton's train proceeded northward. When they reached the Cheyenne river, they found it to be dry, but after digging into the sand of the river bed, pure, cool water was discovered a foot and a half below the surface. There was ample for all the stock and men, but they were obliged to bail it out with dippers.

As the train was preparing the meal that night, a number of buffalo were seen grazing a little distance to the east. Finn took his gun, and started out to try to get one for supper. He ran down the creek bottom, crouching below the banks until he reached a point close to them from which he brought down a young calf with a well-directed shot. The rest of the herd stampeded.

When Finn approached the dead animal, he discovered three arrows sticking into its hide, which indicated the presence of Indians in the vicinity. He lost little time in getting back to camp.

Several others then went with Finn, and assisted in cleaning the carcass. The arrows had been shot but a few hours before, so the meat was unspoiled, and was brought into camp and consumed.

The next camp was at Brown's Springs, and there water was difficult to procure. After digging a hole into which the liquid slowly seeped, the teamsters again were obliged to take turns dipping from the hole to a pail. It was after midnight before the stock had been satisfied.

Next day, camp was set up on a tableland where the Bozeman trail entered the dry fork of Powder river. This high land formed a steep bluff beside the fork, and Finn stood guard at that point for a part of the night.

Returning to the wagons when relieved, Finn started to build a fire in the sheet-iron camp stove. Outside the enclosure he found some dry wood in the dark, and proceeded to whittle some shavings for his fire.

Suddenly, a sharp stab of pain shot along the left side of his head, as an Indian arrow sped from the bank to cut the hair cleanly along a furrow over his ear. Finn jumped into the corral and waked everyone with a shout. In his excitement, he had left his carbine outside, but he still had his pistol and with this he joined in the volleys which the half-dressed teamsters directed at the banks of the tableland.

There was no further trouble. Whatever Indians had been there quickly disappeared. When daybreak came, several arrows were found sticking in the ground around the corral and a few in the wagons, but no one had been seriously hurt. The tracks of twenty-five Indians were discovered in the sand, one of the marks being the largest human footprint they had ever seen.

That night, they reached Fort Reno, and drove down through the little lane between the thickets of the river bottom and the edge of the steep bank below the stockade. Here, apparently, they were safe from Indians, being in the shelter of the fort. A sentry could be plainly seen walking his post along the top of the embankment. So, they built a huge bonfire with cottonwood logs and sprawled about with a perfect sense of security and well-being.

Suddenly, a line of Indians burst from the narrow path below the fort, to come charging straight at the surprised and defenseless teamsters. Right under the sentry's nose they had ridden, and now their bullets sped into the fire, and through the camp.

The teamsters who were sitting about the blaze, all turned backward somersaults out of the light at the sound of the first shot, and in a moment they were vigorously working their guns as the Indians galloped on down the valley yelling with derision.

Next morning, word reached Fort Reno that Major Van Vosey and his escort of soldiers with an ambulance had been ambushed and massacred near Brown's Springs the day after Finn's party had passed. Fifteen soldiers with Tony Addinger, who was a Frenchman, and Finn Burnett, rode to the scene. The bodies of all the soldiers were still lying amid evidences of the most desperate fighting, but there was no sign of the remains of Major Van Vosey.

An extensive search of the vicinity was begun, and a trail was soon discovered which led to where the ambulance had been wrecked. From there the ground showed that something heavy had been dragged away.

The soldiers followed this new trail, expecting to find the body of the major, but, instead, they discovered a small safe rolled into a draw east of the ambulance. This safe was of the type which was used to carry valuables on all the old overland stages. The Indians had evidently dragged it with lariats to the boulder-strewn draw, where they had attempted to knock it to pieces by pounding on it with large rocks. They had not succeeded in opening it, however, and the detail took the safe back with them to Fort Reno, and turned it over to the post commander. The body of Major Van Vosey was never recovered.

When Wood paid Finn a few days later for herding

his mules on the trail, the young man counted up his
money and remarked, "You haven't taken out for the
mule I killed."

"Well," Wood laughed, "I'm glad to lose one mule
and have the rest well cared for."

Which was a proper attitude, for the nights had
seemed endless to Finn as he herded the animals, and
it had been his eternal vigilance which had saved the
train from greater losses on several occasions.

After supplying the sutler's store with a portion of
their goods, the train hitched up again and drove to
Fort Phil Kearny where the remainder was unloaded.
Here, Mr. Leighton discovered for the first time that
John Dale had lost his mule herd, so plans for continuing to Fort C. F. Smith were obliged to wait until a
strong wagon-train went by, going in that direction.

During this period of waiting, Finn herded mules for
the quartermaster. His duties were not difficult as he
was obliged to stand guard but twice a week.

One of the bright spots of Finn's sojourn at Fort Phil
Kearny was his friendship with Mr. and Mrs. Washington. This couple had built a cabin northeast of and
150 yards from the fort. They were excellent shots, and
lived through those dreadful experiences of 1866, 1867,
and 1868, without having to go to the fort for protection
in a single instance. At first, Indians had crept up to the
cabin, but they soon learned of the deadly accuracy of
the occupants, and that any redskin who came within
range of that isolated little building got a bullet in his
blanket. The Washington's home was as safe a retreat
as was the fort itself.

Mrs. Washington was a tall, splendid type of frontier
woman, and possessed the additional charm of being a
wonderful cook. Whenever a soldier at the fort received

any money from home, he would go straight to Mrs. Washington's cabin, and there sit down to a welcome relief from the ordinary rations. On pay-days, her home was thronged with soldiers from early dawn to late at night, all of them reveling in her fine home-cooking.

The Washingtons left that part of the country in 1868, and moved to South Pass and later to a road ranch at Black Rock Spring, on the Rock Springs road.

South of the fort, across Little Piney, there was a prominent point which was called Lookout Station, and there a squad of soldiers was picketed every morning at daybreak, to watch and give the alarm in the event of surprise attacks by Indians.

General H. W. Wessels had taken over the command of the fort, relieving Colonel Carrington who suffered for Fetterman's disobedience by being obliged to return to the East where he received unmerited humiliation and censure. During the entire period of General Wessels's administration at Fort Phil Kearny, he gave absolutely no assistance to those who were attacked outside the stockade.

The first day that Finn was herding the mules, he was assisted by Tony Addinger, the government wagon-master, and six other men. They drove their charges across the Little Piney and let them graze below Lookout Station. The soldiers above them on the hill watched the surrounding country with field-glasses, and at intervals wig-wagged "all clear" to the herders.

The stock had been feeding for about an hour when Addinger happened to ride higher up the hill, from which place he could see a long distance up the creek. There he discerned a war-party of more than a hundred Indians approaching.

Tony shouted to Finn to go above the mules and drive

them in, but by the time the teamsters had gotten the herd started, the Sioux had ridden between them and the post. Addinger called to the men to leave the mules and make for the safety of the fort. The white men charged headlong down the hill, firing right and left as they went, and the stockade was reached safely. The mule herd was never recovered.

That was not the greatest raid which occurred at Fort Phil Kearny, however. The last time that Finn was ever destined to herd the stock at that historic old post, he, with a number of other men, lost 600 animals, and barely escaped with his life.

There was another well-remembered attack on the mules at Fort Phil Kearny in June. General John E. Smith had succeeded General Wessels as post-commander at the time, and Finn with eight teamsters had taken the herd out one Sunday morning to a grassy spot about three-quarters of a mile west of the post.

Four teamsters returned to the fort after helping to drive the mules to grass and assisting in hobbling them with drag chains. Four remained to ride herd, Finn Burnett, Tony Addinger, Edward Gibson, and Charles White. They rode to a low ridge and dismounted, to watch the herd from that more shaded place.

A large number of mounted Indians suddenly broke from a thicket and raced yelling at the herd in an effort to stampede it. Being hobbled, the mules did not respond.

The four white men on the ridge lay on their stomachs and began to fire into the Sioux, killing one pony and wounding two bucks. They immediately turned from the mules and bunched together, preparing to attack.

They had just begun their rush, when the gates of the fort crashed open, and out came the cavalry, pouring across the plain, with General Smith in the lead, attired in dressing-gown and slippers.

At the first sound of firing from the four herders, General Smith had been sleeping in his quarters. He had jumped out of bed, ordered his bugler to blow "boots and saddles," had raced out in his dressing-gown and slippers calling "the first one out is the best man," and had galloped through the opened gate with the foremost of the garrison. Most of the soldiers were riding bareback, with halters on their mounts.

"Sourdough Charlie" White, a short, little man, had been detailed to watch the gulch behind the ridge to protect his three companions from a rear attack. He had evidently not been very attentive to his job, for Indians had crept up the ravine which he was supposed to be guarding, and had fired arrows into the air at random, hoping that some of the missiles would hit the men on the other side when they came down. There were at least two dozen arrows sticking in the ground around the three men when the skirmish was finished.

The beef herd was grazing a half mile north of this little engagement. A teamster named Healy was with them, sitting on his mule, and watching the fight in apparent safety.

At the moment that the Indians were put to flight, a number of Sioux suddenly sprang up around him, and commenced to attack. He spurred his mount over a steep bank, rolled to the bottom and escaped.

One Indian, on a nearby hill, then began to amuse himself by shooting arrows into the beef herd. Another redskin sat beside him on a pony, watching. Finn saw the situation, and lay flat on the ground to get a careful aim at the sportsman. His first shot tumbled the marksman from his horse, and it was the longest "scratch" hit that Finn ever made. From that time on, the young man was jokingly referred to as the "crack shot of the out-fit."

A few days later, "Dad" Snell drove into the fort with a train. He had two of Leighton's mules, and Finn was able to rig up a four-mule outfit and to join a large train of soldiers under General Bradley who were going to Fort C. F. Smith to take over that post.

The wagons of the detachment were heavily freighted, and on going up the hill west of Peno creek, the teams had to be doubled for every load. The escort was divided, one half going to the top of the incline to protect those vehicles which had been pulled up, with the remainder acting as a rear guard at the bottom. All but two of the wagons had been safely drawn to the top, when the rear guard, believing all danger to be past, went up the hill.

The last load was "Dad" Snell's, and was drawn by six mules. It contained, among other things, two cases of Winchesters for the supply store at Fort C. F. Smith. The other wagon was driven by Healy, the short, black-haired Irishman who had escaped from the attack on the beef herd a few days before.

Both wagons began the climb up the hill, when a war-party of Sioux burst from the willows. Snell's wagon-mules wheeled in fright, and ran away down the creek to be lost with their driver and all the stores.

Healy, perceiving "Dad" Snell's predicament behind him, excitedly prodded his mules with the stock of his Spencer carbine, which was loaded in the breech with seven cartridges.

The gun exploded, and the soldiers raced down as he fell from the wagon. Healy was bleeding profusely, and was calling on his saints to save him when they reached him. On examination, however, it was found that a shell had exploded in the breech of his gun, and a splinter from the stock had grazed his face deeply enough to make him bleed freely. It was difficult to convince Healy that the entire side of his head had not been torn away.

That night, they camped on the Tongue river. After corralling the wagons, and leaving some men to arrange camp and start the cooking, the teamsters and soldiers accompanied the mules to an adjacent grazing spot.

It was fortunate that they had been so careful, for scarcely had the animals begun to feed when a party of the Sioux attacked. The soldiers quickly formed a line which drove them off, while the teamsters bunched around the animals.

The Indians then withdrew down the valley about three-quarters of a mile, and congregated on a high, alkali bluff sitting amid badlands in a bend of the river. There, they began to make gestures, ridiculing the soldiers, imitating their military wig-wagging signals with blankets, and striking many derisive poses.

The soldiers then set up a twelve-pound howitzer, and fired it. The Sioux had had experiences with similar cannon in the past, and knew that they were not in danger. The discharge of the gun served but to redouble their mirth.

The detachment, however, had been issued a new steel, nine-pound, rifled gun, a weapon not known to the frontier before this time. Its gunner was a man who was known as "Uncle Tommy," and he had been squinting at the Sioux for several minutes, sizing up the situation. Finally, he asked for the permission of his commanding officer to try out his new gun. This was granted, and he took plenty of time setting it properly, and figuring out the elevation and deflection.

He fired, and the soldiers watched the butte with interest. A second after the gun's discharge, a great ball of smoke burst five feet above the heads of the Indians, showering them with a hail of flying death. In the twinkling of an eye, the group of gesticulating warriors was reduced to a mangled pile, from which a pitiful few weakly pushed aside their dead comrades, to tumble down the sides of the bluff and stumble to their ponies.

Leighton, Lieutenant Macauley, and a squad of soldiers rode over later to see the destruction, and they returned with the news that the top of the butte was a mixed-up mass of mangled Indians, feathers, and horses.

Word of the range and execution of this new gun soon spread across the range, and from that time on no Indian would stop for a moment within sight of the detachment.

There were no further Indian troubles on the road, and Fort C. F. Smith was relieved without other incidents of interest.

The Battle in the Hay Fields

The Battle in the Hay Fields

Shortly after his arrival, Mr. Leighton secured the contract to furnish hay for the fort, agreeing to a set price of fifty dollars a ton. He then decided to begin cutting in a natural meadow three miles down the Big Horn river.

Fort C. F. Smith, as has been already stated, was situated on a tableland east of the river. Four miles to the southward was the gap known as the Big Horn canyon, from which poured the river, to flow north past the post and on to a bend. Beyond this curve, the valley widened into a large, grassy meadow, fringed on the southeast by the willow thickets along the banks of Warrior creek.

In that grassy meadow two and one-half miles below the fort was erected a strong corral by the soldiers and teamsters, and there, as well, was to be fought the greatest Indian battle in Finn Burnett's experience. And, while it was greater by far than was the well-known Wagon-box fight near Fort Phil Kearny, yet it remained practically unknown and unrecorded for over sixty years. Government records and reports seldom reflect any lack of initiative or courageous determination on the part of their writers, and post commanders made all reports from their respective forts.

A large detail of soldiers under Lieutenant Stromberg proceeded with the teamsters to the meadow, and forty feet west from the banks of Warrior creek they commenced the erection of a strong, square corral.

The eastern line of this enclosure ran north and south, with the only gateway on the south side. It was foreseen by all that the corral would have to be stoutly built, and that it must be erected in such a manner as to serve as a makeshift fortification in time of attack.

Two heavy posts were thereupon set upright together, and other pairs were planted deeply all about the corral at intervals of six feet. Logs were then laid on the ground between them, and heavy pole bars were hung half way up with another on top of the uprights. These horizontal poles were lashed securely to the posts with pliable green willow branches, which tightened on drying. Finished, the enclosure was an admirable little fort, with heavy, close-set protecting bars.

No gate was placed at the lone entrance on the south side, but a wagon gear was run across the opening, and at night the front and rear wheels were chained tightly to the gate posts, eliminating any opportunity for Indians to push aside the obstruction during the night.

With the corral completed, the wagon-boxes with their canvas-topped shelters were lifted from their gears and set in a line inside the enclosure along the west side with the three army tents which housed the soldiers. Across the center of the corral was erected the picket line from north to south, with a huge barrel for drinking water at one end.

Next, the situation outside of the corral was closely studied. To the south, forty feet away, Warrior creek straggled along between deep willow thickets, with a high bank running parallel to its far side. The willows grew close to the southwest corner of the enclosure, leaving barely enough room for a wagon to pass through, and there was stretched a tarpaulin to shelter the kitchen with its long, rough table.

To the south, the creek ambled away through rough country, with long, jagged draws and gulches hacked sideways into the hills, while to the west was a high bench about sixty yards away, and eastward stretched the meadow.

Lieutenant Stromberg then ordered his soldiers to dig three half-moon trenches, thirty feet long, at the northeast, northwest, and southeast corners of the corral. Then, with all defenses erected, an entire day was spent stepping off the various distances to the benches, and the probable points of attack. This information was to prove exceedingly useful to the defenders later, during the Hay Fields fight.

Altogether, it was a remarkably strong position when finished. There were ample defenders, armed with the latest guns for which they had an abundance of ammunition.

Indians had made their appearance from the first day that the detachment arrived in the meadow, and none of the white men had drawn an easy breath until the corral and the trenches had been completed.

Then, when the hay-cutting operations began, the Indians harassed them daily. The timothy could be cut, and not a redskin would molest the workers, but, when the sun-cured hay would be stacked and ready for loading on the wagons, trouble would immediately develop. Down would come the Sioux upon them from some hidden draw in such overwhelming numbers that the soldiers and teamsters would be obliged to withdraw to their corral, to watch as the redskins burned every wisp of the dried hay.

None of the detachment knew of the peril which was developing daily beyond the horizon. Thirty miles to the east, on the Rosebud river, Chief Red Cloud was

preparing diligently for a great, concerted drive to erase
all the forts from the Bozeman trail.

For months, he had been gathering together every
available warrior of the Sioux and the Cheyenne and the
Arapaho, concentrating them in huge villages on the
Rosebud. He was haranguing them daily with his ferocious eloquence, firing them all to a savage intensity of
feeling that would shortly spew them forward over the
country in a deadly, savage frenzy.

The forts were in a pitiful condition. Weak garrisons,
poorly provided for, promised an easy prey for the
thousands of well-equipped warriors who awaited their
chief's command. Red Cloud as a final gesture promised
a lasting peace among the tribes, and a frontier-wide
readjustment of existing treaties and areas for hunting
grounds, which brought to his cause the support of all
the warriors west of the Missouri river. This was the
only incident in all the years of frontier warfare when
an Indian chieftain united the western tribes into one
concerted effort, and had it progressed to its fruition it
undoubtedly would have been successful.

But the one factor which served to minimize the
efforts of Red Cloud, and which eventually destroyed
his plans altogether, was an aspiring warrior in his own
ranks. This chieftain was known as a Miniconjou Sioux,
which has the Indian meaning of Missouri river, or
"muddy water." He had gained a considerable reputation among the Indians in Missouri for some successes
against the whites, and it is to be conjectured that his
coming to the Rosebud at this time was imbued with the
hope that he would be chosen as the supreme commander for the campaign.

At any rate, the supreme council day arrived, and all

the chieftains sat in blanketed rows in the midst of Red Cloud's lodges on the Rosebud.

The final stages of planning had been reached when the negotiations became deadlocked. Red Cloud advocated an attack on Fort Phil Kearny first, using his entire force. Afterwards, he would sweep back upon Fort C. F. Smith. For some reason, the Miniconjou Sioux objected, arguing that the procedure should be reversed, that Fort C. F. Smith should be immediately destroyed, followed by the elimination of Fort Phil Kearny. The arguments of the two chieftains became violent, and the council was fast getting out of hand.

Red Cloud pondered, slowly puffing at his pipe, then suddenly sprang to his feet, and walked to the far side of the council fire.

"Hear me," he shouted to the huddled mass of warriors. "All who agree to go with me to Fort Phil Kearny first, come to me, and all who wish to join this Miniconjou Sioux remain on the far side of the fire."

There was an immediate alignment of chiefs who espoused each cause. It appeared that the opinions of the council were evenly divided. A count was begun of the number in each group.

It is a well-known fact that an Indian could never count up to one hundred. From that number onward, calculations became especially vague, and, as such throngs had flocked in this instance to both leaders, the result was still undecided.

Finally, after more argument, a compromise agreement was reached. It was decided that Chief Red Cloud would lead his supporters against Fort Phil Kearny, and the Miniconjou Sioux chieftain would proceed with his adherents to attack Fort C. F. Smith. All the chiefs were jubilant at the outcome, and hurried to their respective camps to arouse their thousands, daub their faces and bodies with gleaming war-paint, and prepare for battle.

At this time, the Crow Indians were at peace with the Sioux as well as with the whites. A number of them visited frequently forth and back between Red Cloud's villages and the forts, and now they wasted little time in warning the posts of the impending campaign.

Galloping up the meadow, they roused the soldiers at the corral, and urged them vigorously to return to the protection of the fort, stating that there were more Indians congregated in Red Cloud's villages than they had ever seen in one place before, and that within a few days a veritable avalanche of warriors would arrive to attack the post.

Had their warnings been heeded, the Hay Fields battle would never have been fought. But, for some time those at the corral had had the impression that the Crow were averse to the cutting of the hay in the meadow, and it was believed that the warnings were actuated by the desire of those friendly Indians to have the hay fields vacated.

So the usual routine continued. Four or five Indian raids were repulsed every day until on the evening of the 29th day of July, 1867, twenty Crow scouts rode into the enclosure at a gallop.

They stated that they had that day been to the great Sioux camp down the valley, five miles away, and that a general attack would be launched by thousands of redskins on the morrow. They begged and pleaded with the soldiers and teamsters, asking them to believe their report and to flee from the insecurity of the corral.

None would heed them. Finally, seeing that further

argument was useless, they departed toward Fort C. F. Smith, bidding each white man a fervent and sorrowful farewell which was so sincere that several men were silent and exceedingly thoughtful for the remainder of the evening.

On the following day nothing unusual occurred. All worked until after dark loading a number of hay wagons which were to be sent to the fort under escort the next morning.

The first day of August broke bright and sunny. The lazy haze of early dawn hung about the valley as breakfast was eaten at the kitchen outside the corral. Mules were hitched to the hay wagons, mounted soldiers grouped about them, and all started away for the fort, leaving Lieutenant Stromberg with eight soldiers and nine teamsters at the enclosure.

The men who remained took things very easily during the early morning, awaiting the return of their comrades before venturing into the meadow. The teamsters fed and watered the thirty-one mules at the picket line and aired their bedding, while the soldiers played cards and wrote letters.

The teamsters presented an interesting group, there being Al and Zeke Colvin, Al Stevenson, Robert Wheeling, Robert Little, George Duncan, William Haynes, a man named Hollister, and Finn Burnett. Each was to perform his individual part in the great drama which was shortly to begin.

About nine o'clock, Finn called to Bill Little.

"Say, the Indians haven't paid us their usual morning call," he said. "I wonder what's the matter."

"Oh, well," returned Bill, "from what the Crow said, they'll probably blow us a lively horn for dinner."

Scarcely had the words been uttered when a picket

on the point of the bench, seven hundred yards below the corral, fired his gun and came galloping in. Everyone rushed to the gate to question his alarm.

"For heaven's sake, look at the Indians coming up the valley," shouted someone, pointing, and all eyes left the picket to peer off toward the northeast.

It was a sight filled with dreadful possibilities which met their gaze. The entire lower valley was a solid mass of advancing warriors. They were riding slowly and confidently, presenting an impenetrable front of pinto ponies, moving inexorably forward in numbers which held the threat of riding over and completely submerging the little corral.

Suddenly, they began a great screeching and whooping. Hands were upflung, holding aloft war-clubs and tomahawks which their gestures promised to stain with the blood of white men that day. War-bonnets waved from hundreds of heads, and feathers streamed from horses' manes. Splashes of red and yellow paint on faces and breasts lent hideous unreality to the horrid clamor. The handful of defenders in the enclosure promised for them but a quick skirmish before the desperate battle at the fort.

"Man the rifle pits," called Lieutenant Stromberg, and the soldiers hurried to the barriers of the corral with guns in hand. But, before they could climb through the bars to obey the order, the foremost line of Indians had charged and were between the trenches and the enclosure.

In a moment, every man in the corral had thrown himself upon the ground behind a log, and had pushed his gun forward to open up a rattling fire at the redskins, who now entirely surrounded them.

Finn Burnett found himself at the southwest corner, facing the kitchen, shooting into the willow thickets to attempt to reduce the number of savages who had concealed themselves there, and who had now commenced a sniping fire.

Everyone had been in his position but a moment, when a Sioux warrior dashed from the meadow to the southeast, holding aloft a burning torch of dry hay. Galloping to the enclosure, he started to thrust the flames among the dry willows on the railings, when Zeke Colvin fired at him.

The Indian was so close that Zeke could not shoot the warrior, but wounded his black horse in the breast. The animal fell against the corral logs, imprisoning his rider's foot, and it was several seconds before the Sioux could release himself and attempt to dash away. By that time, Zeke had reloaded, and the torchbearer fell dead with a bullet in his back.

Echoing volleys were now being delivered from every side of the enclosure. So solid were the masses of redskins outside that every shot was a hit, and the number of dead and wounded on the ground spoke of deadly execution. The air above was aflicker with a dense swarm of arrows that whispered and whistled across the top bars to fall into every corner of the enclosure and among the tortured mules along the picket line.

Like swarms of hornets, the Sioux swept again and again upon the corral, and at each effort they were flung back upon the mangled, shattered remnants of previous charges which lay upon the ground. The dead were literally in piles after the first five minutes of fighting.

Lieutenant Stromberg was a fine soldier, but he was inexperienced in Indian warfare.

"Stand up, men, and fight like soldiers," he shouted to the troopers as he sprang erect by the wagon at the gate, and fired over the hay-rack into the Indians.

"No! No! lieutenant," Finn yelled. "Lie down. Don't expose yourself like that!"

The words had scarcely been called when the officer fell. Finn crawled to where he lay on his face struggling, and on putting his hand to the dying man's head he found it to be completely crushed by the force of a bullet which had entered above his right eye.

As he turned to go back to his place, Finn beheld one of Al Colvin's mules struggling at the picket line badly wounded. Fearing that the struggles of the animal would stampede the other mules, Finn made his way over to the beast and untied her rope. She reeled back, stumbled in a circle and toppled over on top of the lieutenant, and they died there together.

Now, for a moment, came the first breathing space. The Indians withdrew down the meadow, and to the banks and hills surrounding the corral, to reorganize for another effort. The unsuspected strength of the defenders had quenched a great part of their enthusiasm, but they were now doubly anxious to wipe out the stigma of their losses with the blood of all those in the enclosure.

The sun blazed hot upon the backs of the men who crouched behind their log breastworks. The dust raised by the frantic mules choked the mouths of everyone.

Finn slipped back to a wagon for his other gun and for additional ammunition. He was well prepared for this battle, having now a Spencer carbine, and a ten-gauge, double-barreled shotgun, with plenty of shells for each of them.

Looking around the corral, Finn saw that Zeke Col-

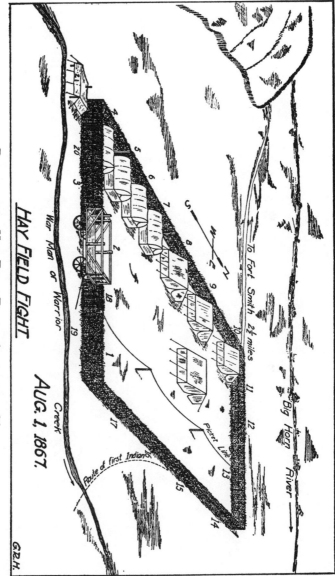

PLAN OF THE HAY FIELD FIGHT, AUGUST 1, 1867

Figures indicate positions of fighters. (1) Capt. Colvin (2) Lt. Stromberg, killed (3) Al Stevenson (4) Finn Burnett (5) George Duncan (6) Man located here who lost his nerve and never fired a shot during the battle (7) Robert Little (8) Hollister, wounded, died next day (9, 10, 11) Soldiers (12) Soldier, killed (13) Soldier stationed here who lost his nerve and threatened to commit suicide (14) Soldier wounded with arrow (15) Zeke Colvin (16) A sergeant, wounded in shoulder, fought bravely throughout battle (17) William Haynes (18) Soldier (19) Sioux chief killed here by Capt. Colvin (20) Soldier known as "Scotty," wounded; fought desperately through engagement (21) Cook tent at lower left, outside corral.

vin was defending the southeast corner, his brother, Al, was at the northeast corner, and Al Stevenson was facing the east at Finn's left, while George Duncan and Bob Little watched the west and south from between the wagon-boxes. The soldiers had chosen places at intervals all around the enclosure.

Zeke Colvin had served as a captain under Price in the Southern army during the Civil war. The gun which he was using that day was an Enfield muzzle-loading musket which he had taken from a dead soldier on the battlefield at Wilson creek, in Missouri.

Al Colvin, Zeke's brother, peculiarly had been a captain in the Union army, serving under Buell, and now, Lieutenant Stromberg being dead, he assumed command of the defenders. Under ordinary circumstances, Al had proved himself to be a jolly, good-natured fellow, with a joke ready for every event. He had rather a thick lower lip which was always sore and cracked. Every time he told a joke, he laughed, and his lip would always start to bleed.

During this desperate day, however, he shot like a devil incarnate. The lives of all the men in the corral were to a great degree in his hands, and he fought with every ounce of his courage to bring them through. Armed with a sixteen shot Henry rifle of .44 calibre, he had a thousand rounds of ammunition laid out beside him on the ground, and was taking unusual care not to waste a shot. Throughout the fighting, he slowly and systematically mowed down the Indians, and none of his comrades ever saw him miss his mark. Now he was calling to the men.

"The probabilities are," he was saying, "that we will never get out of here alive, but let's make these Indians remember this day as long as there is a Sioux alive."

The savages had seen the officer fall, and, heartened at the thought that the defenders were leaderless, they charged down again from all sides. Straight from the hills they hurled themselves recklessly at the corral, to be met by a flashing stream of lead that swept them back again.

Time and again they reached the enclosure, and their hands and moccasins flashed on the rails as they attempted to climb over to mix in hand-to-hand conflict, but in every instance they were blown back to add their bodies to the heaps outside.

This second attack was short, and the Sioux again retreated to hold another pow-wow, and to reorganize. The defenders now found that a soldier had been killed, while a sergeant and the teamster named Hollister were badly wounded.

The soldier had been stationed on the west side, and had found himself in a desperate situation with two Indian snipers engaging him in a cross-fire from a position sixty yards outside.

Armed with a .50 calibre needle gun, he had continued firing at them until, in response to one of his shots, his assailant jumped up fatally wounded, and fell over backward with his feet toward the corral. He continued struggling, and the soldier feared he might get up, so he shot the Sioux again. Then, evidently forgetting that he had two snipers to contend with, the soldier sat up carelessly to reload his gun. He was immediately shot through the head, and was dead before he hit the ground.

The man, Hollister, was a fine young fellow from Kansas City. He had been armed with a double-barreled shotgun, and had crept over to Finn during the second attack asking how to load the weapon, as he was unaccustomed to that type of gun. A shot had crashed through the bark on one of the fence posts, filling Finn's eyes with splinters, and had hit Hollister in the stomach. The defenders moved him into a tent, where he remained in terrible agony for the rest of the day.

The other injured man was a sergeant, who had a gaping wound in his left shoulder. He was carried into the tent with Hollister, but a loaded revolver was kept ready for him, and throughout the day, at every attack, he stumbled out, to fight beside the others. Then, when another lull would occur, he would be helped back into the tent, exhausted.

Victory

Victory

The second phase of the battle now commenced. Evidently the losses sustained in the two previous attacks had taught the Sioux the need for caution, as they now encircled the corral and poured upon it a raking fire. Every bank and boulder, every thicket and bush, held its deadly menace, and it became absolute suicide for a defender to raise his head.

The entire force of the Sioux now settled down to the business of obliterating this little enclosure. All plans for continuing on toward Fort C. F. Smith were temporarily put aside until this determined band had been wiped from their path.

One well-fortified group of Sioux snipers lay on the bluffs to the west, shooting into the corrals with a precision so well calculated that it threatened to kill every mule along the picket line. Others fired from the thickets, making chips fly from the horizontal poles of the fence, and honeycombing the tents and wagon-tops with their searching bullets and arrows.

Finn noticed that Al Colvin was being particularly singled out by the enemy for attack. He was withstanding a sharp cross-fire from both the east and the north, but was replying carefully and accurately. Fearing that he might be hit behind his inadequate shelter, Finn crept back and got an end-gate from a wagon. With this in hand, he crawled to Al's position, and set the added barricade up on one side, which made the position much more secure. Al's curly hair was already filled with chips and dry willow leaves which had dropped from the rails above him.

On returning to his corner, Finn noticed an unusual movement in the thicket back of the kitchen. He remained quiet and watched closely. The cook had left the cleaned metal dishes setting on the table as usual after breakfast, with the tin cups piled neatly beside them.

As Finn waited, an Indian coup-stick appeared from the thicket. It was extended forward by an unseen hand toward the cups on the table, and worked softly among them until a handle had become engaged. Then, raising the stick, the cup slid down its length into the thicket where probably it was pounced upon eagerly by an Indian souvenir hunter.

One by one the cups disappeared in this manner. Those closest to the thicket were taken first, but as those farther away were sought after, the holder of the coup-stick was obliged to display more and more of his arm.

"Say, Al," Finn called to Stevenson, "can you see that Sioux getting our cups?"

"Sure can," answered Al. "Can you get him?"

"Wait till I see his shoulder," cautioned Finn.

With that, they settled down to watch, and finally the red, painted shoulder showed for a moment from its concealment. Instantly, Finn's gun spoke, and the sound of an awful thrashing and groaning was heard in the bushes.

"Darned if you didn't kill 'em all," yelled Stevenson, excitedly.

Finn did not understand this remark, but on investigating later, he found that his shot had almost cut the cup-fisherman in two, and the thicket looked like a slaughterhouse.

After this shot, there was a momentary silence in the thicket, then a Sioux gave a signal which imitated a frog, and a number of Indians left the bushes to race away. Stevenson and Finn fired quickly into them, and managed to bring down two before they disappeared.

A small, dark complexioned soldier, holding a 45-70 needle carbine in his trembling hand, now crawled to Finn's side.

"It's no use, Burnett," he whined. "We're going to be overrun here in a few minutes, and then – oh, my heavens, what they'll do to us. They'll torture us, Finn, they'll carve us until we die. I can't stand it. I won't stand it, I tell you. I'll shoot myself first."

"Oh, now, wait a minute, soldier," Finn soothed. "You just lie down here with me and help me fight awhile. You'll get over this all right."

"No, I won't," went on the craven trooper. "There isn't a chance. I'm going to kill myself, I tell you."

"How will you do it?" asked Finn, interested.

"With my ramrod, that's how," was the answer. "Here, I've taken it out, and all I have to do is hold the muzzle up to my head, and work the trigger back with the ramrod."

Finn's attention was diverted at this moment by some firing on his right which he assisted. When he had time to look around again, the soldier had made his way over to Zeke Colvin, to whom he was telling the same story.

Zeke wasted no time with him. He jerked the coward's gun from him, and stripped him of his cartridges.

"There, now," Zeke snarled. "Go over and hide in that hole that the dogs dug yesterday. And, if I hear another word out of you, I'll save you the trouble by blowing your head off, myself, and I'd get a lot of pleasure out of it, too. Get!"

Nor was this the only instance of cowardice among the white men. Two others, a soldier and a teamster, were showing their lack of manliness, and were proving to be a total loss in the defense of the corral.

The soldier had been slightly wounded in the second attack. Lying prone on the ground, an arrow had hit him horizontally in the legs, passing slightly beneath the skin of both calves. He set up such a clamor at his pain that everyone believed he had been wounded more seriously, and he was helped into the tent, to lie between the sergeant and Hollister.

There he began to groan and cry out until the Indians heard him from outside the corral, and directed their firing at the tent until it was hanging in ribbons.

Finally, the sergeant leaned over him, gun in hand.

"Listen, you," he growled. "I want to hear just one more yelp out of you for an excuse to kill you. Now, shut your mouth, or you will get it."

There was silence in the tent from that time on.

The teamster who was showing yellow was the man named Wheeling. He was a big, ruffianly fellow who had swaggered around the camp with two six-guns belted to his hips. Everyone had been more or less afraid of his bluster.

At the beginning of the battle, he had thrown himself down at the northwest corner of the corral, and no one had had time to take any notice of him. It was finally discovered that he had barricaded himself behind a heap of boxes and harness, and there he was lying, crying like a baby. Although he was armed with a Spencer rifle, and plenty of ammunition, neither he nor the soldier in the dog's hole fired a shot all that day.

A little after noon, the firing from outside died away. With the cessation, the fighters realized their thirst, and also that the water barrel was empty. The wounded were beginning to beg for water, and the sun was pouring molten heat into the corral.

All the pans and pails which were intact were gathered together, and a number of men prepared to dash to the creek for water. The soldiers were concentrated along the south fence to cover their attempt with heavy firing, and, a few moments later, the men crawled out from under the wagon at the gate and made their run.

They were surprised to find that not a shot was fired at them. All made the dash to the creek and back several times, until the barrel had been filled to overflowing. The Sioux, in retiring for lunch, had lost another opportunity for adding to their enemies' discomfort.

Unknown, of course, to those in the enclosure, their plight had been detected at Fort C. F. Smith. During the morning, Captain Hartz, a Civil war veteran, had left the post with a wood-train and had climbed high into the mountains. On looking over the surrounding country with field-glasses from that point, he discerned the enclosure hemmed in by a dense mass of Indians, and the desperate battle that was going on.

The captain galloped to the fort, and reported that the corral was surrounded by at least 2,500 Sioux. He furthermore asked that he might go with three or four companies to their relief.

There were seven companies in the post, but General Bradley was mindful of his responsibility for the safety of the fort, and, fearing a massacre, ordered everyone into the stockade and closed and locked the gate. The men in the corral were left to their fate.

The defenders used this noon respite to good advantage. Employing knives and plates – anything that they could find – they dug holes for their bodies behind the ground logs. More ammunition was passed around, clogged guns were busily repaired, and a hurried bit of food was divided among them all.

A few minutes before the fight was resumed, Finn discovered an Indian chieftain riding on a sorrel horse across the creek. He stopped in plain sight, stood up in his stirrups, shaded his eyes with his hand, and peered toward the corral.

It was too good an opportunity to miss. Finn ran for his gun, took careful aim, and fired. At the report, the sorrel jumped back, and his rider fell into the creek to lie there strangling and gasping in three feet of water.

"That Indian is drowning," Finn exclaimed to Al Stevenson, who happened to be watching.

"I hope he lasts all day, then," returned the teamster.

That sounded harsh, undoubtedly, but every man knew the cruelty of the foe. All had talked the situation over during the lulls, and not a person there but believed that the enclosure would be overrun by nightfall. Each had resolved to keep one shot for himself at the last, and to take as many Sioux with him as was possible.

Then, like an avalanche, swept down the whooping tide again. From the west side this time the attack was the most ferocious, led by a Cheyenne medicine-man who wore a waving war-bonnet with double tails reaching almost to the ground on each side of his horse.

Around and around the mounted Indians raced, firing from positions flat along their ponies' backs, dropping off with shrieks of agony here and there as they were hit by the volleys from the corral.

Finn found little to do at this time in his corner, so he slipped over to the west side to help Duncan there. Noting the medicine-man, and his leadership of the

Indians, Finn turned to Duncan, and pointed to his new Winchester rifle.

"George," he yelled amid the clamor, "get that medicine-man the next time he comes past. Don't miss him!"

A moment later, and the Cheyenne chieftain rode by again, leading a swarm of his supporters from the hills. Whooping, and waving his arms about, he proved to be an easy target for George Duncan, and he fell with a bullet in his head.

There ensued a wild yelling and jabbering, as a number of warriors charged in, picked up his body, and fled to the top of the bench. There, those bodies which had been recovered, together with the wounded, had been brought, and hundreds of squaws were busy with bandages and herbs, keeping up a continual howling and death-chanting.

On laying the medicine-man upon the ground, the Indians were astonished to see him come to life and sit up. The bullet had hit him in the forehead, and had in some surprising manner followed along his skull under the skin, and had emerged at the back. He had been merely stunned.

He immediately perceived the advertising value of his predicament. Spitting on the ground, he took up the mud and slapped it to both holes in his head.

"See, my children," he howled. "See my medicine. The bullets of the white men cannot harm me. Come with me and let us overrun these white fiends together."

Something went wrong with this plan, however. Either he was too weakened to continue, or his followers had lost faith, for he did not make his appearance in front of the corral again that day.

The keen zest for the fight had long since departed

from the Sioux. They had pounced upon the apparently defenseless corral that morning, believing that the elimination of this handful of white men would be but a passing incident on their path to a greater victory. But they had up to this time been whipped unmercifully.

Piles of dead were lying before the enclosure, in the thickets, and upon the bench. Discontent was becoming apparent in their ranks, as was attested by the manner in which they withdrew into little, disgruntled groups which sat arguing sullenly and casting dark, vengeful glances toward the defenders.

There was intermittent firing going on, however, on all sides, and Finn continued busy in his corner, keeping the Indians far back in the thickets. Then, as most tragedies have their elements of humor, so did a phase of this battle bring a smile to the grim lips of Finn Burnett.

While he had been working for the government, he had followed the usual procedure of drawing clothing from the quartermaster. A few days before this battle, he had been issued a pair of trousers, and had found them to be much too large about the waist. He had gathered them together, and had tied the excess waistband into a bunch at the back.

Now, as he lay flat behind the bottom log at his corner of the corral, he frequently became conscious of a peculiar tugging sensation behind him. He investigated, and found that whenever he raised himself a trifle to shoot, the bunch on the rear of his pants was revealed above the log. Some hidden marksman was taking unjustifiable liberties, in his somewhat prejudiced opinion.

Finn began to observe from whence the shots came. Keeping his eye to a crack in the log, he cautiously raised his hind quarters a trifle, and was rewarded with a sharp pull at the bunch, and the sight of gun smoke from behind a cottonwood stump, forty yards from the corral.

It had been a bit of excellent shooting, and Finn was careful. The stump behind which the marksman was concealed had been gnawed by beavers years before, and now appeared to be somewhat rotten and untrustworthy.

"Hey, George, watch me get me another Indian," Finn called to Duncan.

Then, setting his sights carefully on the spot where the Indian would appear, Finn slowly humped himself. There was a movement by the stump, and, at the instant of the tug behind him, Finn fired.

"You shot too low. You didn't get him," roared Duncan.

Finn said nothing. He had perfect faith in his marksmanship now, and when he investigated later, his belief was justified.

Following that bit of diversion, Al Colvin crept to every man in the corral, and shifted most of the defenders to concentrate his entire force along the south side. He seemed to sense that the next attack would come from the direction of Warrior creek, and he planned to meet it with a terrible fire which would end the battle.

His foresight was admirable. The Miniconjou Sioux had been directing his force from a distant bluff, fairly frothing at the mouth as he saw charge after charge of his great army thrown back, bloody and defeated. Now, he came strutting angrily into their midst, south of the creek.

"Listen, you chiefs of the Sioux. I will show you how

to kill these despised white men. I, myself, will lead you. Order all your warriors to leave their ponies and follow me to victory on foot."

Every Indian on the banks whooped, and joined his host of braves. Down to the stream they ran, with the Miniconjou Sioux in the lead.

Al Colvin, in the corral, lay watching.

"I'll kill the first Indian that crosses the creek. You can have the rest," he yelled.

The Indians plunged down the bank and splashed through the water. Hundreds of leaping, hideously-painted maniacs they were, shrieking with frenzy, brandishing war-clubs and knives, painted with all the mingled colors of carmine, yellow, and slate blue.

The Miniconjou Sioux, a magnificent figure of a man, strong and deadly with purpose, was the first across the stream. He lunged up the bank and began to race toward the corral.

"Fire," roared Colvin, and he pressed his trigger. As the crash of the most concerted volley of the day rang out, the Miniconjou Sioux seemed to wither and shrink in upon himself, the glisten in his eyes turned to glaze, and he fell like a log, headlong to the dust.

From every foot of the corral fence came volley after volley which blew the Indians to pieces as they fled back across the creek. Back they came again, and yet again, in heroic efforts to regain the body of their chieftain, but at every effort, Al Colvin and his men piled them up in shuddering, bloody heaps upon the ground.

"I'll hold that chief there if I have to go out and sit on him," remarked Colvin once, as he blew the smoke from his Henry rifle. Then he grinned, and his lip bled.

That attack marked the end of the battle, and every-one knew it when they saw the heaps of dead and

wounded, many of which were but an arms-length from
the posts of the corral. Such deadly accuracy of concentrated firing was more than any human beings could
sustain.

Soon could be seen bands of mounted Indians riding
far down the valley, converging on the outlet, and
moving homeward. Evidently, they were commencing a
general retreat to the Rosebud, believing that if they
could not overcome a handful of white men in an open
corral, they could not hope to engage successfully the
several companies of soldiers within the stockade of
Fort C. F. Smith.

All through the day, one of the soldiers had been
pleading with Al Colvin for permission to ride to the
fort to beg for relief for the beleaguered corral. Now it
was decided that he could make the attempt, as but a
few snipers were being left behind the main body of
the Sioux.

It was found that one horse only remained un-
wounded at the picket line, and this the soldier hastened
to saddle while Colvin wrote a message to General
Bradley.

This letter should have been preserved as one of the
most priceless messages in American military history.
He wrote that he had dead and wounded in the corral,
and that he was unable to care for them properly because after dark all the survivors would probably be
obliged to leave the enclosure. He stated that the Indians had been so severely punished that they had left,
with only a few snipers remaining behind them, and
that if he, General Bradley, was a man, he would send
relief, but that if he wasn't, he could go to hell where
he ought to be.

This peculiar appeal was given to the messenger, who

set out, after belting on two pistols for protection. Colvin cautioned him to go quietly until he had reached the point of the bench which hid the fort from sight. Then, if any Indians had discovered him, they would probably cut in behind him, and he should gallop into the post from there.

The men in the enclosure saw that he was not accustomed to riding horses, as soon as he started out. They tried to call him back, but the brave fellow refused to listen, and rode quietly on to the point, as he had been directed, but, instead of galloping from there, he continued on at a walk.

Those in the corral saw thirty Indians start out along the foot of the hills after him, and all yelled and fired their guns as a warning, but he took no heed, and ambled on easily until the warriors overtook him about 700 yards from the fort.

There is a divine providence which seems to undertake the special care of fools and innocents, and in this case the fact was most apparent. There was a deep gulch crossing the road at the spot where the Indians overtook the messenger. He promptly fell from his mount into this gulley, and rolled unharmed down the sharp incline all the way from the road to the river.

The soldiers in the fort had been aroused at the sight of the Indians, and all had poured their fire at them, without seeing the messenger at all. He, under cover of their volleys, kept below the bank until he arrived opposite the post, where he forded the river, and was met by the entire personnel of the fort at the gate. He gave the message to General Bradley, who ordered out two companies to go to the corral immediately.

The men back in the enclosure feared that the rescuers would turn back when they met the Indian snipers on the way. They packed up, made stretchers for the wounded, and prepared to make a dash for the fort in the event the relief did not get through.

Their fears were justified. At the first shots from the snipers, the major who commanded the foremost company halted the column, and prepared to retire. The lieutenant in charge of the company behind him, then rode up and told the major to go ahead or get his men out of the way before he had to march over them.

The two companies then fought through, and reached the corral at sunset. The first act of the soldiers of the relief, was to cut off the head of the Miniconjou Sioux for a souvenir.

On looking over the battleground, they found plenty of evidence of how desperate had been the fighting. The end-gate which Finn had set up to shield Al Colvin had been literally shot to pieces, and, although his clothes were cut and torn by bullets, he had not received a single wound.

Of the thirty-one mules which had been tied along the picket line, only one was unharmed. The wagon-boxes along the west side of the corral had been riddled to splinters, and the soldiers' tents were in ribbons. Armfuls of arrows were scattered about the enclosure, and the ground was covered with cartridge shells around the little dug-out positions that the men had defended throughout the day.

Outside, the thickets and the grass in the meadows were filled with the remains of shattered redskins. Many of the bodies were so close to the corral that they had been powder-burned. In some instances, there was evidence that more than one Sioux had been killed by a single shot.

The major was anxious to get started back to the fort.

Finn found two of his mules apparently not badly wounded, and they were hitched up. Into the wagon he piled all the property which he wished to carry along, for he knew the Indians would return that night, and would destroy everything that was left.

Others found a few mules which could travel, and were busy loading up another wagon.

The major was hurrying everyone. Finn was doing his best, when the officer stepped up to him and swore at him, telling the young man to get on his wagon and to start for the fort, half loaded. Al Colvin heard this, and went over to them.

"Major," he drawled, "if you're afraid to stay here long enough for Burnett to gather up his employer's property, you'd better take your outfit and go on without us. We've fought Indians all day, and I guess we could fight our way back to the fort all right now."

Then, as they started, Finn noticed that one of his mules was trembling violently. He got down to look her over, and found blood to be spurting from her side. A bullet had gone through her breast, scraping her heart, and at the first pull of the load, the blood had begun to flow with every pulse beat. She bled to death in her tracks.

Finn found another mule to take her place, and the trip to the fort was made without further incidents.

Next day, on returning to the corral, it was found that the Indians had wrecked everything. They had taken their spite out on the wounded mules, by cutting and hacking them until they died.

For several days after the Hay Fields fight, as it was called from then on, Crow Indians kept riding into the fort with interesting information. They said that the Sioux village on the Rosebud was filled with wounded, and that they were continually carrying away newly-dead from the lodges. Day after day, they said, the squaws were keeping up a hideous howling and lamentation.

Colonel Green reached the fort with two companies of cavalry two days after the fight, and when the Crow told him of the great numbers of the Sioux that had been killed, he expressed some doubts. The Crow then offered to take him to the spot where the Sioux buried their dead.

It was customary for the plains Indians to shroud the bodies of their dead in blankets or buffalo robes, and suspend them in trees or upon scaffolds. If, however, no vegetation were nearby sufficient for their needs, the sides of cliffs were excavated, and caves were used for repositories. These Crow guided Colonel Green to a sandstone ledge some distance east of the corral, and told him that the numbers buried there were small beside those which were to be found in another location a longer distance away and which they were prepared to show him.

Colonel Green was astonished at the execution which had evidently been wrought, and stated that he was satisfied. There was a large party of Sioux in the neighborhood, so he returned to the fort, and consequently no one ever was to know the true number of Sioux who died as a result of that fight.

At the fort, the day after the Hay Fields fight brought shame to the cowards who had shown their weakness in the corral. The soldier who had threatened suicide and the one who had been slightly wounded in the legs were obliged to march through the post with placards tied to their breasts and backs, marked "COWARD." In addition, each carried a heavy log over his shoulder.

Wheeling, being a teamster, escaped such punishment, but he was ostracised by everyone, and his situation was made so embarrassing for him that he left soon afterwards for other parts.

The major refused to recognize Finn at any time after that, fearing that his timidity at the corrals would be advertised. But, although Finn came in contact with him frequently several months later at Fort Washakie, the young man never divulged his character to anyone.

Hollister, wounded in the stomach, was operated upon by post surgeons the next day, but did not live past nightfall.

There is one important point to bring out before closing the account of this episode. Following the argument between Chief Red Cloud and the Miniconjou Sioux on the Rosebud, the forces had been equally divided. The Miniconjou Sioux had advanced on Fort C. F. Smith, and on meeting a decided reverse at the hay fields, the survivors had returned to their main camp.

It is probably one of the most peculiar coincidences of all frontier history, and one whose results held far-reaching benefits for the white cause, that Chief Red Cloud proceeded with his force on the longer trail toward Fort Phil Kearny, and on August 2nd, on the day following the Hay Fields fight, ninety-one miles away, met a small wood-train in his path, stopped to wipe it out, and was there repulsed with such losses that he, too, returned to the Rosebud without attacking his main objective.

Both chieftains, then, with equal numbers in their commands, suffered defeats from small forces in their paths, and both armies returned discomfited to the village, to give up their plans for general devastation.

The battle at Fort Phil Kearny was called the

Wagon-box fight. In this battle there were thirty-two men who fought from behind a circle of wagon-boxes for three hours until relieved by General Smith.

But, although the Hay Fields battle was fought by only nineteen men from an open corral, and no relief was sent to them all day, the reports which were received in Washington were curiously silent about this battle.

General Smith relieved his wood-train at the Wagon-box fight, and reported it fully. Full recognition was given to its gallant fighters. General Bradley, on the other hand, did not relieve the defenders of his hay corral, and therefore made no report of the incident. So, the Hay Fields fight has not to this day received the recognition which it deserved.

Two days after the battle, Finn moved back with an escort to the meadows, and there a new corral was built a half mile farther out into the valley, away from the hills. Uprights were set in the ground, with logs laid in crotches, and sod was stacked up underneath to form a solid breastworks.

But they were never attacked by any large force of Indians again, and the hay contract was filled within the next two weeks in comparative safety.

"Big Bat" Poirier, a half-breed, and Louis Richards acted as guards and scouts, supplying the corral with fresh meat. A full company of infantry with a twelve-pound howitzer also insured protection against a repetition of that desperate day of the Hay Fields fight.

Running the Big Horn Canyon

Running the Big Horn Canyon

With the hay work finished, Mr. Leighton next secured a contract to deliver wood at Fort C. F. Smith for $27.50 a cord, and saw-logs at $50 per thousand.

For several days, all the driftwood along the banks of the Big Horn river was gathered. Then it was decided that the crew should cut logs over the mountains to the southward, and attempt to run them through the Big Horn canyon to the fort. A boom was thereupon built across the river close to the post, and Leighton's wagon-train started for the logging country.

A sixteen-foot boat had been constructed at Fort C. F. Smith, and this they hauled with them on a wagon, up the Bozeman trail and through the Pryor mountains to a place close to the mouth of Stinking Water, above the canyon.

Here were found thick forests, and all hands set to work, felling the pine trees, lopping the limbs, bucking the logs, and rolling them to the river.

After several weeks of such labor, the store of provisions began to get low and conversations were heard among the men relative to the possibility for a boat to negotiate the thirty-mile-long canyon to the fort.

Crow Indians who visited the logging-camp were asked for their opinion, and all declared that such a venture would result in disaster for the participants. They stated that no one, red or white, had ever run the gorge successfully; that there were falls and rapids to be met with at frequent intervals; and that a boat or raft would be broken up before a mile could be negotiated. They furthermore declared that from the tops of its cliffs they had seen one spot where the river plunged into a subterranean tunnel which gave forth dreadful sighings and groanings.

Al Colvin, Al Stevenson, and Finn Burnett were undaunted by these adverse reports, and decided to take the boat and attempt to be the first human beings to go through the canyon. They believed that the roar of the falls and rapids which they would meet would give them ample warning of their peril, and that they could portage around most of the difficulties.

The three adventurers then slid the boat to the edge of the river, and placed a sack of provisions within it. As an extra precaution, they took a rifle, plugged its tube and breech with tallow, and tied it fast where it could not be lost in a possible upset.

All the men in camp then worked an entire day, pushing most of the accumulated logs into the river and starting them on their way through the gap toward the fort. This completed, the three men bade farewell to their comrades who were preparing to hitch up and travel the long, roundabout route back to Fort C. F. Smith.

One old man named Harwood was to be left at the camp until their return. He was told to wait for ten days, and after that length of time had elapsed, if none of them had returned to the logging camp, he should roll the last of the logs into the river and make his way alone to the fort.

Next morning, the boat was launched, and the great adventure was begun. To the south, behind these voyagers spread out the beautiful Big Horn basin, with its watershed of 22,000 square miles which emptied into this mighty river. Before them, was the winding canyon of the Big Horn river which promised unknown dangers.

For a little distance, they drifted easily into the southern end of the gorge. The banks were scarcely thirty feet apart, and the limestone cliffs rose on either side. Here the water was black and moved slowly, evidently being of great depth.

Beyond these first narrows, the river widened, and little pastures appeared on either bank, with gently sloping ridges covered with sage and scrub pines. Floating gently through this hidden paradise, they found themselves swept around a curve which circled the base of a towering red cliff, as they entered the impressive gateway of the main canyon.

Here the walls ascended vertically from the water to a height of 2000 feet. The frail boat was threatened with huge boulders and ledges of rocks which had toppled from above in past centuries, and over which the water cascaded in a foaming torrent. The three men barely had poled and pushed their craft past these dangers when a deafening blast of noise sounded a warning ahead.

Colvin glanced around quickly for a landing place and saw a sand bar convenient to their need. Beaching the boat, the three made their way along the edge of the water to view the difficulty ahead.

Here proved to be what is referred to as a "bottleneck," where the narrowing walls of the canyon held back the river, to allow it to spew onward with terrific force and pandemonium. In the little space between the cliffs, the sound of this liberated water reverberated upon the ears of the three men like the blasting barrages of giant artillery.

The danger to be met in traversing the course, however, appeared to be slight at this time, for, although the current was narrow and swift, the infernal noise promised to be their worst hindrance.

After successfully running these narrows, the voyagers found their journey to be a continued demand upon their vigilance. The river twisted and turned between shouldering walls so swiftly that seldom could they see farther than two hundred yards before them. The air in those depths was forbidding and chill. Sun penetrated to the river but a few minutes of the day, then lingered only upon the topmost pinnacles, to kindle their splashes of red and crimson to a maze of brilliant pigment.

The adventurers floated on, sometimes speeding along between the cliffs on the bosom of the swift waters, at others floating quietly on the widened stream to gaze with intense interest at flats and little, wooded creeks which bubbled and leaped their way to the river from either side.

At the mouth of one of these tributaries, they stopped for the night, beaching their boat on a sand tongue which thrust itself out into the current. Here a huge gorge struck off diagonally from the Big Horn river, and through it flowed an icy mountain stream, fed by the glaciers of the distant peaks.

At this point, the walls of the canyon proper were at least 2000 feet in height. The river had torn at the base of the cliffs until in many places they overhung the water.

Next morning, the travelers started on again, in the

cold, moist dawn. Mile after mile through the canyon they swept, watching with eagle eyes for the upshooting rocks ahead, poling their way carefully around the curves, drenched with flecks of splashing water, and chilled to the bone in the gloomy depths of the deafening inferno.

For awhile, the cliffs became lower, and they passed through a flatter country. Then, beyond, as they entered another phase of their endeavor, the walls of rocks again pushed in upon them.

Suddenly, they reached a sharp bend. Colvin braced his pole against a solid wall of granite that appeared directly before him, and pushed the bow of the boat around. The current swirled them ahead sideways, and in a flash of speed they found themselves in the midst of a boiling, leaping cauldron which lifted them and hurled them upside down into a froth-covered whirlpool.

The three were good swimmers, and each struck out through the icy water for the nearest bank. Fortunately, there was a wide shelf of rock along the water's edge at this point, and they emerged together, to hoist themselves dripping upon this refuge where they could look about them and take stock of their situation.

They discovered that they had been tremendously fortunate. The boat was found floating around and around in an eddy nearby, and when recovered proved to be undamaged. One oar was softly nudging the far cliff, and the other had been flung upon a pile of driftwood, fifty feet down the stream.

When these had been regained, the light was fading, and they decided to make a fire and remain there for the night. They were wet, chilled, and thoroughly miserable, but after dry driftwood had been collected and a fire started with their flint and steel, the welcome heat brought back their optimism.

All the provisions had been lost, however. A moist loaf of bread was all that had been found floating in an eddy, and this they divided for their supper.

Then the miracle happened. All were sitting glumly around the fire, hungry and wondering about the future, when Al Stevenson chanced to glance up at the cliffs above. He sprang for the boat and began to tear frantically at the ropes which secured the gun. The other two men gazed at him wonderingly, and then looked upward. There, in plain sight, on a ledge directly over them, stood a large mountain sheep.

Hours seemed to pass before Stevenson released the gun, hastily cleaned away the tallow, and aimed at the animal. As he fired, the sheep slumped a moment, then slowly straightened out and fell from the ledge, to land almost in the center of the campfire.

It was with a cheer mingled with amazement at their good fortune that the three men pulled the fat, young buck to one side and in a few minutes had him skinned and cleaned. Soon they were sitting in a circle around the blazing logs, roasting huge steaks until their hunger had been appeased.

Next morning, after a broiled breakfast, the voyagers started on again, taking with them ample meat to use for the remainder of the trip. That day brought to them a succession of fourteen rapids with short distances of swift, dangerous water between. The canyon walls continued high and overhanging, and mist which rose from the churning waters lingered overhead throughout the day.

That night was spent above the worst rapid of the

entire trip. Camp was made amid beautiful surroundings, where dense thickets of cottonwoods grew to the bank of the river, and vines and bushes were green on every side.

Next morning, refreshed and with plenty of good sheep steaks under their belts, the three adventurers shot the rapids. The stream swept in a torrent through a maze of jagged boulders which threatened at any minute to tear great holes in the bottom of the vessel.

Colvin in the bow worked frantically to keep the boat clear. Then, to avoid disaster, he gave a desperate heave at his oar to miss a pointed rock, and the craft swung broadside to the current. In a moment, the water had poured over the gunwhales, and all were in the water vainly struggling to gain the shore.

Several hundred yards below the scene of the accident, the current lost its grip, and the three men were able to wade ashore. The boat was found to be still unharmed, and it was cleared, and all set out again.

There were a few more rapids which were negotiated successfully, and at three o'clock in the afternoon, the three travelers emerged from the canyon's mouth, and saw Fort C. F. Smith awaiting them. They had been the first human beings to go through the great gorge of the Big Horn river.

For several days after their arrival, Colvin, Stevenson, and Finn Burnett alternately rested and watched the river intently. No logs had yet come through, but on the fifth day, something black drifted out from the mouth of the canyon. Finn called to his friends that the logs were coming, and all ran to the boom.

The floating object slowly resolved itself into the form of old man Harwood. He had run out of food, and, despairing of anyone reaching him before he starved to death, he had pinned two cottonwood logs together, and had ridden them down.

All plans for driving logs through the canyon were then discarded. Logging operations were started on the mountains closer to Fort C. F. Smith, and the contract was filled in record time.

Louis Richards, the scout, left the Big Horn country at this time, and Frank Berthune took his place as camp guard and hunter. Indians never attacked the wood-train, and the timber work proved to be uneventful.

Leaving the Indian Country

Leaving the Indian Country

In October, 1867, Finn returned to Fort Phil Kearny with the Leighton train. There he went to work for the quartermaster again, caring for the beef herd.

Word had been sent to the Sioux, Cheyenne, and Arapaho during the latter part of October, asking them to come to Fort Phil Kearny, there to assist in drawing up a treaty between all belligerents which would insure a lasting peace.

On the arrival of the Indians, they grouped their lodges in a great village along the Big Piney creek. As an act of courtesy, General Smith ordered the quartermaster's department to take provisions to them, and the clerk, Smith, and Finn Burnett loaded up a wagon with the food.

The two men started out for the Indian camp at nightfall, with sugar, flour, bacon, and coffee piled in the wagon. Both of them were extremely uneasy, as no treaty had been negotiated as yet, and the Indians whom they were approaching were still technically on the warpath.

News of the approaching peace conference had been received with little confidence by the garrisons and frontiersmen on the plains. The entire idea had been born in the unknowing minds of the board of Indian commissioners in Washington, which consisted of three men who themselves did not care to undertake the risk of meeting with the Indians, but who had delegated their authority to the army officers at Fort Phil Kearny, or-

dering them to prepare and sign a preliminary understanding which would be acceptable to the tribes. Later,
the formal treaty would be drawn up and ratified.

No one on the frontier had the least confidence in the
integrity of any promises which the Indians would
give; everyone believed that any treaty which might be
made would be an empty gesture.

Consequently, the two men driving toward the Indian
camp with a wagonload of provisions recognized their
danger, and, on leaving the gates of the fort behind,
Smith remarked to Finn, "You take care of the horses,
no matter what happens, and I'll see that the provisions
are unloaded."

Nearing the Sioux village, the two white men found
themselves entering an atmosphere of weird pandemonium. Dances were being held around a hundred campfires; drums boom-thong-boom-thonged everywhere;
dark, wild-acting, knife-stabbing shapes jumped and
pranced in and out of the firelight.

As they approached the lodges, the terror of the horses
rose correspondingly, until, when they had reached a
point fifty yards from the outskirts of the village, they
became absolutely unmanageable, and notwithstanding
Finn's efforts to control them, they wheeled about and
started to run toward the fort.

"This is as close as I can get," Finn yelled to Smith.
"Throw the grub out."

The clerk began to dump everything over the end-
gate as they bumped madly over the prairie, and when
the runaways reached the fort gates, provisions were
lying on the ground all the way to the village. The Indians came out later and gathered them up.

The preliminary treaty was signed next day. General
Smith, General Dandy, and all the commissioned offi-

cers of the fort met with the Indian chieftains on the Big Piney, about 500 yards from the stockade.

The quartermaster clerk, Smith, took down the treaty and all the speeches in splendid, legible longhand. The agreement stipulated that Forts C. F. Smith, Phil Kearny, Reno, and Fetterman were to be abandoned; that all soldiers would leave the country north of the Platte river, and west of the Black Hills of Dakota. In return, the Indians guaranteed to cease all hostilities, and to live quietly and peacefully on their reservations.

Later, the Sioux, Cheyenne, and Arapaho would meet at Fort Laramie with the board of Indian commissioners, and there would accomplish the final signing of the treaty. Until that time, the posts would be slowly dismantled.

Following this agreement, the winter of 1867-1868 was spent in demolishing Fort Phil Kearny, and it was during this period that Finn worked himself into a new job. Before this time, the mail had always been carried between the posts in an ambulance drawn by a six-mule team which was guided with a jerk-line. Trouble had been encountered repeatedly with Indians, and many mules had become exhausted and lost on the trail.

One morning, Burnett and Al Colvin were standing in front of General Dandy's office.

"I tell you, Finn," Colvin was saying, "I've only got three mules left out of the best lot of teams in the post. I have lost one or two every trip."

Finn smoked a moment, thoughtfully, then turned to Al.

"Why don't you rig the team up the way a stage outfit is rigged, with a jerk-line?" he asked. "You could make better time on the road, and have a lot less trouble."

General Dandy's voice surprised them from behind.

"Do you know how to rig up a team that way, Burnett?" he asked.

"Yes, sir, I do," answered the young man. "And I think that George Breckenridge, the master of transportation, does, too."

"I don't think that Breckenridge knows anything about it," returned the general. "If he did, he'd have arranged his teams that way before this. He knows what trouble we're having on the road. I'll tell you what I want you to do, Burnett. You take the mules you need from among the government teams, and rig them up as you suggested. Try driving the mails through for awhile. We'll see what luck you have."

Finn selected the best mules, put them in a separate stable in charge of a competent man who would give them proper care. Then he fitted an ambulance with seats which ran parallel with its length, and with a boot in the rear which would hold the mail and baggage.

From the time he began to drive with the mail, using the new rigging, Burnett never lost a mule, although, as was to be expected, the cavalry which acted as his escort lost several of their horses. The ambulance proved to be so comfortable that his trips became the occasions for outings by the officers and their families, who made the round trip frequently between Fort Phil Kearny and Fort Laramie for the pleasure of it.

Starting out from Fort Phil Kearny, after leaving the adjutant's office, his ambulance passed through an opening into the quartermaster's corral, then through the east gate, to start down the road along a grade, to cross the bridge of Little Piney and pull up the long hill to the summit of the divide that runs between Little Piney and Shell creeks.

Generally, after reaching the summit, the mules settled down and made excellent stage time. There were frequent attacks along the road, of course. Sometimes an Indian sniper would fire into the escort from bluffs or thickets, and the soldiers' horses were often wounded.

These mounts were always killed if they were too badly injured to travel, lest they be recovered by the Indians, healed, and used in later years against the whites.

Whenever a shot was heard, Finn had orders to slow down, and stop if the circumstances permitted. Shortly afterward, if a horse had been wounded, a cavalryman would always ride up carrying an empty saddle which he would place in the ambulance. A moment later, and another soldier would gallop up with the trooper who had lost his horse mounted behind him. The extra rider would climb into the ambulance, and all would then dash on down the trail.

When spring came to the plains in 1868, there was great activity along the Bozeman trail. Soldiers in every fort were busily engaged at dismantling the buildings and loading the supplies. Major David Gordon's company was ordered to Camp Stambaugh, a post near Atlantic City close to the head of the Sweetwater river, where he would be under the command of Colonel James Brisbin.

In March, some Arapaho Indians came in to Fort Phil Kearny with eighteen head of work oxen which they had captured from General Porter during the preceding summer. They offered to trade the cattle for flour, and Finn, sensing a bargain, agreed to take the animals, paying a hundred pounds of flour for each.

General Dandy sold Finn the government flour at $30 a hundredweight, but, as the young man did not have that amount of money, he got two men, Benjamin Heater and "Doc" Wilson, to go in with him on the deal.

The three partners then salvaged everything that they needed from the remains of the dismantled fort. Every sort of equipment, furnishings, and implements were heaped inside the stockade. Wagons, yokes, and chains were found, and when all had been assembled, they had three three-yoke teams with two wagons hitched to each team. These six wagons they then loaded with the beef hides which had accumulated at the fort ever since its occupation, and which were lying there waiting for anyone to take. They would sell for a high figure in Cheyenne.

When all were loaded and ready for the trail, Finn went to General Smith.

"General," the young man said, "in your opinion, would it be safe for us to make a trip through from here to Cheyenne without waiting for an escort?"

"Yes, if you start early," the officer answered. "If you go now before the grass becomes rich, and before the Indians' horses can get strong enough to be used in fighting, you will probably get through all right."

"There's another thing, general," Finn went on. "These oxen that we bought from the Indians still have General Porter's brand on them. I'm afraid that our title will be questioned when we try to sell them."

"The government has already paid General Porter for the cattle," answered the general. "But, to make everything perfectly in order, I'll draw up a paper for you, stating all the circumstances of your legal purchase of the cattle with my consent. I'll have General Dandy, Captain Ten Eyck, and Captain Gordon sign it with me."

About the first day of April, 1868, the three partners, "Doc" Wilson, Benjamin Heater, and Finn Burnett joined a wagon-train owned by a man named Callaghan who, with five others, was going to Cheyenne.

The day before they started, John Miller with six men in his train, left for Fort Fetterman. They encountered some Sioux as they camped on Sage creek, a day's drive from Fetterman.

As they were breaking camp in the morning, a Mexican employee of Miller's left to chase an antelope. He had been gone but a few minutes when a war-party of Sioux rode in and demanded something to eat. Miller and his companions held their guns ready and put up a brave front, stating that they had no food to give away. These Indians parleyed and threatened awhile, then rode away over the ridge in the direction which the Mexican had taken earlier in the morning.

The train waited for some time for the hunter's return, then a number of the men began to search for him. When they reached the top of the ridge, they could see his body lying in plain sight a short distance below them. He had been caught, killed, and scalped by the Sioux, after which his head had been cut off and used for a football.

When Burnett arrived with his wagon-train at Fort Fetterman after an uneventful trip, he found an atmosphere of great uneasiness and apprehension existing in the post. Miller had arrived with his outfit, and had camped on the banks of the Platte under the protection of the fort. There he stated that he was resolved to stay until travel in the country had become safe again.

The situation in the Platte valley was desperate that spring. Following the dismantling of the forts along the Bozeman trail, the Indians had begun to demonstrate an arrogance and an intolerance for white men which had not been foreseen by the war department. As a result, it had been decided that Fort Fetterman would not be discontinued until all Indian difficulties had become dissipated, and now that post sat, a lone refuge, in a valley that was daily being overrun by a treacherous, murderous horde.

With absolute disregard for the dangers which surrounded them on every side, Burnett and his friends rested for one day before starting on to Cheyenne.

Their first indication of trouble was found when the Fetterman road entered the Oregon trail at "One Arm" Judd's ranch below the natural bridge on La Prele creek. Judd had had a flourishing business in wintering ox-trains in his pastures, but now his establishment was found to be a smouldering ruin.

The house and barns were afire, the haystacks had been consumed, and the corrals were demolished. No living person was around the ranch, but there was every indication that a large war-party of Indians had swept through the valley that morning, burning ranches, and running off all the stock. Subsequently, it was learned that Judd had escaped, but of his men and cattle, nothing was ever heard.

The little wagon-train, warned of its danger by the destruction in evidence at Judd's ranch, proceeded on down the valley in a pouring rain, taking every precaution against ambush or surprise attack. These nine were the only men who traveled on the trail that week, to brave the horrors of massacre. Four men drove, keeping the four wagons close together, while five men marched beside them with guns ready across their breasts, watching every bush and tree, alert for the appearance of the black scalp-locks of waiting Sioux.

Every ranch from "One Arm" Judd's south to the Bordeaux ranch on the Chugwater had been burned to the ground. Each showed evidences of hurried departure, of sudden attack, of fiendish savagery.

Occasionally, Indians were seen watching this lone wagon-train that proceeded on so seemingly indifferent to the wasted country. But Indians seldom attacked anyone unless they had the element of surprise with them. If a redskin knew that he would encounter a desperate defense from the first moment of onslaught, he would usually withdraw and wait until he could fling himself upon his unsuspecting prey at a more auspicious time.

So this wagon-train plodded on slowly in the rain, watched by crouching Sioux from behind the surrounding hills and clumps of sage. As they progressed, the caution of the whites increased until, by the time they arrived at the canyon west of Horseshoe Station, through which the trail ran, they had reached the point of extreme watchfulness.

This defile was narrow and promised to be a place of unusual danger at such a menacing time. Scouting ahead before allowing the wagons to proceed through it, Finn found indications of the recent passing of the Indian war-party. In the trail at one place, the tracks of their ponies could be seen clearly where they had been made but a few minutes before, as was proved by the displaced mud which had not yet settled back into the hoof-prints. In another place, the grass and weeds which pushed close to the trail still dripped with the muddy water which had been splashed upon them by the passing of Indian ponies.

Returning to the wagons, and warning the drivers to keep their outfits closer together, the five scouts looked to their guns, and started afoot through the canyon, a hundred yards in advance of the first team.

Every step was taken with unusual caution. Every cliff and ledge, tree and bush, and the gray fallen logs which lay criss-crossed among the tangled vines and brush, were submitted to a sharp and suspicious scrutiny. Slowly, foot by foot, they worked their way down the valley, stopping repeatedly to allow the scouts to reconnoitre around the sharp corners ahead. Undoubtedly, their extreme caution and care brought them through in safety, for the gulleys and ravines about them were apparently filled with Sioux.

Finally, the vigilant band approached the southern end of Horseshoe canyon, and there they beheld the stage station and trader's store ablaze across the creek from the trail. Knowing that Indians still lurked in the shadows anticipating that those in the train would dash for the buildings and thus divide their forces, Burnett and the others paid no attention to the burning settlement.

They corralled their wagons quietly on a well-protected knoll, tied the mules and oxen in the center, and cooked their supper of bacon, fresh meat, bread, and coffee.

It was dark when the meal had been eaten and the dishes washed. Then, Callaghan and Finn decided to do a little scouting of their own to determine if there were any wounded whites hidden around the station.

Each took a blanket and wrapped it in Indian fashion about him, knowing it to be a sufficient disguise in the blackness of the night. They crossed the creek carefully and began to investigate, finding that the store had been gutted, and its goods scattered in the grass of the clearing. Several head of horses and cattle lay dead in the corrals, but scalped or wounded human beings were not to be found.

Had they known of the whereabouts of the dug-out close to the trader's store, they would have found there three dead men, scalped and mutilated after a terrible siege. John Smith, the trader, had escaped with two others by fighting a desperate running battle, during which they gained a high saddle-shaped bluff southwest of the station. Here they had managed to repel the Indians until nightfall brought them an opportunity to slip away. These three survivors then made their way afoot to Fort Laramie, twenty-five miles away, and arrived almost dead from exhaustion.

Next morning, Burnett's party started on. Here they left the trail as it turned eastward toward Fort Laramie, and the train proceeded directly southward for the mouth of the Chugwater on the Laramie river. The ranch on the Cottonwood was found to be burning, as was the one on the Little Laramie river. When they arrived at the Bordeaux ranch on the Chugwater they found it to be unharmed, and filled to overflowing with traders and ranch people who lived in the vicinity and who had fled to its shelter for sanctuary. Fortifications had been made on all sides, and everyone was ready to make a desperate fight against the war-party which had laid waste the lower end of the valley.

The cattle and horses of these refugees had been left outside the breastworks with the Bordeaux herd. As it had been felt that every man was needed to guard the ranch, this stock had been unguarded when a band of 175 Sioux swept down upon them.

Finding that the white men were well fortified, the Indians had been content in this instance to make a slight demonstration against the settlement and then had gathered up most of the herd. This stock they had run eastward over the divide toward Horse creek.

This raid was made in the latter part of April, 1868. It will be remembered that the agreement which had been signed at Fort Phil Kearny in October of the preceding year had stipulated that the forts along the Bozeman trail would be abandoned, and that the Indians would cease hostilities. Now, during the spring of 1868, the forts had been dismantled, but the Sioux continued their depredations.

Continuing on southward toward Cheyenne, Burnett's party camped one night on the divide between Crow creek and the Chugwater. They had a tent with them, but the night was pleasant and they unrolled their beds and slept in the open.

During the night, Finn was awakened by snow which was pelting him in the face. He drowsily drew his tarpaulin bedcover over his head, and went back to sleep.

Next morning, the party found that they had been slumbering in three feet of snow. The storm had come from the northeast, and the stock had drifted with it. Finn started out to look for the animals and found them behind a sandstone ledge about 500 yards from camp, huddled close together.

Arriving in Cheyenne without further trouble, they sold the beef hides for seventeen cents a pound, and Finn Burnett bought several teams of oxen and mules, and two wagons with his share. His days along the Bozeman trail were over, and he found that he must begin a new phase of life.

The Union Pacific railroad had built to Dale creek, west of Cheyenne. There a trestle was being flung across a canyon, and the young man decided to become a "grader."

Grading on the Union Pacific

Grading on the Union Pacific

A few days of work at Dale creek convinced Finn that his teams could produce better profits for him elsewhere. All of his money had been used to pay for his oxen, and he had no more with which to procure scrapers.

So he drove on westward to Laramie. There he became acquainted with a Mr. Butler who was constructing a ferry boat on the Platte river, a half mile above where the Union Pacific crossing was to be in later years. Mr. Butler hired Finn to haul the lumber from a sawmill at Cooper lake.

With that job finished, the young man secured the contract for transporting the piling and bridge timbers from Elk mountain for the first bridge which the Union Pacific built near Fort Steele. Finn put his train in charge of Al Colvin for this job while he helped to build the ferryboat for Mr. Butler.

About four hundred yards above the site of the proposed ferry was a ford which was used by the emigrants on the Overland trail. It provided a very dangerous passage, and one outfit composed of surveyors and their assistants had been drowned at that crossing a few days before Finn's arrival.

Superintended by a Scottish ship carpenter, Alec McIntyre, the ferryboat was completed, and then it was found that Finn was the only man available who could operate it. Mr. Butler hired him to run the boat until the fall, when the flood waters would decrease.

During this time, he worked day and night ferrying emigrant trains across to the west bank, as well as the wagons hauling supplies ahead for the railroad.

By the first of July, Finn had accumulated a little money, and he sold his oxen for an excellent figure to his old friends Benjamin Heater and "Doc" Wilson. He immediately invested every cent of his profits in mules, horses, and scrapers, which enabled him to work on the railroad again as a grader with his own first-class outfit.

The work on the right-of-way was being done by contractors who took over the construction and grading of portions of the road work, hiring men like Finn Burnett, who had their own outfits with which to do the work.

His first job was under a contractor named Henry Sisson, who had come west from Finn's neighborhood in Missouri. Many of the men in this group had been boyhood friends of the young man, and he enjoyed his work tremendously.

It was while he was grading with Sisson's men that Finn became a victim of the last raid that the Sioux made upon the Union Pacific right-of-way.

This was about the last of July, 1868, when camp had been made on a flat across the river from Fort Steele. The Indians attacked without warning at dawn, and killed several graders before running off most of their horses and mules. Finn's loss in this engagement amounted to more than half of his stock.

When that section of the right-of-way had been completed, Finn moved westward to work first for M. S. Hall on Bitter creek, and then for other contractors who were eager for his services.

While he was grading for Hall, Finn received a letter from A. C. Leighton. The old sutler informed him that he was opening up a store in Atlantic City in the newly-discovered gold country of the upper Sweetwater valley. He offered the young man a place with him, and Finn left his teams in charge of Tom McCoy while he went to look the situation over. He decided, however, that there was more money to be gained at grading work that year, but, as the railroad was rapidly nearing completion, he promised Mr. Leighton that he would return in the spring to work for him.

It was while he was employed between Black Butte Station and Point of Rocks that Finn lost the remainder of his teams. A gang of horse-thieves had made their rendezvous in the mountains south of the railroad, from whence they descended regularly upon the camps of the graders to take a great toll from the herds along the right-of-way. These stolen animals were then driven into Colorado where they were sold.

The thieves raided the camp at night, and ran off almost the entire herd. Finn joined William McKin and a number of other graders in a pursuit which followed their trail for fifteen miles before they overtook the outlaws.

As the posse approached a large, rocky draw, they were met with a volley from ambush. McKin and Finn ran from their horses, and began to return the fire from behind the boulders in the ravine, but the thieves outflanked them, and made their position so dangerous that the two were obliged to retreat slowly back to their mounts and race for their lives.

This raid practically ruined Finn, but he borrowed some money, bought more mules, and continued with his work, moving on to Edward Creighton's outfit which was working between Rawlins and Green river.

Here he found the most efficient work being accomplished that he had ever seen. The track-layers were immediately behind the graders in this stretch, laying the rails as fast as the dirt-movers could level the right-of-way ahead of them. In one day, they laid more than nine miles of track, and all by hand, a record which was said never to have been equalled.

West of Rawlins, the grade entered the territory of Chief Washakie of the friendly Shoshoni tribe of Indians. This great, old chieftain had guaranteed that the contractors of the Union Pacific railroad would never be molested in that portion of the frontier which was under his jurisdiction, and the promise was never broken.

The graders then contracted for a piece of work across the east line of Nevada on Grouse creek, and moved to that point. Before they had completed the job, they were ordered back to assist in the unusually difficult grading work at a promontory west of the Salt lake.

They had a very interesting experience on their way to the new location. The outfit stopped in Ogden to rest, and boarded at the only hotel in the town. This hostelry was owned by Bishop West of the Mormon church, who had sixteen wives. Nine of these fortunate women ran the hotel under the leadership of his ninth wife who was a middle-aged, splendid woman. As she was much more intelligent than were his other wives, Bishop West had made her his general counsel, and had given her his utmost confidence in keeping his hotel and wives in order.

A short time before the arrival of the graders, however, the bishop's youngest wife, a handsome girl of sixteen, had fallen in love with the division agent of the Overland Stage company, in Ogden. They were both well aware that rumors had been whispered of a gentile who had but a few weeks before this time attempted to elope with one of a Mormon's miscellaneous wives, and that the couple had been pursued and killed on the west side of the Salt lake.

Notwithstanding all this, the two lovers decided to escape to Sacramento, in California. They had in some manner gained the confidence and assistance of the bishop's ninth wife, and she had joined in the plans for their departure.

The Overland Stage company had sent a span of its finest thoroughbred racing horses to Ogden to be used in the initial dash, and at the stations which were dotted across the country all the way to California specially fed horses were awaiting the exciting day.

To assist in their speed, a light-weight, single-seated spring buggy had also been taken secretly into Ogden, and everyone anticipated that they would effect the quickest trip in frontier history.

Finn was told of the scheme, and was asked to assist with the other young dare-devil graders in guarding the road leading out of Ogden, to turn back any Mormon pursuers. This he agreed to do, and received the hearty accord of his friends.

On the designated night, all were in readiness. The thoroughbreds were harnessed and champing at their bits in the darkness of their stable; the graders lay along the road on the outskirts of Ogden with their guns ready. At every stage station west of the Salt lake, hostlers were awake and waiting, peering into the eastern night for the sight of the galloping teams.

The lovers slipped quietly through the dark to the barns. In a moment their baggage was stowed away, and they were hoisted into the seat by willing hands. The prospective groom grasped the reins, whispered a quick word of thanks, the doors were thrown open, and the race was on.

Down the streets of Ogden they sped past silent houses, and westward across the prairies. Behind them, the graders closed in upon the road, to lie there with ready guns to turn back any who gave chase.

On the lovers sped. The hoof beats of their racing horses echoed far ahead, and at every change station the lights were on, and eager groups of men were waiting to spring to unhitch the traces and replace the lathering thoroughbreds with others champing to be away.

There was no pursuit. The elopement had been so shrouded in secrecy, and so efficiently planned, that the young agent and the bishop's wife were in Sacramento, and far beyond the influence of Bishop West before their absence was detected.

The completion of the transcontinental line approached rapidly. The Central Pacific railroad was building from the western terminal, while the Union Pacific was pushing its rails westward. Both railroads were rushing their construction with utmost speed, for it had been agreed that the point at which the rails of the two contestants met would mark the end of their respective lines.

A peculiar side-light of that spectacular race is revealed in that the Central Pacific employed Chinamen almost exclusively for its labor, while the Union Pacific hired Irishmen who worked as though the welfare of the entire railroad rested on their shoulders.

After the rails from the east and west had joined,

however, a compromise was agreed upon between the two railroads, and the "golden" spike which should have been hammered in at the point of juncture, was driven instead at Ogden, fifty miles to the east.

The last day was the scene of a great celebration. Together, the superintendents of the Union Pacific and Central Pacific put in place the polished tie that would mark the exact spot of the union of the two railroads.

Then came a squad of Irish track-workers of the Union Pacific railroad, clean and shining for the occasion, with a pair of rails upon their shoulders, while, from the opposite direction came a similar group of Chinamen bearing the other pair of rails which would complete the track. Amid a roar of pride, the last fish-plate was tightened, and various officials drove their silver and golden spikes.

Thomas A. McCoy and Finn had been hauling crooked juniper and cedar wood from the hills for the locomotives, as there was a scarcity of coal. On the day of the festivities, Tom and his wife attended the ceremonies with Finn, watching the driving of the "golden" spike, hearing the sonorous speeches, and joining in the dancing and merrymaking.

Thus, in a grand burst of entertainment and amid a scene of hilarity, ended Finn's grading days. And, as the passing of every experience leaves a sense of loss in the heart, so Finn departed for the gold country with a sense of loneliness.

Had he but known, he was passing on to a new wealth of adventure, and to the sweetest romance of his life.

Mining and Matrimony

Mining and Matrimony

South Pass, or "Southern Pass" as it had been originally named, was not a deep defile through the mountains
as its name implies. It was, in reality, a gently sloping
meadow, a wide, untimbered valley which offered a
welcome passage through the Rocky mountains for the
emigrants on the Oregon trail.

Already, it had attained a measure of popularity in
the hearts of those travelers who journeyed to Oregon
and California, for it marked exactly the half-way point
on the trail from Independence to Fort Vancouver.
Grim-faced men in buckskins, and clear-eyed women
in sunbonnets and ginghams stopped at South Pass with
a weary sigh of relief, and were wont to peer ahead at
the latter half of their journey with an eagerness born
of anticipation.

Now, gold had been discovered among the mountains
on the borders of the pass. The bustling mining town
of South Pass, with its population of 10,000 inhabitants,
had grown up on Willow creek seemingly overnight late
in 1867. The little community of Atlantic City was
started soon afterwards on Rock creek, six miles to the
northeast of South Pass, while eight miles still farther
to the north, the town of Miners' Delight came into
being.

The inhabitants of these three temporary towns of
boom activity soon found the continued menace of Indian depredations all around them, which their proximity to the new Camp Stambaugh on the Sweetwater

did not relieve. They, accordingly, became closely knit in mutual interests as well as for their better protection against the frequent war-parties of their common enemy.

When Finn arrived in South Pass, he found the population to have dwindled a little, for at that time the total number of inhabitants in the three communities numbered in all but ten thousand, as was attested by Judge Amos Steck, Colonel Bright, and John Mowers.

History has shown that seldom in the lawless boom towns of the gold countries was it possible to find individuals who were proficient in legal matters and who were willing to assume the dignity of becoming magistrates, due in a large measure to the doubtful length of time that they would be allowed to enjoy the honor. The reckless element of mining camps has always professed that its greatest pleasure was in the shooting of buttons from the vests of those in authority. A justice of the peace who wore no vest was thereupon called to her duty.

Mrs. John Morris was the first woman in the United States to be duly elected to the office of justice of the peace. She was a modest, sedate, well-educated mother of two sons, and conducted her office with far more dignity, and acquitted her position with greater credit, than would have been possible for those of the male population who ridiculed her.

Eastern sporting papers of the times, notably the *Police Gazette* and *Day Doings,* printed cartoons of Mrs. Morris which represented her as being a formidable type of fanatic who sat with her feet on the magistrate's desk, and who conducted her court with a cigar between her lips, the while she whittled a heap of shavings with a huge jack-knife. The absurdity of such ridicule was so apparent and met with such disapproval that these cartoons soon ceased.

Finn went to work for Mr. Leighton in Atlantic City and found spare time to prospect in the neighboring hills. His efforts met with little success, as most of the country had already been gone over thoroughly.

He lived at Mrs. Stewart's boarding-house, and at the first meal that he ate in her establishment, he became aware of the flashing eyes of little Eliza Ann McCarthy.

That morning, Finn lowered his head and began to eat, but he was constantly aware when she came near him. Forth and back she hurried between the kitchen and the tables, helping Mrs. Stewart to feed the hungry men who lived at the frontier hotel. Her dark, brown hair was soft and wavy, and once when from across the table she looked squarely at him, Finn discovered that her eyes were as blue as the heaven that she awoke in his heart.

That night, without a word being passed between them, she slipped him a second helping of pudding at supper-time, and Finn felt a hope down in his breast that perhaps she knew the same sensations that he was knowing.

At breakfast, next morning, the young man hurried to his place with his eyes alight. The big dining-room was athrob with conversation and the rattling of dishes and utensils. Then Eliza Ann slipped through the kitchen door with a heaped-up tray upon her shoulder. Immediately, her eyes searched for his, and Finn knew.

He was purposely late for the noon dinner, and everyone had filed from the dining-room before he had finished. Eliza Ann was busily gathering the empty dishes upon her tray and was hurrying them to the kitchen. Her strong, little body swung back and forth across the tables as she reached here and there for the cups and plates, but her eyes were demure and downcast.

Someway, in some manner that only sweethearts know, they began to talk, first in halting, self-conscious words, then with growing confidence in each other, and when Finn strode happily back to the store that noon, he had her wish that he would call at Mrs. Stewart's living-room after supper.

Eliza Ann McCarthy's path had not been one of ease. She had been born upon the sea as her Irish father and mother were emigrating to New York. There had been a childhood of slaving labor, and then her father had died, two years before she came to South Pass.

Shortly after this catastrophe, a hard-drinking Welshman had appeared upon the scene to become her stepfather, and conditions had become so unbearable for the girl that she had left her home to brave the frontier with her mother's friend, Mrs. Stewart.

When their first visit had ended that evening, they had reached an unspoken understanding, and when they rose to part, Eliza came close to Finn and touched his shirt-front tenderly.

"Finn," she whispered, "your shirts need buttons here and there. Won't you bring them to me to wash and mend?"

So began for Finn a life which before had been unknown to him, and as the months went by he grew to lean on her advice, and bit by bit she took over the washing and mending of all his clothes until he knew that he needed her even as he was needed.

Frequently, they went to dances in the town, and to card parties with their friends, the Irwins, the Stevensons, Mrs. Pelky, the Dalys, and the Anthonys.

Then, although they had but little in money, this pair

decided that the future held a paradise if they could be together. So they were married by Dr. James Irwin, a justice of the peace, at his home in Atlantic City. Dr. William Stevenson and his wife, who was Dr. Irwin's oldest daughter, were present.

The newlyweds had a pitiful outlook before them if viewed by later more affluent generations, but they were of the stuff that builds frontiers and prepares the way for softer feet to tread.

They selected a strong, well-built little cabin for their residence, and found that it contained a single room, a sod roof, a dirt floor, and one six-paned window. This building was close to Hoffman's general store, and was assured of pure, icy water from the creek, seventy-five yards away.

It was a happy day when they began to furnish their first home with the little that they had. Finn found a dry-goods box, and made a cupboard while Eliza took the plates and pans, scrubbed them with ashes and damascened them with a cloth. Their dishes were of tin, and their knives and forks were of cast-iron, with handles japanned black. But they thought that they had the most beautiful cupboard and dishes in the world when they had finished.

Then Finn found a length of four-by-four timber, and some inch-boards a foot wide, with which he made some stools, and with poles he erected a bedstead in the corner. There were quaking-asp trees growing near the cabin, and one of these Finn cut down and fashioned a seat from the trunk, and rockers from the branches, making a rocking-chair for his Eliza Ann.

The dirt floor was leveled in the room by wetting and packing it hard with a maul.

The price of the poorest ingrained carpet which could

be bought at Hoffman's store was far beyond their means, but recently Mr. Leighton had received a consignment of bedding, and Finn had saved the burlap wrappings from the goods. Now he carried this sacking to the cabin where Eliza sewed it together into a carpet, underneath which they spread papers, and nailed it down tightly with wooden pegs.

The price of cook-stoves also being beyond their reach, they searched Atlantic City for one which they could buy second-hand. They were fortunate in finding a Charter Oak, number eight, which they bought from Mrs. Pelky.

Eliza went with Finn to help in carrying this new treasure. Half-way home, the entire stove collapsed in their hands, and Finn, when he spoke of it in later years, often declared that the two of them "could have sat right down and cried."

Then, collecting the fragments of their courage, they gathered up the pieces of the stove and found, on closer observation, that the rod which had held it together had been burned completely in two, but otherwise everything was in good condition. So they went to E. F. Cheney, who ran a blacksmith and wagon shop. He made new rods for them, and put the stove together until it stood as capable of good service as it had ever been.

James Leighton, the young bachelor brother of the sutler, was now put in charge of the business in Atlantic City. He owned a nicely-hewed log house with shingled roof. It contained three rooms, the sitting-room and bedroom being carpeted, and the kitchen having a considerable reputation in the community for its beautiful equipment. There was even wall-paper on the walls, while brown muslin curtains hung at the windows.

There he lived alone and many thought it a pity that he had not married, to give one of the attractive girls of Atlantic City an opportunity to share such a comfortable home. His meals he took at the hotel.

One morning he came into the store and sank dizzily into a chair. His face was gray.

"Finn," he groaned, "the poor food at the hotel is killing me. I'm getting chronic stomach trouble. I'm sick half the time, it seems to me."

"I can handle things all right, here," Finn sympathized. "Why don't you go home and lie down, Jim. I'll manage all right."

So the young bachelor slowly stumbled out of the door with his young clerk watching his progress with thoughtful eyes.

At dinner that noon, her husband was so quiet that Eliza began to watch him intently.

"What's the matter, Finn?" she asked. "Did something go wrong at the store?"

"Yes, Jim's sick again," returned Finn. "He complained that the hotel food is doing him harm. Let's have him in to supper tomorrow night."

"Why, he wouldn't be satisfied with the food we have," she exclaimed. "I would have had him over before but I never thought for a moment that he would like what little we have. Invite him by all means, if he'll come."

So the following evening, James Leighton had supper with Finn and Eliza Burnett. They were surprised when he exclaimed with great satisfaction at the venison steaks, canned tomatoes, and potatoes that they had, and were gratified when he pushed his chair back from the table with a sigh of contentment and began to com-

pliment Eliza not alone on her cooking but also on her
ability as a housekeeper.

Suddenly he stopped, and frowned in thought.

"Say," he exclaimed, "I've got an idea. How would
you two consider a proposition to move up to my house?
Your care of the place and your cooking, Mrs. Burnett,
would more than compensate me for your board."

The thought hit Finn and his little wife like a bomb-
shell, and, after an hour of excited planning, it was decided that they would move the next day.

The newlyweds found themselves safely sheltered in
the neatest little cabin in Atlantic City. There was,
however, a pang of remorse in their hearts when they
left their first home without moving a single piece of
its poor, hard-won furnishings. Someone who needed its
shelter soon moved in.

The year 1869 proved to be a golden year for South
Pass and its sister communities, Atlantic City and
Miners' Delight. Meadow Gulch produced more than
$1,250,000 worth of the precious mineral from its va-
rious holdings.

The principal mines near Atlantic City were the
Caribou, Mary Ellen, and the Soles and Perkins. Most
of the gold taken from these holdings was handled
through the Leighton store.

Two Montana men from Virginia City, named Pease
and William Taylor, owned the Caribou, which was a
specimen mine and which produced free gold to a depth
of one hundred feet. The holdings produced $40,000 for
them, and then they sold out to Mr. Poiree for a like
figure.

The roaster was located on Rock creek, and when
the rich ore was hauled from the mine, one of the part-

ners always rode with the driver to keep passers-by from picking specimens from the load.

The Mary Ellen paid well, but it was a small-veined and difficult mine. The foot and wall rock were very hard and therefore the mine was expensive to operate.

Finn grub-staked several miners at different times, but he received little in return. In one such instance, together with Chris Smith and George Donald, he became a partner in the Duncan mine. This holding was a ledge from three to six feet in length which was easily mined and which yielded from eleven to sixteen dollars worth of gold to the ton. They had worked this mine but a short time when a Colorado company offered to buy them out for $50,000.

Donald Smith refused the offer, and afterward they bonded the property away until eventually the partners lost all title to it. Finn later sold his interest to a George Thompson for $300. He received half of the amount at the time of the sale, and was never paid the balance.

In the spring of 1870, however, Finn had his first piece of financial luck. With Charles and James Oldham, and Dr. Stevenson for partners, he discovered a placer claim just below the forks of Atlantic Gulch which paid from fifteen to forty dollars a day to each of them.

The rich pay extended from fifty to sixty feet. The gold was coarse and most of it composed of nuggets which were worth from fifteen cents to forty dollars apiece. As the work in this mine continued, it was found that these nuggets contained more and more crystallized quartz until finally the pay strip played out entirely when it reached an age-old river bed that cut diagonally across the formation of the country.

Indian raids were a common occurrence during these mining days. As early as 1866, when the Carissa Ledge and Gulch had been discovered, hostile savages had become so active in the South Pass country that the gold-hunters had been obliged to abandon their location until the following year.

Then, in 1869, when many miners began to perceive that the pass was worked out, and when, as a result, the population of the three towns began to dwindle, Indians began their depredations more than ever.

In 1870, Frank Irwin, the son of Finn's old friend, was employed in Miners' Delight. Every Saturday evening he walked the eight miles to visit his parents in Atlantic City over the week-end, returning to his duties early on Monday mornings.

On one such occasion, he was walking back to Miners' Delight through the early dawn. The darkness was being pushed back into the distant canyons, and the rising sun was splashing the heaped-up pinnacles of the mountains with brilliant red. He was sauntering along with his eyes drinking in the beauty of his surroundings when he reached a point half way between the Big and Little Atlantic Gulches.

A shot tore from the bushes on the right side of the road, and Frank felt the burning shock of a slight flesh wound in his shoulder. Evidently a war-party of Indians had hidden themselves to surprise lone white men who might pass.

The young man had no weapons, and he turned and began to flee back toward Atlantic City. A group of mounted warriors raced after him, whooping and yelling with delight. When they overtook him close to Atlantic Creek they knocked him down, kicked and abused him until he was almost dead.

Then he was pulled to his feet, was stripped of all his clothes, and was told to go home. He started down the road and had gone but a few steps when the savages fired three arrows into his back.

A while later, a man on the outskirts of Atlantic City saw him staggering over the ridge that divided Little Atlantic from Slaughter House stream. Calling the alarm to miners who were near-by, he ran to Frank's assistance and helped him to reach his home.

James Oldham and Finn heard of the ambush as Frank was being brought into town. Both ran to Slaughter House Gulch, but the war-party had disappeared with the exception of one lone Indian who peered at them from behind a pile of rocks. Oldham shot at him, but the savage dodged back and the bullet missed.

Finn then ran across the gulch to get behind the redskin, but when he had found a place on the far hill from whence he could shoot to advantage, he saw the Indian gallop away. The young man shot at him, but, at the instant that his gun exploded, the redskin's pony stumbled in a snow-bank, sending his rider over his head, unharmed.

Fourteen men were killed in this raid which brought tragedy to the Irwin family, and not one Indian paid for his actions. All of the victims had left their guns at home, believing it to be too early for savage depredations. Every one of the dead had been scalped and mutilated, and in most cases were found with their miner's picks driven through their eyes on into the ground.

Frank Irwin's father was a physician and surgeon, but all his efforts were of little benefit, and the boy died the following noon. It remained a mystery why he had not been scalped.

The same party of Indians went on to attack the mines

farther down the valley on the following day. They killed a number of miners, and ran off eighty head of mules belonging to William Smith.

John Anthony and Charles Oldham had left Atlantic City on the evening before this raid, to go to the Anthony sawmill on the head of Mill creek. This was the mill, by the way, which later sawed all the logs for the first agency buildings on the Shoshoni reservation.

The people of Atlantic City feared that the two men had met the Indian war party, and sent a group to Camp Stambaugh for military help to find them. Walter Hagen, James Leighton, a man named Thompson, Finn Burnett, and four others set out for the post heavily armed and watchful for trouble on the road.

Colonel Brisbin, the commanding officer at Camp Stambaugh, detailed a sergeant and six privates to aid in the search. They started out, and near the head of Red canyon they surprised a party of fifteen Indians, chasing them for miles, but never getting within gunshot of them.

Continuing on down the road, they came upon a number of soldiers from Camp Brown who had come in response to the report of E. F. Cheney that he had found the remains of a desperate battle at that place.

They had discovered that the Indian war-party had attacked and massacred Dr. Barr, Harvey Morgan, and Hugh McLean, between Willow creek and Camp Brown.

The three men had been veteran Indian fighters and had lost their lives only after a prolonged battle during which they overturned their wagon, and heaped a round table, boxes, and piles of sacked stuff around them to form an excellent barricade. The Indians were in such numbers, however, that they had literally shot the breastworks to pieces, and when the soldiers arrived, the three white men were found dead. The table had been shot through and through in several places.

Dr. Barr was discovered lying on a pile of exploded cartridge shells, face up, and with the wagon wrench driven through one eye and into the ground below. He was buried as he was found, with his two comrades.

John Anthony and Charles Oldham, mounted, and with a pack horse apiece, had kept to the trail along the foot of the mountain, until it met the main road at Deep creek, traveling at night, as they were aware that they were in hostile country. They had watered their horses at the creek, and after a short rest, Charles had mounted to start on.

"Say, Charlie," Anthony called, "I want to go on the road. Some way or another, I've got a presentiment that we'll get into trouble if we follow the trail."

"Oh, nonsense," Oldham answered. "It's not half as dangerous on the trail. If there were any Indians in the country they'd be watching the road."

"Well, just the same, Charlie," returned the more experienced man, "we'll take the road. I know we would have trouble on the trail."

At that moment, the Arapaho war-party of 175 warriors was camped a few hundred yards ahead of them down the valley, with scouts stationed on each side of the trail. The two white men were less than half a mile from them as they argued, and had they disregarded this remarkable instance of presentiment that night both of them would undoubtedly have been slaughtered.

They had continued down the road, however, had passed the Barr party in the darkness without seeing them, and had arrived at Camp Brown unharmed.

The quantity of gold taken from the mines around

South Pass and its sister communities began to dwindle at this time, so, as hopes faded, disappointed men began to prey upon their fellows.

An old man named Davis had discovered the Rock Creek Gulch mine below Atlantic City, and the location had proved to be a very rich one for three hundred feet. He had two partners in the enterprise named Tom Cook and Jo Powers.

Subsequent investigations indicated that the murder of Davis had been carefully planned by these two partners, and that Bob Wheeling, the cowardly two-gun man of the Hay Fields fight, had been hired to do the deed. It was universally believed that it was he who secreted himself behind a log house and shot the old man as he came past from town.

At any rate, Davis was murdered, and Cook and Powers worked the claim in the face of wide-spread suspicion and public condemnation, and later they left the country with close to $50,000 in gold.

On Strawberry Gulch, there was a rich placer ground which was owned by Lorenzo Davis and "Dutch Tom," but it never proved to be as rich as those locations farther north.

In the Miners' Delight mine, rich free gold was discovered from the grass roots down, which yielded its owners, Jack Holbrook, Frank McGovern, and Johnson Pugh, a million dollars. The three were wild drinkers, and inveterate gamblers, and soon squandered their proceeds.

The Miners' Delight Gulch below the mine was very rich in placer gold for several hundred feet, as was Meadow Gulch northwest of it.

Bolivar Roberts, who reopened the Carissa mine near South Pass took out a half million dollars worth of free gold. Mr. Amoretti located the Bonanza mine on one of the Hermit creeks which proved to be small but so rich in precious mineral that he retired after a few months with a fortune.

Finn continued prospecting and hoping for a "break." "Pony" Steel discovered the Oriental mine, and it proved to be small and composed mostly of decomposed quartz. Donald and Chris Smith went with Finn and Steel, working this new venture, and they mined down to water level at which point all the mines in the territory gradually became base metal ore with very little gold.

The four partners hoisted the ore in a ten gallon pail, and each bucketful yielded them approximately seventy-five dollars in gold.

One afternoon, Finn was prospecting slowly through the lower ridges, when Eliza came to find him.

"It's time for supper, Finn," she called. "You'd better quit."

Finn was picking over a ledge of quartz about four feet wide, and at that moment had noticed on the north a narrow strip of decomposed quartz that was full of free gold.

"Come quick, mom," Finn cried. "I've got something."

Before them was a layer of transparent quartz through which a pocket of gold could be plainly seen, like a promise of paradise behind a glass panel on a wall.

The quartz was soon picked away, and there appeared to the excited couple a little shallow hole which was filled with rich gold. Some nuggets were two and three inches in length.

Until darkness fell, Finn and Eliza Ann raked up the gold into their hats and pockets before returning home.

There, they weighed up what they had, and found its value to be $150.

At dawn next morning, they hurried to the scene of their rich discovery. Finn climbed into the hole and, at the first dig of his pick, he struck into solid quartz again, which meant the end of the gold in that spot. The "pay-streak" had run across and then straight down the east wall, and the little pocket of gold which they had found the night before was all that they were destined to discover.

In the fall of 1869, soldiers moved to Atlantic City, and camped in Big Atlantic Gulch. They had been there but a few days, and the Indians were still unaware of their presence, when a man named Bennett, who lived in Miners' Delight, awoke one morning to find his span of mules gone from his barn.

He started out through the hills toward Atlantic City searching for his animals, and had gone about four miles when he was surprised by a large band of Arapaho who sprang up all around him.

Bennett tried frantically to escape, while his captors formed a circle around him and hit him with their coup-sticks, laughing and whooping at his efforts. Finally, he broke free and began to run toward Atlantic City, with the Indians running beside him, hitting him with blows which rapidly sapped him of his strength.

As they topped the ridge and started down into the gulch, the Arapaho suddenly found themselves confronted with the soldiers' tents and an excited group of guards who sent a volley among them.

Bennett staggered alive into the camp, while the troopers raced to their horses and gave chase to his late captors. There was a large number of Indians killed that day. First-sergeant Moore of Captain Gordon's

FORT FETTERMAN
From a contemporary sketch.

company told Finn afterwards that he had knocked over two, himself, during the morning.

The remnants of this band of Arapaho re-formed later in the day, and began to search the hills for isolated miners and small groups of whites. Only the thrilling torture of a pain-maddened captive could drive their late humiliation from their minds.

Their first encounter was above the mouth of Red Canyon creek on the Little Popo Agie. Here they came upon Jimmy Goodson and an old scout named Billy McKabe. Attacking this pair of old tartars was the second mistake that those Indians made that day, for when they retreated there were three "good" redskins lying in sight before the temporary breastworks, and several others lay dead in the brush.

That evening, Chief Washakie with a number of his friendly Shoshoni was camping on the outskirts of Atlantic City when Jimmy Goodson and Billy McKabe sauntered in and told of their battle, in a somewhat off-hand way.

Chief Washakie was very anxious to view the bodies of the Arapaho, who were the traditional enemies of his tribe, and Billy rode back with the chief and a number of his warriors to the battleground. When they returned, they brought a number of scalps, and a great scalp-and-war-dance was held afterwards in the Shoshoni camp for the benefit of the white spectators.

That night was the first time that Finn had ever seen Chief Washakie. He proved to be a fine-looking old chieftain with impressive bearing, and his reputation for wisdom and honor had placed him among the foremost leaders of all the tribes upon the plains.

General Armstrong, a great student of Indians and their history, was later to tell Finn that in his estimation Chief Washakie had proved himself to be undoubtedly the greatest Indian friend that the white men had ever encountered on the western plains.

In 1852, when he was a lieutenant in the 2nd Ragoons, the general met Chief Washakie for the first time at Fort Bridger. Army officers were contemplating an expedition through the mountains in the following spring.

They wished to procure a large number of Indian ponies which should be delivered at Fort Laramie on a certain date early in the year, and Chief Washakie had agreed to bring guides and mounts to the post on the designated date.

The winter which followed was unusually severe. Spring opened late, and blizzards swept the plains, burying the country in huge drifts, as the date approached which had been set for the arrival of Chief Washakie with his ponies. Many of the officers at Fort Laramie frowned at the weather and began to voice doubts that the chief could meet them at the specified time.

An old trapper in the post heard the soldiers speculating.

"Did Washakie promise to be here on that date?" he asked.

"He did," they answered.

"Well, he'll carry out his promise, and he'll get through some way if he's alive," said the trapper, confidently.

On the appointed day, Chief Washakie with his outfit and pack horses filed into the fort. To the day of his death, no man ever knew him to fail to keep his word.

First Days of the Shoshoni Reservation

First Days of the Shoshoni Reservation

On the first day of May, 1871, Finn Burnett was offered the position of "boss farmer" at the Shoshoni reservation in the Wind River valley. Dr. James Irwin had been appointed agent, and Finn's old friend prevailed on him to leave the dying town of Atlantic City to undergo those extraordinary experiences which were to be encountered during the transition of the wild savages into civilized agriculturists.

Finn and his wife accepted their new responsibilities, and moved down the valley with their baby son, Jim, to Camp Brown where the city of Lander was established later.

His salary was fixed at $65 a month, and the government furnished his provisions, home, fuel, and light, the latter being tallow candles and coal oil. Furthermore, it was understood that he would be allowed to purchase clothing, blankets, and equipment from the commissaries at cost.

It was clearly realized from the beginning that the task which lay ahead of these first white men on the reservation would be one of infinite labor and danger. Thousands of untamed Shoshoni were to be more or less confined to a restricted area and there they would be obliged to submit to a regular routine which was absolutely foreign to either their wishes or their instincts.

From the time of their earliest knowledge, these Indians had been nomadic hunters, traveling thousands of miles in every direction, and enjoying complete freedom from restraint. Now, limited to the area of their reservation, outbursts of disinclination toward agriculture were anticipated, and it was feared that even the stern discipline of Chief Washakie would not always overcome universal unrest in his tribe.

Furthermore, the Arapaho had not submitted to the white man's laws. From time beyond memory, this troublesome people had warred with the Shoshoni, and the mountains in the vicinity of Camp Brown and the agency were dotted thickly with their war-parties, eager to destroy Shoshoni and whites alike.

It was planned in Washington to reorganize the Shoshoni into a self-supporting, agricultural people. Irrigation projects were to be undertaken, large tracts were to be plowed and seeded, and gradually as their education was assimilated it was believed that the redskins could regain the farming traits which their ancestors had cast aside before coming to the plains.

Two weeks after the arrival of the Burnetts at Camp Brown, the commanding officer, Captain Torrey, notified them that soldiers would be transferred to the agency within a few days. The little group of employees moved immediately to the site of their future labors and proceeded to erect those buildings which they would require.

They found seven log houses awaiting them in various stages of construction. Six four-room units had been placed in a row for the employees, while a larger six-roomed establishment for the agent, which stood at the west end of the alignment, had been completed the year before.

Finn was assigned to the house next to that of the agent, and found the new home to be built of logs, with four rooms, one of them being a living-room with a big stone fireplace. Finn and his wife were pleased at the comfort such a residence promised.

All set to work to complete their houses, and to furnish them before taking up their other work. With these completed, they proceeded with the erection of a substantial fort for their protection. This stronghold was built just west of the dwelling-houses, and the walls were made of blocks of sandstone, two feet in thickness. Roofed with lumber upon which dirt had been thrown to the depth of more than a foot, it also had above its center a strongly-built sentinel's box, eight feet square with a ladder leading up to it.

The walls were pierced with loopholes on all sides, and the only door, which opened to the east, was made of five thicknesses of two-inch planks. A well was sunk under the floor to provide ample water in times of siege, and sufficient provisions to feed the entire community for a month were stored along the walls.

For two and one-half months the soldiers delayed moving from Camp Brown, and during that time those who worked at the agency were without protection. Then, on August first, the troopers took up permanent quarters at Fort Washakie.

Their arrival, however, did not promise any measure of protection. They had received strict orders on no account to fire at any Indians unless obliged to do so in self-defense, and that no demonstration of force should ever be made by the military under any circumstances until orders to do so had been received from Washington.

The telegraph station nearest to Fort Washakie was at South Pass, fifty miles away, which fact made it apparent to those at the agency that no help could ever be expected from the soldiers in an emergency. Black

Coal, chief of the Arapaho, was raiding up and down the valley almost daily, and the employees went about their work with carbines ready in their hands.

At night, everyone slept in the agency fort, with four men taking their turns at standing guard on the breast-works overhead. Beds were spread upon the floor, and everyone lived a closely-knit community life until 1874. Every morning displayed moccasin tracks around the cabins and dwellings, proving that there had been skulkers in the night.

In later years, Finn was to ask Black Coal why his warriors had never burned any of the agency buildings during those times, and was to be met with the answer that it had not occurred to them.

Finn, during those days of construction, built a stable close to his dwelling for his four mules and two horses.

After building the walls like those of a stockade, with logs set upright in the ground, and after covering the roof with a deep layer of sod as a protection against flaming arrows, he made a huge door with several thick-nesses of two-inch planks, and welded some old wagon tires together into a heavy bar which was padlocked across the entrance.

Many a night, when all was dark and still, the guards on the fort roof could hear Indians pounding with rocks and hatchets in their futile efforts to hammer away the bar, and gain access to the stock.

Once, the Burnetts had a bad scare. They had worked hard around their home putting their furnishings in place, and although several hostile Indians had been seen darting through the brush during the day they had decided to sleep in their own cabin that night.

They had retired, with Finn's six-shooter scabbard

hanging close to his hand. During the night Eliza woke her husband with the warning that an Indian was peering in at them through a window.

Finn reached for his pistol, and found it gone.

"Where's my gun, mom?" he hissed. "It's not here."

"Oh, Finn," she apologized, "I was afraid that Jimmy might catch hold of it, so I put it on the shelf over there."

Exclaiming with the usual husbandly expressions so common in such instances, Finn made his way to the shelf and found the weapon. Turning to approach the window he stumbled over a frontier utensil in the center of the floor, and dropped the pistol squarely on a corn. His yell of agony was so mingled with ferocity that a guard at the fort later remarked that "it was doubtful if that Arapaho would ever be seen in these parts again, the way he was getting away from there when I saw him."

On another occasion, Mrs. Burnett woke her husband in the night and pointed out a dread, black shape at a window. Finn was not sure where Eliza might have put his gun this time, and made the quick decision to strike the skulker's face through the glass, which would fill his eyes with splinters.

Finn struck with all his strength, and his arm crashed through to his shoulder. Then his wife began to laugh. During the previous afternoon, Jimmy had broken the window. Eliza had crammed an old hat into the hole and had then forgotten it. Finn had struck the hat, had cut his shoulder, and then listened to his wife's subsequent mirth with the dawning realization which comes to every husband that a woman is a remarkable creature.

With the dwellings furnished and prepared for occupancy, and the fort securely prepared, the government next ordered that twenty-four log houses should be erected for the use of the Shoshoni.

These dwellings were to be built in groups; six to be constructed one and a half miles west of Fort Washakie, which were to be called the Washakie Houses; six to be placed half way between the fort and the agency, to be known as the Sinclair Houses; and six which were given the name of the Bazil Row were to be erected nearest to the agency.

When all the buildings had been completed, attention was directed to the agricultural development on the reservation.

In 1870, 320 acres of prairie northeast of the agency had been fenced and John Anthony had broken it under contract for seeding at that time, and again in the fall of the following year, as the necessary equipment did not arrive until too late for planting in 1871.

In the spring of 1872, this land was sown with wheat, oats, and barley, and the resulting harvest was to yield the first wheat crop that was ever produced in what was later to be Wyoming.

The seeding was of unusual interest that spring, for it marked the first attempt of the Indians to learn the rudiments of agriculture. An irrigating ditch site had been selected in the foothills, and it was decided to complete it after the Shoshoni had departed for their summer hunting.

The long-awaited plows and harness arrived for the use of those on the reservation. On an appointed day, the Shoshoni began to arrive at the office of the agent to learn the white man's methods of plowing.

The entire proceeding was amusing to the Indians.

Helped by the white men, they finally had the horses harnessed to the plows, and all drove to the field where they formed a long line.

It was a most interesting sight that morning to see the manner with which those braves went about their labor. There was being enacted a scene which symbolized the transition of a great nomadic people to their heritage of agriculture. To the west, north, and south lay the foothills, stair-stepping up to the lower fringes of the pines and the thickets of quaking-asps. High in the mountains behind them flashed the radiance of lingering snow upon the peaks. Here on the little plain stood the wild men waiting in a long, restless line.

Here and there, a squaw with the zig-zagged design of her blanket showing bright about her, and with two long braids of black, shining hair hanging to her waist, sat hunched upon the back of a plow-horse. In some instances, these Indian mothers had their papooses upon their backs, with their little ebon, button-like eyes peering with wonder at the excitement around them. And, occasionally, there could be seen a Shoshoni warrior riding his plow-horse, while his squaw stood waiting between the handles of the plow.

Finally, all was ready. Each unit was informed that at a given signal it must cut a furrow straight ahead across the field. Every Indian grasped his handles and his muscles tensed.

There was a yell, and all started at the sound. There was pandemonium everywhere. Here, a pony balked; there, a plow bit too deeply. In another place, three teams came together in a crashing mess of flying straps and whirling handles, while beyond the mix-up could be seen a dozen pairs of horses running away with broken harness flying, and plows leaping and jumping behind them. Clouds of dust rose on all sides.

The Shoshoni were treating the spectacle with great amusement. Laughing uproariously, they were betting which team of runaways would be leading at the farthest limits of the field.

It was several hours later when the order to begin was given again, and the plowing of 320 acres commenced. Slowly at first, and then more and more of the native sod was turned as these red-skinned students learned the knack of driving, and of handling the plow. That spring, ten acres were planted with oats, forty with barley, two with potatoes, and the remainder with wheat.

When this had been accomplished, the Shoshoni packed up their belongings, hitched their travois behind their ponies and departed in a body to pursue their annual summer hunting. Far away in the mountains, and among the foothills, they would find great herds of deer and buffalo which would replenish their winter supply of food.

After their departure, Finn went with the other men, and began the work of completing the irrigation canal. It was believed that this would require but three or four weeks of their time, but they reckoned without the hazards.

It was an "open" spring that year, that is, the snows melted from the prairies and foothills early, with few late storms. The drifts in the valleys and canyons thawed quickly, leaving the trails open, to add to the dangers from Arapaho raiders. Scarcely had the ditch been started when large war-bands began to annoy and harass the white people. As the Shoshoni had all departed, the handful of officials and employees at the agency were left unprotected, to fight off these hostile groups. Frequently, Finn remained with the other men close to the fort throughout the day, as the situation was too menacing outside.

At other times, after an hour's work had been done on the canal, a shower of arrows would come humming from the bushes, and the whites would be driven into the brush, to ride back to their homes for the day.

At lunch-time, one of the ditch-diggers stood guard on a prominent point while the rest ate.

On one such occasion, no Indians had been seen for several days, but Tilford Cutch was taking his turn, watching from a spot across the creek while the others sat eating. The stream at this place divided to leave a strip of land about forty feet in width, and it had already been decided that in the event of attack, this island would serve as a secure refuge.

The men were squatting in a circle on the bank, each with a tin cup filled with steaming coffee in one hand, and sandwiches or pie in the other. Here and there a cheek swelled out and in with the movement of a grim jaw. Conversation had languished. The noon sun bathed the little group with a welcome languor, and eyes became sleepy and inattentive.

"Hey! Look there!" came the cry from one of them.

Tin cups clanged, coffee splashed to earth as the men came alive. Hands shot instinctively to guns, and all turned to face the spot across the creek where through the thickets could be seen the flitting forms of approaching Indians.

Within the space of a minute, all had splashed across the twelve-foot, shallow stream to the island, and all had spread themselves among the choke-cherry bushes and willows, with guns ready.

For some unknown reason, the Arapaho did not attack, and the men emerged to return to work unmolested. It had been discovered, however, that Cutch had wet but one moccasin when he crossed the creek, and he underwent an unmerciful joking at his leaping abilities in time of danger.

The ditch was completed on the 15th day of June, and was the first irrigation canal that had ever been attempted in Wyoming up to this time. Water was immediately turned into it, and the seeded fields were given their first thorough soaking. After that initial wetting, the ditch was not used again that summer. The Arapaho developed a sense of malicious pleasure from tearing holes in the banks which rendered the project useless.

Notwithstanding all these difficulties, a splendid crop was harvested. Acres of golden grain billowed like a gently rolling sea across the meadow lands. The potatoes were large and smooth and moist in their cool nests. Finn declared at that time that the soil was proving to be the best that he had ever seen, and for sixty years it was to continue to produce the same rich returns.

Ed St. John measured the grain when the threshing was completed, and declared the yield to have been seventy-five bushels to the acre.

That fall, Finn cut hay with "Uncle Billy" Rogers. The hay field was known as the Warm Spring meadow, as it was watered continuously from the warm water of a spring which emerged from a hill above it. Below this field was a creek, hidden with clumps of wild rose and bullberries, with choke-cherries, wild raspberries, and cottonwoods above and behind in dense thickets.

Frequently, the redskins lay in concealment along

the creek, watching the two men with their mowing-machine clattering forth and back across the meadow. Finn, as he sat on the seat, clasped a carbine between his knees and a heavy six-shooter hung to a belt of cartridges around his waist.

As swath after swath fell to the rear of the machine, and the two men drew closer to the creek, there were many times when a flicker of sunlight on a buckle, or the unnatural flutter of a bush, warned the workers of their danger, and they would dash for safety in the brush. The two men were the objects of many fierce attacks that fall, and in every instance proved themselves victorious.

Rattlesnakes were found to be of even greater menace than were the Arapaho. On Crooked creek, a small stream between Fort Washakie and the agency, so many horses and cattle were bitten that stock was kept away from that section entirely. These reptiles were found to be of an unusually wicked disposition, being short, slender devils which fought man or beast to the death whenever their domain was invaded.

Those rattlesnakes in the Warm Spring meadow were not so vicious, but they were far more numerous. The soil thoroughout the hay field was composed of the loose sediment from the spring, which had become honey-combed with rattlesnake holes. On any warm, sunny day when the noisy mowing-machine clattered at its work, a continual rattling could be heard underground where the reptiles lay disturbed in their burrows.

The knives of the mower cut hundreds of them to pieces as they passed, which left in their wake an added menace. A rattlesnake without its rattles, lying broken and venomous, capable of striking without warning, provided a constant threat for these hay-workers.

When the time came to take the hay to the agency, John Kingston hitched up his hay-rack and went with Finn and "Uncle Billy" to the meadow. Kingston had been a prisoner in Andersonville prison during the Civil war, and scurvy had left him absolutely deaf.

Finn and "Uncle Billy" worked on the ground, throwing the hay up with their pitchforks from both sides to Kingston who distributed it evenly on the rack.

"Hey! There's a rattlesnake on this load," he cried.

Finn and "Uncle Billy" laughed.

"You couldn't hear one rattle if it was right beside you," answered "Uncle Billy."

"What's that?" roared Kingston.

The two men stopped their work to shake their heads and point to their ears.

"Well," returned the deaf man above them, "I may not be able to hear a rattlesnake, but I can smell one. They have a scent like a green cucumber."

Finn and his comrade continued to fork the hay up until the rack was piled high. Then "Uncle Billy" climbed upon the wagon-hounds in front to pass up the pole which was used to bind the load. As he reached up to secure the tie-rope, he gave a yell and fell backward off the rack, to land between the oxen.

"Say, there's a rattlesnake up there," he gasped as he scrambled clear. "It was almost against my nose when I saw it."

A few probes with a fork brought the reptile to light, and from that time onward everyone at the agency believed John Kingston when he scented green cucumbers.

While they were eating their lunch one noon in the shade of the trees, Finn noticed some bushes loaded with black currants and wild gooseberries. He filled his lunch-pail with them, and took them home to Eliza. She was enthusiastic over the thought of preserving a quantity of the fruit, and made her husband agree to take her with the haying crew next morning. She took Dr. Irwin's housekeeper, Lizzie Askir, along to help gather the berries.

The men had scarcely begun to work in the field when they heard a shriek in the bushes. With guns in hand, they ran toward the creek, and beheld emerging from the thickets at one place the two startled, wild-eyed women who were running toward them, and, about a hundred yards beyond, a brown bear was racing for the tall timber as fast as his legs could carry him.

The two women had commenced to gather berries, when Eliza saw a movement close to her. She turned to look closer, and the bear raised his head. Both women were badly frightened and neither would go berry-gathering again.

Finn was working in the fields on the first day of October, 1872, when word was brought to him that he was needed at home. He saddled a mule and went in.

His second boy, Frank, was born that afternoon, the first white child to be born in the Little Wind River valley. The mother and infant were attended by Dr. Grimes, the first physician to be located at Fort Washakie.

That year, the government had purchased a herd of Indian ponies for the use of the cavalry at Fort Washakie, and these they kept in a corral which was situated below the high bank of the river, and under the eye of a sentinel at all times. As an extra precaution against nocturnal visitors, bars were placed across the exit, with a chain running through the ends, and padlocked.

Nevertheless, one moonless night, an Indian slipped to the gate, and, disregarding the sentry who appeared at intervals above him, he set to work to cut a hole noise-lessly in each bar to release the chain. Quietly and care-fully he released the cross-pieces one by one, and led the ponies out and away to waiting friends. When dawn came, the guard looked down into an empty corral.

As the time drew near when the Shoshoni were to return to the agency, it was decided that some new build-ings should be erected during the winter to keep every-one busy. Dr. Irwin, Dr. Stevenson, Charles Oldham, Frank Trumble, and Finn set out for the mountains to select the necessary logs.

Late in the afternoon, this group completed their survey, and rode over to a ranch owned by Thomas Orton and George Smith on the north fork of the Popo Agie river. Here they were to eat dinner, and as they approached the cabins at the ranch, a cloud of dust was discerned across the hills to the north.

After a fine meal, the agency men started homeward, and night had set in when they crossed the gulch west of Boulder Flat.

As they rode up to level ground, they heard the ap-proach of a large body of Indians, and all crowded into a depression, and prepared for trouble. Soon, their po-sition was completely surrounded by the sound of trot-ting horses, jabbering Indians, squalling papooses, and dragging travois clattering through the darkness.

Suddenly there came a yell of alarm from some war-rior who had discovered the presence of the white men, and there was an immediate scurrying in the night. There was a tense moment of waiting.

"What's the matter up there?" called the voice of Chief Washakie.

Dr. Irwin chuckled, and called out his name, as the sound of laughter began to ripple from all sides. A moment later, and the noise of their continued march was heard again.

The old chief rode up, and squatted beside the men of the agency after gravely exchanging greetings with each of them. He reported that the hunting had been very successful in the mountains during that summer, and that the tribe was on its way back to the reservation loaded with ample meat for their needs.

That morning, the hostile Arapaho had attacked the Shoshoni camp on Trout creek. A boy had been killed, and several head of horses had been stolen before Chief Washakie and his warriors started in pursuit. Evidently the dust cloud which the white men had seen from the North Fork had been made by the escaping Arapaho.

Dr. Irwin and his men trotted on to the agency surrounded by the squaws and the loaded ponies of the Shoshoni, while Chief Washakie with his warriors started toward Little Popo Agie, taking with him a few days' supplies, and a number of tepees. He caught up with the Arapaho war-party late in the afternoon, and threw a guard around their camp, but they managed to slip through the cordon by using an obscure and unguarded draw to escape into the night.

When the agency men arrived home, they found every family to be crowded into the blockhouse, mourning. The trail of Dr. Irwin and his party had been traced to within gunshot distance of a war-party which had hidden itself on Juniper Butte. Everyone believed that the little group had been massacred.

Chief Washakie's band continued scouting through the foothills, searching for hostiles, until his force reached the old government road crossing at Mill creek.

Here the scouts rode in to report that an overwhelming force of Sioux were all around them, unaware of the presence of the Shoshoni in their midst, but entirely cutting off any way of retreat. The crafty old chieftain pondered for a few moments, then ordered his braves to cross the divide to Trout creek.

When this move had been accomplished, the warriors found themselves to be in a wide valley out of range of the hills, and within sight of the agency. There, Washakie ordered that the tepees should be set up quickly over the buffalo "wallows" which dotted the meadow at this point.

Since ages long beyond the memory of Indian traditions, vast herds of buffalo had included that secluded valley in their aimless wanderings across the plains. During the hot days of summer, these gigantic beasts had with keen enjoyment wallowed in the ooze of the valley bottom, to emerge caked with mud from head to tail. When the sun had dried them, this coating solidified, and provided an impregnable protection against the stinging deer-flies.

As years went by, these buffalo mud-baths, or "wallows," were deepened and widened as they were used by every passing herd, and now, when the Shoshoni lodges were raised above a number of them, they provided an excellent protection from attackers.

When finally a band of Sioux rode up on a distant hill, it saw an apparently unsuspecting village camped before it. In reality, however, the Shoshoni ponies had been hobbled, and in the shelter of each lodge crouched a group of deadly fighters in a wallow, waiting in obedience to the order of Chief Washakie not on any account to show themselves to the foe outside.

In a few minutes, the Sioux had gathered together a

large force, and this mass of warriors crept closer until they were behind a nearby ridge.

Then, with a whoop, they charged down upon the cluster of lodges, shooting and yelling as they rode. Straight through the village they dashed, with their guns snapping right and left, to emerge on the far side where they crowded together within half a mile of the agency.

The whites had clustered at the blockhouse, and were fearful for the safety of the Shoshoni warriors fighting out there in the face of such an overwhelming number of Sioux. But the squaws and old men of the tribe went about their work with scarcely a glance at the battle. Their faces were untroubled, and their manner reflected unlimited confidence in their chieftain and the victorious outcome of the conflict.

After a short moment for preparation, the Sioux then charged back through the village, without a shot being fired at them, and returned to the ridge.

There they commenced to "make medicine," during which they prepared for the final phase of the slaughter. The silence of the village signified to them that only a few old men and squaws were hiding in the tepees, and now they would charge in and put them all to death. For more than an hour they splashed paint upon their bodies and over the hides of their ponies, continuing a wild yelling and a brandishing of clubs and knives, and stirring themselves into a murderous frenzy.

Then they charged down the hill again. This time they emptied their guns into the tepees before they reached the village, believing that they would not need them in the coming slaughter.

Scarcely had their shots ceased to echo when from the wallows came a volley which literally blew them to pieces. The quiet lodges of the Shoshoni seemed to float upon a swirling cloud of gun-smoke from which snapped sparks of biting death that tore at the Sioux who were carried by the impetus of their rush into the village street.

The Sioux had no bullets in their guns with which to answer the fire which was being poured at them from every tepee. With empty guns, the remnant of their charge dashed on, to run a veritable gauntlet of fire before they emerged torn and bloody on the far side of the village.

Then Chief Washakie called an order, and the scene became as an ant hill swarming with a vengeful host. In a moment, the hobbled ponies had been released and a galloping line of Shoshoni raced out across the meadow in the wake of the escaping Sioux. All the way to Badwater, a distance of thirty-five miles, the Shoshoni continued their revenge, killing the stragglers, wiping out small bands which attempted to make a stand, and completely demoralizing any thought that the Sioux might have had of molesting the agency during the coming winter.

Such was the strategy of Chief Washakie; and with similar instances repeated over a long period of years which brought humiliation and defeat to the Blackfeet, Crow, Sioux, Cheyenne, and Arapaho with every attempt which they made to overrun the domain of this wily leader, it was possible for the weaker band of Shoshoni to continue in possession of their rich domain.

General Bates, who knew as much as any man of the distribution and force of the government troops upon the plains, made the statement, himself, that if the Sioux had had a chief with the generalship of Washakie, the various commands would have been massacred in turn until the entire army on the frontier had been wiped out. The Fetterman and Custer massacres would not then have been among the bloodiest pages in plains history.

The fatal lack of generalship throughout the tribes was best exemplified in the Sioux nation. The scattered groups of white soldiers, never over ten thousand of them, had galloped here and there across the plains with the firm impression that they were "chasing Indians," and that they were exterminating the Sioux tribe which numbered 70,000 braves. Yet, there were many instances when, in reality, the Sioux feared that the white troopers would not find them, and had voluntarily made obvious trails for them to follow. Had this tribe possessed a Chief Washakie, they could have retarded white civilization of the plains for fifty years.

The Mormons recognized early the attributes of the great Shoshoni chieftain. They attempted with every means to induce Chief Washakie to fight those white people who did not accept their faith and whom they called "the gentiles."

They did succeed for a time in alienating the Bannock, who formed one-fourth of the Shoshoni tribe, from their allegiance, and caused them to advance with the Mormon fighters against the troops of the United States government under General Connor. This trouble followed that bloody incident when Porter Rockwell, a Mormon who was the leader of a group which was known as the "Destroying Angels," led his men, disguised as Indians, to massacre a wagon-train of emigrants south of Salt Lake City.

Chief Washakie, when he heard of the deflection of the Bannock, rode with the remainder of his tribe of fighting warriors to Fort Bridger, and there reported to

the commander of that post that the Bannock were fortified on Bear river, and that the Shoshoni were ready to
assist the white soldiers in subduing them.

General Connor, however, chose wisely for the future
of the old chieftain. He sent Washakie home with his
grateful appreciation, stating that he believed he could
subdue the Bannock alone, and that if the Shoshoni
were left out of the trouble the defeated portion of the
tribe would return to their allegiance later.

With the 2nd Californians, and other scattered details
from outlying posts, General Connor had attacked the
Bannock on Bear river, and after fording the ice-choked
stream, he drove the redskins out, destroyed their village, and killed a great number of them. On the day that
General Connor returned to Fort Douglas, near Salt
Lake City, the remnants of this Bannock force were
arriving, shame-faced, at Chief Washakie's camp to
reaffirm their loyalty to his leadership.

Jim Bridger, who probably was more conversant
with the various Indian chiefs than was any frontiersman on the plains, had become an intimate friend of
Washakie in his earlier days.

In 1865, Bridger had remarked to Finn, "Washakie
is only a half-breed Shoshoni really. His mother was a
Lemhi woman."

"Well, how could he have become a chief under those
conditions?" Finn had asked. "I thought a warrior had
to be a full-blooded Shoshoni before he could have
leadership."

"Well, sir," Bridger returned, "it's just because
Washakie is by far the wisest Indian on the plains.
That's why. The best proof of that is the way he figured
about the white men. He saw from the first that they
were to be the rulers of the West, and he always gave
them his friendship and help."

One of the most interesting examples of Washakie's reasoning powers was noted by Finn Burnett at the time that Felix Brunot, chairman of the board of Indian commissioners, spent several months at the agency. With his secretary, Thomas Cree, he was treating with Chief Washakie for the southeastern portion of the reservation.

The southern limits, as they were first designated, had included the Miners' Delight mine, and had followed the Beaver divide between Sweetwater and Wind River valleys. From there it ran due south of the mouth of Owl creek.

Brunot was a splendid, level-headed man, and was regarded with confidence by the Shoshoni. At this time, he warned Chief Washakie against being induced to fight against the white soldiers.

"The white men are as many as are grasshoppers upon the plains," answered the Shoshoni chief. "The time will come when they will overrun the earth. Some Indians are wise, and become great medicine-men in their tribes. But all white men are wise.

"They make water to run uphill, which no Indian can do. They can talk over a long distance, through a wire instead of going over a hill as the Indians do. The white man makes roads through hills for their fire-wagons which go faster than the swiftest horses, which never get tired, and which pull trains of houses which are longer than an Indian can count. A people who can do these things are all great medicine-men. He would be a fool who would counsel his weak Indians to fight such a people."

Later, when Chief Washakie traded the finest piece of land in the country, the Green River valley, in exchange for the Wind River valley, he was presented with a fine suit of broadcloth and a silk "plug" hat.

Then he was taken for his first and only ride on a train. He always roared with laughter afterwards when telling of the incident.

He repeated the tale time and again for the benefit of his marveling listeners around his campfires, of how, when the fire-wagon started, he jumped out and rolled over and over down the bank of the right-of-way.

When he rose, his fine suit was covered with dirt and his new headgear was crushed flat. He had not understood the power of the locomotives or that they could be stopped, so he had jumped for safety.

Never would Chief Washakie go with a delegation to Washington. He always remarked that such a trip would result in little benefit, and that "Washington" would send him word if he wanted anything accomplished. He invariably referred to the president of the United States as "Washington."

His authority was absolute within his tribe. His word was law, and disobedience to his orders constituted a capital offense. It was said that in his earlier days he had killed his wife for refusing to obey him, and his action was readily understandable when viewed by the Indians.

The Shoshoni tribe was numerically weak. Their lives depended on absolute unity. When their chief ordered them to camp, they camped; if he told them to move, they moved.

As a tribe, the Shoshoni were a stubborn and rebellious people, and for Chief Washakie to allow anyone, even his own wife, to disobey his orders, would serve as a precedent for other similar actions.

But Washakie was never a tyrant. He was a good-natured man, sympathetic, generous, and a great lover of children. No chief was ever more greatly beloved or respected by his tribe.

Hunting with Chief Washakie

Hunting with Chief Washakie

In the fall of 1871, the first annuities were issued to the Indians on the reservation. Each brave was given two blankets, one red and one blue, an overcoat, two shirts, two pairs of stockings, a pair of shoes, and a hat.

The squaws were issued enough calico to make two dresses apiece, which amounted to ten yards composed of two patterns. Each was then given ten yards of unbleached muslin, five yards of red flannel, five yards of striped dress goods which was partly wool, two pairs of stockings, a pair of shoes, and a bandanna handkerchief.

The squaws of the plains had always in the past utilized the sinews of various game animals for thread when sewing together their buckskin and hides. Now, they were issued thread with which to sew cloth, and needles and awls. The needles were of two kinds; one for stitching cloth, the other being three-edged for sewing buckskin.

Rations which were issued at this time consisted of a quarter of beef, four times a month to each lodge. The first week a dwelling would receive a front quarter, and in the following week it would be issued a hind quarter. Besides the meat, each Indian received a regular soldier's ration of two pounds of bacon, rice, beans, baking-powder, coffee and sugar, as well as a specified amount of navy tobacco. The clothing and shoes were issued annually; the provisions, once a week.

After receiving their annuities that fall, the Shoshoni

packed up their belongings before starting on their short winter's hunt. Chief Washakie went to Dr. Irwin, the agent, during these preparations.

"I would like Finn Burnett to go with us," the old chief said, in the vernacular. "The country in which we shall hunt has many hostile Sioux and Cheyenne. I wish a white man to go with us to assure the white trappers and hunters whom we meet that we are friendly."

Finn was ordered to go with Chief Washakie, and he took a saddle pony which he had purchased from an Indian, and rounded up five jackasses which had been grazing in the valley without any apparent owners. These he loaded with his camp outfit, provisions, and tent, left his family under the protection of Dr. Irwin, and departed with the Shoshoni.

It was an excellent opportunity for the young man to learn the habits and accomplishments of the tribe. From the start, he was petted and pampered by every brave and squaw in the band. The best cuts of every kill of game were brought to him. Every morning, when orders were given to break camp, a detail of squaws was always ready to pull down his tent, and to load his outfit on his donkeys. In the evening, another group unpacked everything, put his tent in perfect order, and piled dry wood close to a new campfire for him.

On leaving with a hunting party in the morning, Chief Washakie always put a squaw on guard at Finn's tent, and on his return, everything would be cleaned and put in place. Even his supper would be simmering on the fire.

The first buffalo they saw were on the head of Muddy creek, later known as the Government meadows. But it was on the third day out from the agency that they crossed the Owl mountains and camped on Owl creek, close to the main herd.

Looking over the country from the mountain-top that morning, the valley appeared to be swarming with thousands of buffalo. Below, in every direction, in groups of fifty, and bands of hundreds, they scattered everywhere, feeding and wallowing in the cool, moist, bottom lands.

Next morning, Finn packed up to accompany the Shoshoni braves on a several days' hunting trip, and for two weeks they went from place to place, killing buffalo during that time, and several mountain-sheep, elk, and deer for the winter larder.

When the hunters returned to their main camp on Owl creek, Finn discovered that his tent had been completely burned during his absence. Chief Washakie immediately presented him with a fine, new lodge made of dressed buffalo skins, which was more spacious and comfortable than had been his little tent.

That trip proved to be a period of great education for Finn, and showed to him that the Shoshoni were without doubt the best people whom he had ever known. He found the braves to be truthful and courageous, and the squaws hardworking and moral.

In all his experience, he never knew a Shoshoni to steal anything from a white man, and the only two lewd women of the tribe were ostracized to lodges outside the village.

The tribal punishment for infidelity was the cutting off of the woman's nose, though it was also lawful for the husband to kill his wife for her offense. Men who were unfaithful were ridiculed and shamed by the tribe, but suffered no other punishment. In almost every instance when squaws had been mutilated for this shameful reason, they wandered away into the wilderness to commit suicide or to die from hunger and exposure.

Finn knew of but one woman, the Bannock wife of an Indian named Kag-e-vah, who suffered the loss of her nose, and who lived to be an old woman, retaining the respect of her husband, and bravely continuing her life in the face of public ridicule.

She told Finn that when she was a young girl, a playful child had thrown a kettle, and that it had cut her nose off. As she recounted this story, other Indians within hearing demonstrated their disbelief by laughing and winking. But Finn knew her always as a good woman and a faithful wife.

Several times during the three months that they were hunting, the Shoshoni were attacked by war-parties of Sioux, Cheyenne, and Arapaho who attempted to steal the horses. Finn went with the pursuers, learning their mode of warfare, and their methods of trailing and scouting.

When the marauders were overtaken, their dead bodies were scalped and mutilated. The ears, hands, and other portions were cut off and borne to the Shoshoni village in triumph, where the squaws would gloat and exclaim over the trophies.

That night, around a great fire, the tribe would hold a scalp-dance, during which the warriors would boast of their bravery and prowess, and their squaws would recite instances of the courage of their men in past battles. All of them would dance until morning, when all retired to sleep through the day.

If they were not dancing at night, they gambled. The squaws played with hand-made dice which they rolled from a flat basket upon a blanket. The stakes usually consisted of a horse, buffalo robe, elk or buck skins, or clothing of exceptional value. One of these items was won in each game. For instance, a horse was decided upon as the stake. Each squaw around the campfire then selected a designated number of short sticks which she placed in a pile before her.

Sides were chosen, and one squaw then started the game. She rolled the dice around in the basket before casting them before her on the blanket. The spots on the top sides of the dice were counted, and all the other players passed her that number of sticks.

The basket passed to the player to her left, and the same manner of play continued on and on around the circle until one squaw had won all the sticks of the players. She was awarded the horse, another stake was selected, and another game began.

The men amused themselves with a ring which was six inches in diameter and covered with rawhide. A smooth piece of ground was selected and all brush and weeds were chopped away from it until a square of 100 yards had been cleared. Sides were chosen, stakes were declared, and sticks were gathered for counters in the same manner as was done in the squaws' dice game. All stood in line, and, while one rolled the ring across the ground, the rest attempted to throw their spears through it.

Seldom did anyone succeed in casting his weapon through such a small, rolling hoop, but most of them hit it. The warrior whose spear lay closest to the ring after all had taken their turn, won a stick from the other participants. This game continued until one had obtained all the counters.

The squaws had another amusement which was universally popular, and which was called a ball-game.

Two spheres made of buckskin were nailed one to either end of an eight-inch stick. When ready, it resembled a modern dumb-bell.

Two goal lines were made about 100 feet distant on either side of a central line on which this dumb-bell had been placed.

Sides were chosen, and each squaw, after having gathered her counters, armed herself with a crooked stick which was generally used by her in the cleaning of the floor of her lodge, and which was much the same as the hockey stick.

The game started, and showed a crude similarity to the "shinny" so often played by white children on ice. It soon became a general melee, with a whirling mob of squaws hacking with their crooked sticks in savage attempts to drive the dumb-bell across their opponents' goal line. The side which won all the sticks then held an elimination contest, where contestants strove by twos to outwit their opponents.

The men had another game which they called "hands." This was played with either a small bone or a bullet. Opponents lined up on opposite sides of the campfire to sit there watchfully. The first contestant would take the object and would begin to throw it around rapidly, suddenly concealing it in one hand or the other. The warrior across the fire from him was then obliged to guess which hand held the object.

Finn noticed several instances when an Indian started with affluent means to play the games throughout the night, and daybreak would find him to be the poorest brave in camp. They bet shirts, moccasins, horses or any possessions which they owned. Sometimes they gambled for two and three days without stopping, men as well as squaws.

On the march, scouts rode far ahead, and Finn frequently accompanied them. He learned to pull great clumps of grass from the lowlands, to fashion a rude head-dress and creep with it to the top of a ridge, where he could look over the crest cautiously from beneath the safety of this camouflage.

Sometimes these Shoshoni scouts would lie for hours amid a cluster of sagebrush, watching silently the flutter of meadowlarks and turtle-doves where they flew aimlessly amid the yucca and buffalo grass. If any portion in the wastes before them was shunned by the birds, it was an indication to the scouts that some hostile Sioux crouched there, concealed. The Shoshoni hunters always hid far to the rear of the scouts in isolated gulches, until the signal to proceed was given.

Finn was secretly amused at the superstitions of his Indian friends. They explained to him that the meadowlark was their greatest enemy, for he always ridiculed them and sat on the top-most point of trees and hills for the express purpose of revealing their hiding-places to their enemies. Frequently, a lark singing in the sagebrush, or a rabbit or gopher crossing the trail before them, would turn back the entire expedition.

Finally, the hunting was finished, and Finn returned with the Shoshoni to the reservation. All settled down to a quiet routine for the winter.

Frank Trumble ran the flour mill at the agency with Finn acting as the engineer, until the spring. They ground the first wheat that was raised on the reservation, and found the flour to be of excellent quality.

Bazil, Sacajawea's son, visited frequently at the mill. Finn showed him how the engine worked, and became well acquainted with him. Finally, Bazil asked for the name of his new friend.

Now, in Chief Washakie's camp were two old men who acted as the village criers, who went from lodge to lodge calling the chief's orders and proclamations. The name of one was Werengow, which means "He-Bear," and the other, Toopsapaw, which may be translated as "Brown Water."

As a joke, Finn answered Bazil that his name was Werengow, and that Frank Trumble's was Toopsapaw. From that time on, the Shoshoni called the two men by those names.

The Pillaged Valley

The Pillaged Valley

During the winter of 1871-1872, Dr. Irwin began the education of the Shoshoni Indians along legal lines. Many of the Shoshoni villages on the reservation were situated at a distance from the agency, and it was felt that their leaders could handle many of the petty cases among themselves instead of going to the agent in every instance with their minor troubles.

They were taught, therefore, the white man's methods of conducting trials, and were urged to organize their own courts which would impose sentences for misdemeanors. It was explained during the course of their lessons that the penalty for murder was death, and they were told of the other crimes and of their rightful proportion of punishment.

A noted old warrior named Tone-vok was elected to be the Shoshoni judge, and a council of twelve was also chosen to perform the duties of a permanent jury.

The Indians took their lessons very seriously, and Tone-vok returned with his council to the outlying Shoshoni village near Bull lake. They had scarcely reached their tepees when their newly-acquired legal knowledge was called into action.

A young warrior of the village had ridden to Milford where he obtained and absorbed a large amount of the white man's "fire-water." He returned home in an intoxicated condition, and had killed his wife when in a drunken frenzy.

Judge Tone-vok assembled his council immediately. The murderer was brought before him to be tried with all the dignity and pomp possible to assume in an Indian camp. It may even be suspected that considerable excess ceremony was affected by the new judge in an effort to awe the spectators into proper subservience.

The culprit was found to be guilty, and was sentenced to be hanged. Next morning, while drums boomed dismally, he was led to the council-lodge, where he was made to mount a heap of firewood. From above him dropped a rope from the crossed lodge poles, and the end was fastened about his neck.

Judge Tone-vok then strode forward with all majesty, and, after a solemn exhortation to the onlookers, kicked the wood from under the feet of the doomed man.

When the victim of the execution had been buried, a full report, which fairly radiated with expectation of praise at this first legal experience, was sent to the agent.

Dr. Irwin was horrified, and sent for Tone-vok to report to the agency at once. On arrival, the agent informed the Shoshoni judge that the case should have been reported, and the culprit sent to the agency for trial.

Tone-vok answered that there was no reason to bother the agent with the incident; that he understood the white man's law perfectly. The murderer had been tried, found guilty, and hanged in proper sequence, and nothing more could be done about it. Which was true.

It was during that summer of 1872 that the first white settlers took up homesteads in the valley surrounding the little community which they called Lander. Among them, the best known were Ernest Hornecker, John Bonner, Martin Hornecker, John Knott, Henry Lovell,

Harvey Morgan, Mrs. Richards and Miss Hall, Frank E. Coffey, Frank Lowe, John Pelong, Peter Olsen, John McCollum, and Peter Anderson.

Major Baldwin started a mercantile business at that time with the two saloons which formed the nucleus for the new town of Lander.

Four miles west of this settlement, on the north fork of the Popo Agie, Ad Altman started a saloon, Hiram Mealman erected his blacksmith shop, and Benjamin Sheldon introduced a combined general store and saloon. This little community called itself Milford, and for a number of years it was doubtful which of these towns would outgrow and outlive its rival. Lander won.

It was in September, 1872, when Commissioner Brunot made the aforementioned visit to the agency on business relating to the southeastern limits of the reservation.

On the day before his arrival, Dr. Irwin told Finn to drive to Camp Stambaugh with Colonel Williams to bring the commissioner back to the agency. Finn and the colonel started, and on the way they stopped at Murphy's ranch on the Little Popo Agie river, where they were asked to lead a saddle-mule behind them and deliver it to a man in Miners' Delight.

After crossing Twin creek, Finn noticed the fresh trail of forty Indians. They had evidently dismounted a few minutes before, and their moccasin tracks showed that they had led their horses up the road ahead of him toward the mines.

Since leaving the agency, Finn had whiled the time away by recounting to his companion a number of his experiences with Indians. Colonel Williams had become visibly more upset as every mile passed. Now, he noted the intent manner with which Finn watched the road and the ledges around them.

"Is something wrong?" the officer inquired.

"Well, colonel," his companion replied, "do you see those tracks down there in the dust? They're Indian footprints and they were put there less than fifteen minutes past."

The officer glanced quickly at Finn's face to perceive if he were joking, and on seeing the gravity of his expression, he became excited.

"Let's turn around and go back, then," he said. "We are not able to make a fight if they attack us."

"No, colonel," returned Finn. "There is just as much danger behind us as there is in front. But, if you want to take the saddle-mule that is tied behind us, you can ride back."

The colonel was undoubtedly very much shaken at their predicament, but answered gamely that he would go through with his companion.

They were within a short distance from the top of the divide that ranged between Beaver and Twin creeks, when they heard shots ring out ahead of them. Evidently there was trouble to be encountered. Both men cocked their guns, and held them ready across their knees as they proceeded.

Coming down the slope toward Beaver creek, they saw a wagon loaded with hay standing beside the stream, and beyond, several white men who were walking slowly up the trail toward Miners' Delight.

From the tracks in the road, Finn was able to perceive that the team had been stopped half-way down the hill, the traces had been cut, and the horses freed. Then the wagon had been released, to run unguided the half-mile down the steep incline to the creek where it had halted without turning over.

Finn drove on, and overtook the men before he was made aware of the tragic portion of the incident.

He was told that Michael Heenan had been the driver of the wagon, and that the Indians had ambushed him on the divide, and had killed him at the first volley. The redskins had crowded around the wagon, had pulled the body of their victim from the seat and had stripped it of every piece of clothing. They had cut the four-horse team loose, and had allowed the wagon to roll down the hill, while they disappeared into the thickets, leaving the naked corpse behind on the ground.

Miners in Meadow Gulch had heard the shots, and had come out to the scene, and were now carrying the mutilated body to the Heenan home in Miners' Delight. Mrs. Heenan was to give birth to a child that night.

Finn and the colonel whipped their horses all the way to Camp Stambaugh. There, when they reported to Colonel Brisbin, the post commander, and told of the Heenan killing, they were informed that an old man had been killed earlier in the day by the same band of Indians at Cottonwood Springs, and that the soldiers were already out after them.

Next day, when Commissioner Brunot accompanied Finn and Colonel Williams on their return trip to the agency, they were escorted by fifteen mounted troopers. Arriving at Miners' Delight, the commissioner asked them to stop for a few minutes while he called on Heenan's bereaved family. There he left a little pile of money on the table, as a tangible expression of his fine, Quaker sympathy.

These Indian raids brought continued dread and

watchfulness to the plains throughout that winter, and the spring of 1873 proved to be a season of even greater horror.

The men at the agency were obliged to go to the mountains for logs every day during that spring, and the constant killings going on around every settlement in the Wind River valley made them positively afraid to look toward their homes when they drove over the hill at nightfall. Every day held the menace of burned dwellings and massacred families.

John Anthony moved his wife and three children down to a cottonwood cabin at Warm Springs as soon as the snowdrifts began to melt. He had secured the government contracts for fencing-posts and sawed lumber, and several tents for his men were set up close to his cabin.

Not long after he had settled there, "Uncle Billy" Rogers and Finn set out one morning for the hay fields along the river, not very far from Anthony's little settlement.

As they approached the spring, Finn saw a band of hostile Indians on a ridge to the south of them, evidently looking the valley over for a place to attack. "Uncle Billy's" eyesight was not good, and he refused to believe that Finn could see any Indians, and continued to declare that what the younger man saw was probably a herd of game. Finn remembered that Anthony had a pair of field-glasses, and finally influenced his companion to accompany him to get them. He cautioned the older man not to alarm Mrs. Anthony by any reference to the possibilities.

Finn borrowed the glasses, and stood in the doorway of the Anthony cabin peering through them at the hills. Mrs. Anthony watched him.

"For heaven's sake, Finn," she cried, "don't tell me there are Indians out there."

Finn handed the glasses without a word to "Uncle Billy." He took one look, and saw the redskins to be just across the creek on a ridge, watching him. He jumped back into the room yelling, "Indians."

"Oh, my babies! My babies!" shrieked Mrs. Anthony. "They're out there. I'm going after them."

Both of the men restrained her, and helped her to a chair. Her boy of eleven years, and two girls, seven and nine years of age, had gone to the creek to gather berries in a thicket about five hundred yards away.

"You stay with Mrs. Anthony, Uncle Billy," said Finn. "I'll go after the children. Now, don't worry a bit, we'll get out all right."

The Indians were not half a mile away, and were watching the progress of the lone man as he hurried toward the choke-cherry trees. Finn expected them to charge at any moment, but from sheer curiosity they sat quiet on their ponies as he went on.

He was soon hidden from their sight among the trees along the creek, and not until then did he start to run. He could hear the children distinctly as they chattered at their work, picking the wild cherries and berries, and whooping with delight at the discovery of clusters which were especially luscious.

Finn's appearance, with his eyes wide with fear for them, frightened them into silence He cautioned them to be quiet, and herded them deep into the darkness of a thicket. There the children crouched down in pitiful little heaps, with faces unnaturally white and fearful beneath big, red cherry smears on their cheeks.

The Indians evidently suspected a trap. No lone man in his right mind would leave the defenses of a strong cabin to walk confidently into the insecurity of a thicket unless assured of additional support somewhere. They knew that Anthony's men were nearby, but they were not sure of their exact position.

Finn and the children waited for twenty long minutes, listening to every flicker of wings in the undergrowth and each flutter of leaves overhead, with dread tugging at their hearts. Then he decided to make a break for the house.

"Listen, children," Finn spoke quietly. "We're going home now. All of you must clasp hands, and walk quickly. Don't run or look back. I'll be right here, and I won't let the Indians get you. Go on now."

So out they went. Bravery such as those children displayed that day was glorious to behold. Frightened though they were, with teeth clenched together to stifle the screams that rose to their lips, they joined hands, and trooped hurriedly across the grass, straining their eyes ahead toward the open door, where life waited for each of them. With little sunbonnets above their curls, and rude, ragged, calico dresses about their tiny forms, the girls clung on either side of their brother who strove to be so much a man that morning.

Finn crouched waiting, with his gun ready. Each moment seemed as an hour in passing, as he listened fearfully, expecting a burst of firing from the ridge and the clattering dash of approaching ponies.

But nothing happened. The children dashed through the open door to the arms that were outstretched to receive them, and, as Finn sauntered slowly back to the cabin, he could see the distant backs of the hostile redskins as they disappeared down the valley. Had they known of the exact situation that morning, they would undoubtedly have added one more massacre to that long list which they perpetrated during those dreadful months.

"Uncle Billy" and Finn lost no time in loading the Anthony family into the wagon, and in proceeding with all haste to Fort Washakie with them. There, Mrs. Anthony remained with her children, and never returned to the cabin at the spring.

The two men found it to be a dangerous task to work in the fields that year. Indians repeatedly tried to shoot them down. When they cut the hay, Finn drove, while "Uncle Billy" stood in the wagon to watch for attackers. Then, while his companion raked, Finn took his turn as sentinel.

One morning, when they were working in the field, they heard a great commotion among the trees along the river. A fight of large proportions was taking place as was testified by the amount of firing which could be heard by the two workers. They were mystified, as the only persons who would fight Indians in the vicinity were those soldiers and employees who were at that moment safe at the agency. Nevertheless, the two men hitched up the wagon and withdrew to the fort.

That night, the Shoshoni squaws moved into the agency buildings from their villages in the mountains, and later, their warriors rode in.

They told Finn that they had surprised a large band of Sioux which had hidden among the bushes and willows close to the hay fields. The Shoshoni were gleeful as they displayed their trophies of scalps and captured horses, and Finn was doubly pleased, for they had unknowingly saved the two hay-workers from a furious battle, and possible death that day.

There were two women living alone in the valley at that time, their nearest neighbor being Charlie Fogg whose cabin was more than a mile distant from their home.

One of these recluses was a sixty-year-old widow named Mrs. Richards, who owned a fine herd of cattle, and the other was her niece, Miss Hall, who was then about forty-five years of age.

On the third day of July, 1873, all the men in the valley had gone to the mountains for logs and wood, when fifty Sioux warriors swept down upon the cabin of the unfortunate women. At the moment that the savages burst in the door, a man named Lum Williams emerged from a thicket some distance away, and saw what was taking place, but, being alone, he knew it would be suicide to interfere. He ran for help.

The Sioux tortured and abused the women and ransacked the cabin. Then, after taking everything of value, they rode on down the valley, leaving Mrs. Richards's dead body on the ground, a ghastly mass of gunshot and arrow wounds amid the bruises which she had sustained in a vigorous battle to defend herself.

When help arrived, Miss Hall was found to be unconscious in the house, mutilated and bleeding internally from several arrow wounds. She died three hours later.

Word of the outrage was sent to the agency. Mr. James I. Patten, the school teacher, with his wife and several friends went to the scene and removed the bodies to the Indian burial ground.

Later, the war-party of Sioux which had attacked these women rode into Fort Laramie. There, they represented themselves as being peaceful Indians, and attempted to trade Mrs. Richards's watch, together with a number of other articles which were known to have been the possessions of the two murdered women.

Fearing for the safety of their families, Finn and a number of other men of the agency decided to remove their wives and children to Salt Lake City, the nearest town of any size in that part of the country. Accompanied by Dr. Stevenson and the others, Finn loaded them into wagons and took them on the long trip, and returned without incident. These women did not return until the fall of 1875, two years later.

Freed now of the continual fear of massacre for their families, a portion of the men at the agency were able to move and to work farther from their homes. They set to work getting out timber from the mountains, building a stone cabin at the head of Mill creek for a possible refuge to be used if they were attacked, and camping there from Monday mornings until Saturday afternoons, when they returned to the agency for provisions.

As the summer advanced, the raids of the Sioux became more savage and frequent, requiring that a greater proportion of the agency men remain behind to guard the buildings until, finally, no one went to the mountains at all.

Everyone attended church on Sundays, fully armed, as had the Puritan pioneers of an earlier day. Services were held in the log schoolhouse of the agency which stood on the south side of Trout creek, about a hundred yards from the residences.

Bishop Randall visited the agency twice a year, and held services there for all the white people in the valley. He was a little man, with a splendid voice of great volume and eloquence. Before the bishop's arrival on his first trip, Finn was ordered to go to South Pass with Charles Oldham to meet him with a wagon, and to drive him safely back to the agency.

The bishop had heard the account of an Indian raid which had occurred a few days before, when Lieutenant Stanbro had been killed.

"Do you think it probable that we shall meet hostile Indians on the road, Mr. Burnett?" he asked.

"It's not an unusual experience," answered Finn.

"I asked because I'm not accustomed to the use of guns," the bishop explained. "I am a fairly good shot with a shotgun, however, and if you can get one of that type for me, I could help you to stand off the savages in time of attack."

Oldham and Finn found a shotgun, loaded it with buckshot, and gave it to the bishop. No Indians were encountered on the road, but there was no doubt in the minds of either of his companions that the clergyman would have proved to be a courageous ally had they been attacked.

Bishop Randall was a small man of delicate appearance, but his strength of personality was such that had he chosen the military profession instead of that of the clergy, he would have made a remarkable record. There was not a spark of anything timid or effeminate in his entire makeup.

During one of these visits of the bishop's, and during an evening prayer meeting, a war-party of Arapaho surrounded the building. They crept to the windows and peered in, noting that everyone was well armed and prepared.

They did not understand the significance of the meeting, but they heard the bishop's great voice "making medicine." Being intensely superstitious, they did not so much as fire through the windows, but sneaked to their ponies and disappeared into the night.

No one at the agency was aware of the incident until

Dr. Irwin was told of it by an Arapaho at Fort Laramie. The hostiles had believed that any man with such a voice as had the bishop must be a great medicine-man, and feared a trap.

It was during this same summer that James Chambers drove his ox-team to Fort Washakie one morning, with his wagon loaded high with wood for the post. He had been careless when he hitched up, and was more than half way to the fort when he discovered that he had left his gun back in camp. He continued on, hoping for the best.

When he reached a point about a mile and a half west of the post, he saw a war-party of Indians charging in his direction. There was nothing for him to do but attempt to bluff them. With his axe in hand, Chambers jumped from the wagon, threw himself underneath, and sighted along the axe-handle at the approaching savages.

They discerned a man unafraid, apparently prepared to riddle them with bullets if they came within range, so they whooped at him derisively, wheeled their horses far around him, and charged on down the valley to gather up some loose horses of a settler there.

Finn was nearby, and galloped to the fort to join the soldiers in the chase. Lieutenant Robinson, with a company of cavalry, was already in his saddle when Burnett arrived, and all dashed up the government road toward Mill creek.

The raiders experienced difficulty when they attempted to ford the Popo Agie river with their stolen horses, as the water was running flood high. This fact enabled their pursuers to overtake them.

Lieutenant Robinson and Finn arrived first, and after they had fired two test shots, they were able to determine the range to be 700 yards. This advance knowledge enabled the soldiers to adjust their sights quickly on their arrival, and to pour such an immediate deadly volley into the marauders that the stolen horses were abandoned, and the Indians fled.

The soldiers rode down, gathered up the stolen herd, and drove them up the west side of the river, crossing the north fork to warn the settlers of the presence of the raiders.

The hard pace at which the troopers had ridden from the fort proved too much for their mounts. Of poor grade originally, the horses of many frontier posts at this time broke down after frequent use, and in this instance they began to fall dead before they had galloped beyond sight of the post. One by one, they sank to the ground, until, when White Horse Gulch had been reached, the fourteenth fatality occurred.

"There is another horse down," Finn remarked to Lieutenant Robinson. "That makes more cavalry horses that have died since we left the fort than we have recovered."

"It makes no difference," answered the officer. "It is the policy of the government to protect the settlers at any cost."

Lieutenant Robinson was a brave soldier and a splendid gentleman, and his men were a fine group of fighters, but they could never overtake Indian raiders, being outdistanced by the better horses of the redskins. With the orders of the war department stating that they were not to shoot at Indians, it was not surprising that these troops soon decided to continue a policy which kept them in quarters to protect the fort, and not to pursue marauders under any circumstances.

Shortly after this experience, another raid occurred in the valley. This time it was the agency herd which was attacked. It was grazing about three-quarters of a mile from the buildings when the main band of hostiles appeared, and one lone Arapaho left them to ride in pursuit of a lone white man, and then to return to begin to stampede the herd down the valley.

Among the stolen animals was a small, sorrel, bald-faced pony which belonged to Charles Bruit, an employee of the agency. This pony had become the leader of the herd, and when he refused to run, turning instead to gallop toward the agency, the rest of the animals followed him.

Finn ran to the mill with his gun, and when Bruit's pony raced past with the herd, he had rested his weapon along the sill, and was waiting for the Indian to appear. As the redskin followed the horses past the window, Finn fired, but was obliged to shoot high, fearing to hit the horses.

Evidently the Arapaho believed his "medicine" was strong that morning, or that Finn was a poor shot, for he became bolder, and came on after the herd. Finn, thereupon, got a "bead on him" at 300 yards, and shot him neatly through the stomach.

John McCollum had started for his home in the Lander valley about ten minutes before the raid. His wagon had no springs, and it made a loud noise as his team jogged along, so that he was unaware that any Indians were in the vicinity. The Indian whom Finn had shot had gone over the hill after McCollum, before he returned to stampede the herd.

Dr. Irwin ordered Finn to ride along the north fork to warn settlers of the raid, and to find the body of McCollum on his way back.

After warning the people on the north fork, at Milford on Baldwin creek, and along Squaw creek, Finn rode into Lander. There he found John McCollum sitting in his wagon unharmed in front of Jack Parker's saloon. Finn halted his horse and called his warning to everyone. He added that settlers should watch their stock, as Indians were raiding in the vicinity of Fort Washakie.

"That's a mistake," McCollum called out. "I just came from there."

When Finn told him that an Indian had followed him over the hill at the fort, and that it was an unexplained mystery why he was not lying dead beside the road somewhere, McCollum nearly fainted from fright. The noise of his wagon had drowned all sound of trouble.

Later, an Arapaho named Sherman Sage, stated that the redskin whom Finn had killed was a Cheyenne, and none would admit that the dead warrior was an Arapaho.

Sacajawea

Sacajawea

Sacajawea, who was probably the outstanding Indian woman in the West, came to the Shoshoni reservation late in the fall of 1871. Finn Burnett, through more than ten years of living among the Shoshoni, knew her always by her original name of "Sacajawea," which signified "Boat Woman," or "Boat Pusher," although she was known among her intimates as "Wad-ze-wipe," meaning "Lost Woman."

Indian names are frequently selected from the outstanding accomplishments of childhood, and either of these Shoshoni names by which she was known could undoubtedly have come to her from the experiences of her earlier days.

On her arrival at the reservation, she was accompanied by her son, Bazil, and his wife, a daughter named Ellen, another daughter who had married a white man named Adams, Bazil's sons, Andrew and Edrok, and three of her granddaughters.

All of them were given a comfortable house near the agency, located about one hundred feet southeast of where John Burns' store was later erected. There they lived until 1884, when Sacajawea died.

This remarkable Shoshoni woman always conversed with Bazil in French. There were also four half-breed Indians on the reservation named Weech, Weshaw, Moon-ha-Ve, and To-sah, who talked the French language, which they had learned from the early trappers of the country.

As Sacajawea and Bazil spoke English, as well, they frequently acted as interpreters at the agency, and Finn became intimately acquainted with them.

All that he ever knew of the Lewis and Clark expedition, Finn heard from the lips of Sacajawea. She told him of her capture on the Madison fork of the Missouri river; how she was gathering berries with several other Shoshoni girls and squaws when they were surprised and captured by a war-party of Mandans.

She had been adopted by her captors, and became the wife of a French trader named Charbonneau when she was sixteen years of age. Her first child was born two months before Lewis and Clark started up the Missouri river, and when her husband joined with the expedition, she accompanied him with her baby strapped to her back.

She described the boat trip up the Missouri and on up the Madison fork as far as it was navigable. She told of their leaving the boats; that they had no horses; and that all the Indians east of the Rocky mountains, with the lone exception of the Shoshoni tribe, were hostile to those redskins living on the western slopes. The only hope that the expedition had of reaching the Snake river, and so make their way to the Pacific coast, was to establish communication with the western tribes through some friendly Shoshoni.

They scouted through the country, seeking Shoshoni Indians who could aid them in finding friends beyond the mountains. The first warrior of that tribe whom they saw, was evidently hunting. He became frightened when the travelers made signals of friendship, and galloped away, never allowing them to approach close enough for them to explain their needs.

Everyone of the Lewis and Clark expedition was dressed in the typical frontier buckskin garb of the voyagers and trappers of the time. Their apparel was also similar to that of several northern tribes of hostile Indians, and at a distance it had been impossible to distinguish them as being white men.

Several days later, they sighted a party of thirty Shoshoni. The expedition maneuvered for three days before they could get close enough to them to gain their confidence.

Finally, when they had managed to contact these Indians, Sacajawea was overjoyed to discover her brother, Chief Cameahwait, among them. After a joyful reunion, she began to talk the language of her childhood again, and told him that the white men wished to cross the mountains. She explained that Lewis and Clark needed Shoshoni for guides, and a sufficient number of ponies to transport their provisions and equipment to the headwaters of the Columbia river.

Chief Cameahwait took the party with him to the main Shoshoni village, and held a general council of all the chieftains. There was a feast of happy welcoming for Sacajawea, and ponies and guides were given to the expedition when they pushed onward.

They encountered terrible hardships on the western slope. Game was very scarce, and soon the party was reduced to the extremity of eating the dogs which had followed the expedition. The Shoshoni guides were disgusted with the white men for consuming these animals, stating that they would rather die of hunger than eat these camp scavengers.

It is interesting to note that although the Sioux, Cheyenne, Arapaho, and the other plains Indians living east of the Rocky mountains considered dog flesh to be a great delicacy, the Shoshoni ridiculed the fashion, and declared that only dogs would eat their kind.

When the party arrived at the Snake river, they were able to purchase canoes from the Indians who lived in that vicinity, and continued their journey down the stream.

During the years that Finn was to know her, Sacajawea never tired of telling her people of the different tribes and portions of the country that she visited with the expedition.

Her stories were not always believed. Once, she told of a great fish, evidently a whale, which lay on the beach along the coast. It had either drifted there with the tide, or had been killed by Indians along the shore. The Shoshoni at the agency could not realize that a fish could attain the proportions that she related.

"How high was the fish?" one would ask.

"It would reach to the top of this room," she would answer, pointing to the ceiling, eight feet above the floor.

"How long was it?" came the inquiry.

"As long as it is from here to the hitching-rack over there," she answered. The distance measured sixty feet.

"No," the assembled Shoshoni shook their heads. "That is a lie. A fish could not be as large as that."

Then Sacajawea would tell them of the seals which lived in great numbers along the coast. The Shoshoni believed these to be people who inhabited caves under the water.

"Did you see these people?" her listeners would ask.

"Yes, many times," answered Sacajawea.

"Did you ever talk to them?"

"No, when we tried to get near to them they dived into the water."

"Yes, that is all right," agreed the Shoshoni, nodding gravely at each other. They could believe that people lived under water, but not that fish could grow to be as huge as was described by Sacajawea.

There were other Shoshoni at the agency who had seen seals.

"Those people come right out of the water to walk on the bank," they would declare. "They walked like people, but they had long tails."

Sacajawea went on to say that when the boats of the expedition had reached the mouth of the Columbia river, the water had become very rough, and it was with the greatest difficulty that their light boats were kept afloat. Her account of the size of the waves was also disbelieved by her listeners.

Then, she told of their return after a winter spent on the coast; of how the expedition was divided when it reached the Rocky mountains, and, while Charbonneau had guided Lewis with one portion over their original trail to the Madison river, Sacajawea had taken Clark and the remainder of the party across the country to Clarke's fork, and on to the Yellowstone river.

She told of their arrival at Clarke's fork; how difficult it had been to find logs there which were large enough to use in the construction of the usual size of canoe, and of how they overcame the difficulty by making two small boats, connecting them, and decking them over in pairs. In these peculiar vessels, she recounted that they had transported their equipment down the river and had united with Lewis near the mouth of the Yellowstone river.

Her return to her own people several years after the termination of the Lewis and Clark expedition, was a story of great hardship. Several of the Shoshoni women who had been captured with her during their childhood, accompanied Sacajawea, and they had traveled up the Big Horn river, crossed the Big Horn range on the east side of the canyon, and had continued over the route which was known to the Indians as the "Bad trail."

Near the mouth of Stinking Water, the squaws had met a war-party of Crow Indians of whom they were desperately afraid, as those warriors were at war with the Shoshoni. Only after they had given them all of their valuables were they allowed to proceed.

From Stinking Water creek they followed the river to the hot springs where the city of Thermopolis was later located. There, they crossed the river, followed the Owl Creek mountains to a point close to the head of Crow creek, and from there on across the east fork of the Big Wind river to the mouth of Warm Spring creek, and then over one of several trails to Snake river and her people.

Finn was never able to establish definitely the number of years which elapsed between the date of the Lewis and Clark expedition and that of her return to the Shoshoni.

Her tribe claimed relationship to the Comanche, and it is an established fact that both tribes spoke the same language. They had intermarried with the Lemhi, Bannock, and Ute, and it was not unusual for a party of Shoshoni to travel as far south as the Staked Plains.

Thus, it was very possible that she may have visited with the Comanche for a number of years, as her remarks would lead one to believe. At any rate, it was generally known that she was living with her son, Bazil, and his family near Fort Bridger in 1868, at the time that the treaty was made which ceded the present Shoshoni reservation to the Shoshoni Indians.

Dr. Irwin's wife became interested in the history of Sacajawea, and often visited with her, to write down her account, but later, in the agency fire when the office burned, the document was totally destroyed. In this conflagration, Dr. Irwin lost an autographed letter of thanks which President Lincoln had sent him, expressing appreciation for Dr. Irwin's services at Shiloh.

Sacajawea died in 1884, and was buried in the Indian burying ground west of the Shoshoni agency.

Later, some controversy arose over an Indian woman who was buried somewhere in Dakota, and who had been the wife of Charbonneau, and who was therefore supposed to be Sacajawea. She probably had been a girl companion, one of those Shoshoni children who had been stolen from their berry picking by the Mandans.

She might very possibly have been a wife of Charbonneau, as that Frenchman was a great marrying man. Sacajawea had been his third wife. There is nothing to prove that, following the Lewis and Clark expedition, Sacajawea lived with her husband, and Charbonneau's record would lead one to believe that he would not remain wifeless for any extended period of time. The fact that a Shoshoni wife of Charbonneau is buried in Dakota does not therefore necessarily establish her name as having been Sacajawea.

There were older men of the Shoshoni tribe at that time in Wyoming who could establish the identity of the Sacajawea whom they knew on the Shoshoni reservation as being the sister of Chief Cameahwait, and it is a matter of historical record that the sister of this great chieftain was a guide for Lewis and Clark on their expedition. There was never any question of her absolute identity in her own tribe by those who had known her from babyhood.

Finn, during those years on the reservation, was often filled with wonder at the distances which Indians would travel. Entire families would pack, mount their ponies, and trot out of their villages, to be gone for two or three years at a time, journeying to far places. They undoubtedly were the first "tourists."

In the spring, Finn would note a group of Shoshoni preparing to start on a trip.

"Where are you going?" he would ask.

"To Camas Prairie," they would answer, and Finn would think little of it, as their destination was to Idaho.

But, when that party of Indians returned a year or two later, he would notice that their packs contained smoked salmon and roots which grew only along the coast. Subsequent conversations bore out the evidence that they had set their tepees beside the sands of the western sea.

Others who were related to the Comanche, would go south, to be gone for one or two years. On their return they would tell their tribe of camps, the surroundings of which could have been only upon the Gulf of Mexico. These always brought with them southern horses with which to strengthen the strain in their own herds.

On one occasion, Finn described a California earthquake to a Shoshoni Indian named William Washington, and his wife. At every attempt he made to picture the scene, he was answered with the statement, "I know about that."

"How can you know about it?" Finn asked, finally.

"Well, because we have been there," they answered. "We have felt the ground move."

"When were you there?" Finn inquired.

They replied that several years before, they had left the Shoshoni territory to visit the Ute on White river in Utah. After remaining there a few days, they had decided to visit the Piute who were located still farther west. After that, hearing of other friends, they had continued until they had traveled through California, and had returned home through Oregon, Washington, and Idaho. Their trip had taken them a little less than three years.

Leaving Shoshoni country, these earliest "tourists" would move rapidly until they had reached the western slopes of the Rocky mountains. Seldom did they camp for more than a few minutes until they were beyond the reach of their enemies, all of whom lived on the east side of the continental divide.

The tribe became somewhat divided after the coming of the whites. In the vicinity of Fort Hall and along the Snake river, trappers and other white men had married Shoshoni and Bannock women.

Now, perceiving the Shoshoni reservation to be a rich territory, and desiring a portion of it, these mixed families commenced to petition the government for land.

Hearing this, Dr. Irwin, Dr. Stevenson, Frank Trumble, Charles Oldham, and Finn Burnett cautioned Chief Washakie to demand that the reservation be continued as the possession of the eastern band of Shoshoni, only.

This stipulation was included in the treaty of 1872, which was signed by Chief Washakie and by agents of the government, and which arranged for specified numbers of cattle and amounts of money as annuities.

Yet, that most important clause was forgotten afterwards, and was consistently omitted in all subsequent copies of the treaty which were published.

Furthermore, the government went even beyond that, and settled the Arapaho, the greatest tribal enemies of the Shoshoni, upon the best portion of the reservation, and divided all annuity money for leases and stock equally between the two tribes.

In 1877, Governor McConnell, who held the post of inspector, was sent from Washington to treat with the Arapaho, and to move them to the Pine Ridge reservation. This was before any portion of this agency had been sold or thrown open for settlement, and the Sioux tribe had consented to have the Arapaho with them there.

Sharp Nose, the head chief of the Arapaho, agreed at the council with Governor McConnell to move onto the Pine Ridge reservation, but the treaty was immediately suppressed by certain influences in Washington.

Withal the gratitude of the Union Pacific railroad for the friendship of Chief Washakie during its days of construction, and the thankfulness of the settlers and pioneers whose continued existence had been due entirely to the friendship and assistance of these gentle people, the Shoshoni were abandoned by the white man's government, and were obliged to submit to the usurping of over seventy-five per cent of the most arable land on their reservation.

Maladministration

Maladministration

The record of the manner with which the government handled the Shoshoni reservation was one of almost continuous futility. From the time of that first planting in 1872, 320 acres were added to cultivation each year. With the arrival of each succeeding spring, Chief Washakie held back his hunters from the trail, that they might render every assistance in clearing the new ground and in helping to plow it under.

It proved an arduous labor. Beyond the agency buildings, the land of the valley had been covered with boulders, and these the Indians removed and piled in ridges along the boundary lines. Willows were planted to fence little patches of garden stuff, and it soon became apparent to everyone that the Shoshoni were proving to be an industrious people who would become self-supporting if left to their own efforts.

It seemed, however, to be the policy of the government to make the office of chairman of the board of Indian commissioners a political plum with which a victorious administration could reward its faithful supporters. In other words, not content with over-riding signed treaties, and with establishing the Arapaho on the reservation in question, the government placed these Shoshoni Indians who, in the past, had proved to be the most generous and helpful friends that the whites had found upon the plains, in the hands of politicians who had no sympathy or understanding for their needs. In some instances, there is reason to believe that the office of agent for the reservation was given to individuals for the sole purpose of removing them from Washington, and so lessen their troublesome activities.

Most of the Shoshoni Indians displayed a sincere enthusiasm for farming, and had they not been met by mismanagement and disheartening carelessness in their relationship with those in authority, they would have been a self-supporting tribe within a short period of time.

Through all the terms of those first agents on the Shoshoni reservation, Finn worked on, doing his best with what he had, in an effort to help his red-skinned friends. He attended strictly to his own business throughout, and year after year established himself more deeply in the lasting affection of Chief Washakie and his unfortunate people.

In 1874, Dr. Irwin was rewarded for his successful administration of the Shoshoni by being transferred to the Pine Ridge reservation where he was ordered to superintend the Sioux and the Cheyenne. There had been constant friction there, as both tribes refused to occupy that reservation jointly, each demanding a separate portion for its own.

James I. Patten, who had been the first school superintendent in the Wind River valley, took over Dr. Irwin's duties, and continued efficiently along the lines of his predecessor. During his term of office, Felix Brunot was succeeded by another chairman of the board of Indian commissioners in Washington.

It soon became evident that the new commissioner was using his office in a peculiar manner. Agencies throughout the country were now flooded with farm machinery, threshing machines, wagons, plows, and barbed wire, until barns became filled to the doors with these over-supplies, and it became necessary to heap large quantities of these implements outside, to rust and deteriorate in the open.

Mr. Patten requisitioned for lumber again and again, stating that he must build sheds which would protect the unnecessary machinery, or all would become useless in a short time. He was not allowed a single foot of lumber for this purpose, and year after year the miserable pile of machines and wire became more rusted – a monument to mismanagement.

The frequent demands for lumber that had been made evidently displeased the commissioner, for he appointed a major to succeed Mr. Patten.

From the first, those at the Shoshoni agency wondered how such a man as was this major could have been given the position. This question grew in the minds of everyone until finally four of the old employees, Dr. Stevenson, L. C. Bliss, Charles Oldham, and Finn Burnett, wrote to the postmaster of the major's home town in the East, asking him for a statement of the reasons for the officer's appointment.

The answer was very interesting. He stated that the major had been the leader of a glee club which had campaigned through his home state during Hayes's presidential campaign, with a six-horse team and wagon. He went on to say that the officer's trade was that of tailoring, but that being drunk had been his principal occupation for the last few years.

It was during his administration that the agency herd, which had been accumulated for the Indians, was dissipated. Drives from Texas had brought herds of cattle into the country, and the stock which was purchased from them by the agency was identified by the government brand, which resembled a snake.

Although the Shoshoni were away from the agency a part of each year, their regular issues of rations had continued. The number of unslaughtered cattle which belonged to them for their meat issue thus accumulated to their credit until over five thousand head of fine beef steers were grazing around the agency.

It had been forbidden for anyone to sell government cattle before this time. Various stockmen in the Lander country had attempted to purchase some of the herd without success.

With the major's arrival, however, these men invited the new agent to a wet entertainment in Lander, during which he gave them permission to buy the cattle from the Indians. On his return to the agency, he ordered that the herd be divided pro rata among the redskins, and published an order which allowed them to sell their stock.

In less than two years, the entire herd had disappeared. Many cattle were stolen, as thieves knew the stock to be the possession of the Indians and felt that they were not running the risks which attended the pilfering of government property. But the most of the herd was sold for practically nothing to the neighboring cattlemen by the ignorant Shoshoni.

This major was succeeded by another major whose acquaintances considered him to be simple-minded. This new administrator had a fancy for spectacular dress, clothing himself with long stockings, knee pants, short jackets, and an old wool hat in which he placed a feather in an effort to appear war-like. In this garb, he rode about the reservation, ridiculed by the Indians and eyed thoughtfully by the patient employees.

His administration was followed by that of a professor from Georgia, who brought to the agency a

BRIDGER'S FERRY ON THE NORTH PLATTE RIVER

From a contemporary sketch.

number of his relatives and friends who displaced many
of the experienced employees on the reservation. These
newcomers became noted only for their whiskers, as
each of them had grown a tremendous beard.

John Fosher succeeded the Georgia professor. He
was a western man, and a good one, but his experience
in his own business had not followed along the lines of
agency work. He did his best, and made every effort
to overcome the mistakes left by his predecessors, but
he knew nothing of Indian characteristics, of agriculture, or of stock raising.

He was followed by a captain of the United States
army who was understood to have received his appointment at the request of his superior officer, who wished
to be rid of him. He had no friends among his military
associates, and it was commonly known by those who
were in constant contact with him that he was a mor-
phine addict.

During his administration, the Arapaho moved to
the reservation in great numbers. He started this tribe
at farming, but he was a hard master and demanded that
everything be done with military precision, something
entirely foreign to Indian habit. The Shoshoni were
afraid of him, and left their farms to move into the
mountains beyond his influence.

Then, a bright spot in the list of agents appeared in
the person of Captain R. H. Wilson. He proved to be
one of the most successful executives the reservation
was ever to know. He persuaded the Shoshoni to return
to their farms and to cultivate their grain and other
products with renewed enthusiasm.

More than five hundred acres of new land were developed to give an excellent yield, and everything in
his jurisdiction was progressing favorably when the

Spanish American war broke out, and he was called back into the service.

Captain Wilson had been raised on a farm, and during his experience in the army had handled numbers of men, and had constructed several forts. He was an honest, straightforward gentleman, and it was with sincere regret that the agency saw him depart to leave his duties to the able hands of Captain H. G. Nickerson.

During this new administration, the Indians continued to prosper, but Captain Nickerson was soon relieved by H. E. Wadsworth.

During these years of difficulty on the reservation, when agent succeeded agent with every change of executives in Washington, and when the poor and bewildered Indians were so often torn between their honest desire for peace and fear of these politicians from the East who ruled them with policies which were incomprehensible to their traits and characters, the handling of Indian affairs in the capital was becoming most flagrant.

At the time of the appointment of H. E. Wadsworth, the Shoshoni Indians were farming between 1200 and 1500 acres, beside furnishing the cavalry at Fort Washakie with all the hay they needed. All the flour and wheat used at the agency was being raised by these Indians, and the Milford flour mill which was owned by Noble and Lane obtained its supply of wheat entirely from the same source.

Those Indians who worked, received annuity money from the government. Part of this was spent by them for seed, and they obtained alfalfa, wheat, oats, potatoes, and garden seeds for all the land that they could plow and cultivate.

But there were a number of half-breeds on the reservation who did no work, and therefore received no annuities. One of these complained to the Indian Rights association in Washington that many were receiving no benefits from the money that was expended, and that the full-bloods were being made pets by the agency farmers.

The head of the Indian Rights association then complained to the Indian commissioner of this manner of distributing annuities and seed, and urged that these be issued to all Indians alike.

The result was that the lazy half-breeds received a share equal to the worker who had earned it. The amount of seed distributed at a reservation was determined by the amount produced in the past year, and in this instance was given pro rata to everyone. There was not enough seed for those who had cultivated a large acreage.

Each Indian that year received twenty pounds of oats, thirty pounds of wheat, and ten pounds of alfalfa seed, an amount which was entirely inadequate for their needs.

One Indian living west of the agency on Trout creek had been industrious and had plowed forty acres of land for seeding. When he received his small quota he became disgusted and stopped working entirely.

Everywhere, Indians who had been industrious and who had shown a proper interest in farming, refused to continue, saying that the government had been fooling them, that it did not want them to farm, else it would not have refused them sufficient seed after the land had been prepared.

The same half-breed who had stirred up the trouble then wrote another letter to the Indian Rights association in which he charged that the employees at the agency had stolen the grain which should have been issued to the Indians for seed.

An inspector was sent out to investigate this report.

He was evidently adversely prejudiced before his arrival, and had already decided that the employees were thieves, and that Finn Burnett, being the "boss farmer," was the worst of the lot.

Immediately on his arrival, he sent for Finn.

"I want your resignation right away," he demanded.

"What for?" asked the "boss farmer."

The inspector slapped his hand down heavily upon a stack of papers.

"That's the reason, Burnett," he stormed. "There is a pile of charges, every one of which states that the seed has not been distributed properly to the Indians on this reservation."

"Well," returned Finn, "I'll bet that every charge in that pile has been made by a lazy, disgruntled half-breed. I refuse to resign. I have lived with and worked among these Indians for years. I have done the best I know how, to teach them to farm, and to live as the white man lives. I have a few friends in high places, myself, and I refuse to resign or to leave until this entire affair has had a thorough airing."

"All right, then, Burnett, we'll see," was the reply. "In the meantime, I want you to present a report of all the seed grain that every farm has received to date."

Finn started out to investigate. For four days he traveled up Trout creek, and to the farms near the agency, obtaining the required information. Finally, he reached the house of an Indian named Big Bannock, and knocked at his door.

"I want to know how much grain seed you have used on your place," Finn stated.

Big Bannock's eyes blazed.

"Why do the white men keep coming to me every day asking that I show them the little sack of seed that has been issued me?" he snarled.

"Who visited you before?" Finn asked, surprised.

"A man on a white horse was here yesterday," returned Big Bannock.

The only white horse on the reservation was the favorite mount of the inspector. He had evidently been checking up on Burnett's report.

Finn galloped to the agency with white rage in his heart at this proof that his word was questioned. On the frontier, most white men lived and died for the integrity of their simple statements.

The stormy session that Finn enjoyed that afternoon at the agency was the last. The inspector returned to Washington two days later, and his vitriolic report to the commissioner of Indian affairs was a general accusation of everybody with authority on the Shoshoni reservation.

The head of the Indian Rights association visited the agency, himself, and proceeded to interview only the half-breeds and the disgruntled element which he apparently wished to believe. Not once, during his stay, did he interrogate the agent or the employees, and when he left for Washington, he had accumulated a mass of adverse reports.

The board of Indian commissioners, however, sent out its own investigator to check up on the others, and, to the delight of Finn Burnett, this man proved to be Major McLaughlin, who divided the honor with Finn of being the oldest man in the reservation service at that time. They had worked together for years, and had become firm friends.

Finn was standing in front of the postoffice when Major McLaughlin stepped off the coach.

"Well, Finn," he grinned heartily as he shook hands in welcome, "I've got your scalp in my pocket. There have been some terrible charges preferred against you."

After that opening remark, he proceeded to make a thorough and impartial investigation for two weeks. Every farm was visited, every employee was questioned, and every record closely studied.

The day before he left for the east, he sent for the "boss farmer."

"Finn," he stated, gravely, "I thought it would be only fair to tell you that after a complete study of the entire situation here, I find not one fact nor one word of truth in either of the reports made by the last two investigators. I am mighty pleased, my friend, and I believe all will be ironed out for you people soon."

Theodore Roosevelt was the president of the United States at this time. The board of Indian commissioners placed Major McLaughlin's report in his hands, together with those of the other inspectors, with the result that immediate changes were demanded in the Indian Rights association, and the commissioner's office.

President Roosevelt studied the situation carefully, and became thoroughly convinced that the objects of the Indian Rights association had been disregarded by its head who had by his arbitrary methods caused the association to become a detriment to the Indian service during the years of his administration.

The president began to search for a proper man to put in the commissioner's chair. He finally selected Mr. Loup, an old and trusted friend, with the understanding that he would not be interfered with in any way. The office was taken from under the jurisdiction of the secretary of the interior, and Mr. Loup became the absolute dictator of all the Indians in the United States.

The new commissioner had long been a member of the Indian Rights association, and had assimilated a considerable fund of information relative to the Indian character. He visited the Shoshoni reservation, studied the conditions carefully, made excellent recommendations, and proved himself to be a practical, efficient leader.

Previous to this time, commissioners had let contracts for supplies to the lowest bidders. The result had been that manufacturers had unloaded their worthless and obsolete products on the Indian reservations. Six of the reapers at the Shoshoni agency had been so worthless that the employees had never succeeded in running them long enough to mar the paint on them. Finn had put them away under a shed, and never had been able to find an inspector who would condemn them, so that they could be destroyed.

Mr. Loup ordered that they be junked, and nothing but the best of machinery was sent to the agency from that time on. Whatever was ordered, and the kind that was requisitioned, always arrived promptly during his term of office.

There remained but one other difficulty for Mr. Loup to overcome for the agency, and this he did immediately.

The reclamation service had been organized, and a party of surveyors and engineers had appeared at the Shoshoni agency with orders to construct new irrigation canals. Taking the best Shoshoni with their finest teams from the farm work, they had proceeded with their project, cutting through and obliterating the ditches which had been used successfully by the Indians for years.

Later, the reclamation service had reported to Washington that the work was completed, but that the Shoshoni were refusing to farm the land under the new ditches. The commissioner had written to the agent, ordering him to start the Indians at their work on farms which had been allotted to them under the new canals. The agent answered that the Indians had no seed.

The reclamation service had reported to the commissioner the names of all Indians who had worked on their project, and the amount of money which each had received as wages. Using these reports, some of them two years old, for a basis, the commissioner had ordered that the Indians be made to purchase seed with the wages which they had received.

Anyone with the least knowledge of Indian characteristics and improvidence would have understood the ridicule with which this order was received at the agency. In the first place, the Indians were well aware that they were entitled to their required amount of seed without cost as part of their annuity, and nothing could induce them to buy seed with wages which they had earned. Furthermore, not a Shoshoni ever saved a penny of his money. There was an Indian trait which urged them to spend every cent as soon as it was obtained.

The commissioner's report had shown that one Indian had received more than $600 in wages, and it had been a long and difficult task to make the authorities in Washington understand the improvidence of the redskins, and that the receipt of money did not necessarily mean that they retained it for any length of time.

Finally, the employees on the reservation had devised the plan of saving a portion of the Shoshoni grain at harvest time, to store it for the spring seeding. In this way they had encouraged their charges until they had begun to regain their old prosperity.

Mr. Loup had this difficulty explained to him, and promptly took steps to overcome it. From that time on, the Shoshoni Indian reservation settled down to a peaceful life of industry and education.

The Mormons

The Mormons

Five years after the Shoshoni reservation had been established, Chief Washakie with his tribe took the war-path to assist the troops of the United States army against the Sioux. In 1874, 1875, and 1876, this wise old chieftain was on the move continuously with his warriors, putting aside the memory of the white man's disregard for treaties, and giving his loyal service where none should have been expected.

In the fall of 1873, before the Sioux war became plains-wide in its scope, Charles Harrison and Finn Burnett had driven to Salt Lake City in a light wagon to visit their families. Harrison was the agency carpenter, and his wife lived with Mrs. Burnett in a house three blocks south of the Lion House, which was Brigham Young's home.

Mrs. Harrison had been raised in Salt Lake City, and her family were all of Mormon faith. Her friendships in the city brought to Mrs. Burnett a wide acquaintance with many of the most prominent families who lived there at the time.

Ann Eliza Young, the eighteenth wife of Brigham Young, became a close friend of Finn's wife, and they exchanged many confidences. It was this wife for whom the Mormon leader built a magnificent home which was known throughout the country as Ann Eliza's Palace. She later wrote a book which related her experiences while married to Brigham Young.

A daughter, Maggie, was born to Finn and Eliza

Ann Burnett in Salt Lake City in the spring of 1874, and it was a year from the following fall before Mrs. Harrison and Mrs. Burnett returned to the agency.

Finn stayed in the Mormon metropolis for more than six months and was very much interested in the Mormon life around him. He became acquainted with Porter Rockwell, who was said to have been the leader of the "Destroying Angels," and was especially charmed by his beautiful racing pony, a pinto, named Staggering Buck, which was raised on the great Rockwell cattle and horse ranch south of the city.

When the Mormons originally migrated to this portion of the frontier in 1847, they had found it to be owned by Mexico. A Mormon government which declared itself to be supreme had been developed, and the territory was named Deseret.

When the United States eventually included Deseret among its western possessions, the name of Utah was given to that province, and Brigham Young was appointed to be its first governor. During the presidency of James Buchanan, public opinion throughout the United States had turned against the Mormons to such a degree that the Mormon leader was deposed and Alfred Cummings was appointed governor of Utah.

The Mormons declared war, and that condition continued from the summer of 1857 to June of 1858. After a government defeat, and the subsequent preparation for a terrible retaliation, Brigham Young abdicated, and peace was made.

However, there continued Mormon disregard for the national laws until Brigham Young was finally prosecuted and convicted. He died before paying his fine, or serving his sentence.

Some of the Mormons had difficulties with their

numerous wives, as was proved in the case of a man who
lived in an adobe house not far from the temporary
home of Finn and his wife. The husband had made his
first wife agree to let him marry again, and had coaxed
her to visit her relatives for a month while he enjoyed
a honeymoon with his second mate.

After the marriage, the Mormon had bought new
furniture and had redecorated his home until it was far
prettier than it had ever been before.

One morning, Mrs. Burnett heard a terrific noise
down the street, whacking sounds and shrieks and
screeches which told of women fighting.

With Mrs. Harrison, she ran to the scene, to learn
that the first wife had returned home and had discovered the new furnishings which meant to her that her
husband loved the second wife the more. She had thereupon knocked her supplanter down with a well-aimed
bed-slat and was delivering a beating with energy and
thoroughness when Mrs. Burnett arrived.

The younger wife was removed to Finn's home, and
was taken soon afterwards to a residence in a more distant part of the city.

Keene had been appointed by General Grant to be
the acting-governor of Utah territory at that time. He
summoned Brigham Young to appear in court, and
when the Mormon leader disobeyed the order, he was
arrested and taken to Fort Douglas.

All along the road from Salt Lake City to the military
headquarters, men, women, and children followed the
soldiers who escorted the Mormon leader, crying and
wringing their hands.

On several occasions, Finn discussed Mormonism
with Mr. Holt, who was the father of Mrs. Harrison.
His wife's name was Sophie, a woman of great determi-

nation who believed that she was the only wife that Mr. Holt could have. He would have had several mates if left to his own inclinations, but Sophie dissuaded him firmly.

In his conversations, he frequently declared that Brigham Young was infallible, and that he could do no wrong.

"If, in the interest of the church and the Mormon people, he ordered you to cut my throat, would you do it?" asked Finn.

"Certainly, I would," returned Mr. Holt.

They had several discussions about the apostates, those Mormons who attempted to leave the church to flee the country. If these unfortunates were captured they were always killed.

In the spring of 1874, before Finn returned to the reservation, he began to search for a little home for Eliza Ann where she could remain until the Sioux had been pushed far enough away from the agency for her to live there in safety.

He selected a residence belonging to Enoch Corey, with the understanding that Mrs. Burnett could harvest all the fruit in an orchard behind the house.

Shortly after the Burnetts had moved into their new home, and after the fruit trees had begun to bloom, they awoke one morning to find that there had been a heavy rain during the night which had turned to sleet. The trees were covered with ice which glittered and sparkled in the morning sun.

"That ends all hope for much of a fruit crop," Finn remarked to Mr. Corey. "Those buds are frozen solid."

"No, that is a frequent occurrence," answered the owner. "That is what we call a 'silver frost.' It won't hurt the fruit at all."

His statement proved to be correct, for in the fall Mrs. Burnett gathered a fine crop of peaches and apples.

When Finn returned to the agency, he found most of the Shoshoni to be away scouting or fighting against the Sioux, and aiding the white troops with all their native skill.

Captain Bates with his regiment attacked the Arapaho village on the head of Bridger creek in July of 1874. Chief Washakie and his warriors were with him in the battle, and rendered the most valuable of services. A great number of the Shoshoni warriors were killed that day, before the village was destroyed and the lodges burned to the ground.

It was in the spring of 1876 that Chief Washakie took his warriors from the reservation, rode across the mountains, and joined General Crook's expedition against the Sioux.

This was the year of the Custer massacre. In fact, Crook's battle on the Rosebud was fought but a short time before that tragedy on the Little Big Horn river. Edmore LeClaire, a dispatch rider, told Colonel Bates later that two days before the massacre he had carried a message from General Crook to Custer, and had returned with the answer. This statement was verified, and was interesting historically, as it was generally supposed that General Crook's command was never in communication with Custer, and because of that, the ill-fated commander had been unable to call for reinforcements before his attack.

It was during this summer that General Crook attacked the Sioux on the Rosebud, and it was the result of the bravery of Chief Washakie and his warriors that Captain Henry and his company were not entirely destroyed.

The battle had been going on furiously for some time before the superior numbers of the Sioux began to force the soldiers back, and as the fight continued, it became apparent that the entire military force was in grave danger of being completely annihilated.

Captain Henry had been shot through the jaw, but had remained in command of his men until he had fallen from his horse, weak from loss of blood.

His company was cut off from the remainder of the troops by a large force of Cheyenne, Sioux, and Arapaho who shot and hacked at them from all sides in an effort to massacre the command and to gain the scalp of the white leader.

Chief Washakie, Tigee, and several other chieftains galloped to the spot where Captain Henry had fallen and toward which the hostiles were leaping with brandished tomahawks.

Throwing themselves from their horses, these warriors drew their knives and fought off the enemy in a hand-to-hand encounter, until the other soldiers and Shoshoni braves had re-formed and had dashed to their assistance.

General Crook soon reorganized his battered troops, and plunged through the Sioux, to rescue Captain Henry's company, and all withdrew in proper order. The Shoshoni covered the retreat of the soldiers until they reached their supply base on the Tongue river.

The Shoshoni lost a tremendous number of their best warriors in that fight, while nine soldiers were buried where they fell on the battlefield. When a search was made later, in an attempt to remove their bodies for burial in the Custer cemetery, no trace of their graves could be found.

The First Cattle Drive

The First Cattle Drive

In 1877, Finn ended his service with the government and secured the beef contract for Fort Washakie and the agency. In the following spring, he secured a new contract for 500 head of cows, a large order for those days, so he obtained the assistance of two friends, W. P. Nobel and J. K. Moore, who were willing to furnish his bond for $40,000 which was to secure his fulfillment of the contract, and $20,000 in cash with which to buy the stock in Montana.

J. D. Woodruff, Chas. Bruit, Richard May and "Swede John" decided to go with Finn to drive cattle back for themselves, and before they started, Chief Washakie offered to send four Shoshoni guides to select the best route from Fort Washakie to the Crow reservation, and to meet the cattle drive later on the Yellowstone river.

On the 14th day of July, 1878, the five men left the agency with a pack outfit, to travel the long distance to Bozeman City, Montana. Finn carried the $20,000 in a money belt about his waist.

The country was for the most part rough and unsettled, there being but one cabin between Fort Washakie and the Crow reservation. They enjoyed a pleasant trip, however, as the grass was plentiful for their horses, and there was an abundance of game which supplied them with fresh meat.

Arriving in Bozeman City, Finn deposited the money in the Bozeman bank, and with the four men began to make inquiries at the ranches in the vicinity, stating that they wished to purchase cattle. All of the ranchmen who were thus contacted asked too high a price for their cows and after a few days Finn decided to go to Virginia City and determine the value of stock in that vicinity.

He was told by business men, Nelson Storey, and Martin and Myers, of Bozeman City, that the bank was unstable, and when he withdrew his money without question he was much relieved. For safety, he purchased a long, buckskin belt in which he wrapped the bills, and tied it around his waist.

Next morning, Finn started by coach for Virginia City, arriving there after banking hours. He was therefore obliged to wait until the next day before he could deposit his money.

The hotel at which he took a room had evidently been a mercantile business block in past years, for the interior of the great barn-like structure had been divided into rooms by the erection of partitions, the tops of which came only to within three feet of the ceiling.

Finn was very uneasy about the money in his belt, the loss of which would bring ruin upon his friends as well as upon himself. Fully dressed, and with his gun close at hand, the young man lay through the night upon his bed, sleepless and watchful. Virginia City was in the throes of wildness and turbulence, and had anyone of several hundred of the frontier cut-throats who were there at the time known of such a sum of money within reach, there would without a doubt have been a desperate fight that night.

Lying in that partitioned box, with watchful eyes on the ceiling overhead, Finn could hear every move and breath of each occupant of the hotel. It was with a sigh of relief that he finally saw the walls begin to gray with dawn.

After breakfast, he went to see Mr. Thomas who had arrived from Bozeman that morning. Finn began to speak of stock-buying when the man stopped him.

"Have you heard the news from Bozeman?" he asked.

"No, what is it?"

"The Bozeman bank closed its doors yesterday morning just after the stage left," Thomas remarked.

Finn was dumfounded at his good fortune. Then he remembered that J. D. Woodruff had deposited several thousand dollars in the Bozeman bank, and had refused to heed the warnings of his friends. Subsequently, Finn learned that Woodruff had lost his funds and had returned to Fort Washakie.

There were a number of cattlemen around Virginia City who were eager to sell their stock at a reasonable price. Finn bought the herd belonging to Richard Hickman, the mayor of Virginia City, and purchased 150 head from Mr. Loree who owned a ranch just below the mouth of Alder Gulch. Several other ranchmen sold small lots, notably Mr. Southmaid and Harry Wray.

With the full 500 head purchased and ready for Finn whenever he wanted to gather them, the young man began to search for cow-ponies. He found few that he wanted, so he waited for the Shoshoni guides, and sent word to Charles Bruit to go to Wray's ranch and take charge of the cattle there. George Lane, Jack Wilson, and Richard Hickman had agreed to help in gathering and branding them.

On the 8th of August, it was reported in Virginia City that a war-party of Bannock had raided the Raymond Brothers' ranch on Red creek, and had run off a herd of valuable horses.

The sheriff felt that he should warn the surrounding country of the presence of marauding Indians, and called for volunteers to go with him. No one would undertake the venture, but Finn heard that a man named Varney had a number of fine saddle horses for sale at his ranch on the Madison.

"Mr. Sheriff, could you borrow a horse for me?" Finn asked.

"I'll lend you one," called Hickman from nearby.

"I'd like to buy some horses along the road," Finn went on.

"All right," answered the sheriff. "If you will go with me you can have plenty of time for your business."

The pair were soon on their way, and the first settlement which they warned was the Eight Mile ranch out of Virginia City. Here they stopped to water their horses, and while the sheriff told the ranchman of the depredations of the Bannock, Finn idly looked around at the country.

The ranch sat in a little meadow bottom which ran along the creek. On either side, the rocky flanks of the mountains hedged the valley, and grassy flats pierced the ridges here and there with narrowing funnels that ended in clumps of bushes and quaking-asp groves.

Everywhere was cool tranquillity. A bear could be seen ambling clumsily among the berries in one little gorge. Finn watched the animal with interest.

"That must be a pet bear over there," he remarked to the ranchman.

"Where is it?" came the question. "I haven't any pet bears or wolves or Indians. If you see one it's the devil that has been killing my calves. Point it out to me!"

Finn indicated the ravine, and pulled the gun from the scabbard beneath his leg. The sheriff spurred his horse forward, and in a moment the two trotted across the meadow with their weapons ready.

The officer's horse was a fine, little, imported animal from Kentucky strain. At the first scent of the bear, he became frightened and unmanageable, trembling and darting from side to side until he had worked himself into a heavy lather.

Finn's mount which had been loaned to him by Hickman, was an excellent saddle animal, and now showed evidence of having been used for hunting before. The younger man was therefore enabled to get closer to the bear, and managed to get in a shot which struck the marauder in the shoulder, tearing the jugular vein. The bear fell and became a jerking heap which was soon quiet and dead.

The two mounted men rode back to the ranch, and while Finn wiped his horse down with the long grass by the creek, the sheriff made arrangements with the ranchman to have the bear skin sent with a portion of the meat to Virginia City. He seemed to be talking a long time, but Finn thought nothing of it.

A few minutes later, the two proceeded on, to warn other ranchers of the presence of the Bannock. When they reached Varney's ranch, Finn found that the Royal Northwest Mounted police of Canada had recently been through the country, buying up all horses which were fit for cavalry, and stripping all the ranches clean of available saddle ponies.

On their return to Virginia City, Finn found that the sheriff had made arrangements through the owner of the Eight Mile ranch for a banquet of bear meat to be held in the city on their arrival. Someone had evidently been a lover of romance, for there was a full column printed in the Virginia City newspaper telling of the heroic bear fight, and of how Finn Burnett had killed the animal with one well-placed shot. The sheriff kept the bear skin, and Finn got the glory, being the guest of honor at the banquet.

Finn took the stage back to Bozeman City, and continued his search for saddle-horses from there. The mounted police had purchased most of the mounts in that district, as well, but Finn was able to buy fifty head of unbroken ponies from Nelson Storey, agreeing to pay fifty dollars a head for them, and to take the smallest horses that were gathered. He then sent word to George Lane to meet the cavvy at Benson's Landing.

Finn bought a cheap three-year-old mount from George Wheat of the Big Horn river, for his own use, and after he had completed the purchase of the wild, unbroken horses, he drove them to Benson's Landing and corralled them for the night. These animals all proved to have been crossed from thoroughbred sires with Spanish mares.

Next morning, George Lane and Finn let down the bars of the corral gate and headed the bronchos toward Wray's ranch, twenty miles from the landing, on the Yellowstone river. The morning was warm and the herd was wild, and it soon became a mad race to determine whether Finn and his companion could hold them to their course or not.

Lane was a big man, and at the end of five miles of mad effort, he called to Finn that his horse had "played out." There was nothing for Finn to do but keep on after his wild horses. The country was rough, and the Bannock Indians were stealing every mount that they could find. He knew that if the herd was released, it would scatter and become lost to him.

With doubts as to the ability of his cheap horse to carry him through at the fast pace, Finn kept on down the trail. Luckily, the herd dashed across the creek and turned up the road that led toward Wray's ranch. Behind them came their young owner, madly pursuing them in a cloud of dust, and expecting at any moment to have his doubtful mount stagger and sink beneath him.

The pace was terrific, yet Finn spurred after his horses, madly urging his mount to exert his last ounce of speed in an effort to keep up and prevent the herd from making a break for freedom.

Finally, Wray's ranch appeared far ahead, and the herd dashed for it. The corral bars were down, and it was but the matter of a few moments to turn the wild horses into the entrance. Finn leaped from his gasping pony and ran to put up the bars of the gate.

Then he turned, expecting to see his horse dying on the ground. Instead, the wonderful little animal had proved himself that day, as he did in many subsequent years, to be the best mount that Finn ever was to own. Now, he was quietly grazing on the grass beside the corral fence as though the twenty-mile race was but a passing entertainment.

Next morning, Wray, Charles Bruit, George Lane, Jack Wilson, Richard Hickman, and Finn Burnett began the difficult task of branding the herd, and this work took until noon of the following day. The four Shoshoni guides arrived while the branding was in progress, and reported that the best route from that point to Fort Washakie lay across the Crow reservation. Finn had anticipated this before he left the Shoshoni agency, and had received written permission from the commissioner of Indian affairs to follow a trail approximately the same as that reported by the guides. No one had ever driven cattle through that way before.

The herd was started for Benson's Landing next day.

There, the Yellowstone river was running too high to ford comfortably, so the cattle were made to swim across, followed by the bronchos, the gentle horses, and the two yoke of oxen which had been purchased from Mr. Loree and which hauled the wagon-load of provisions.

Leaving Bruit, Lane, and Wilson to purchase and load the supplies, and to start the herd southward, Finn rode with his four Shoshoni guides to the Crow reservation to ask the agent to select the route which the stock should follow.

This official proved to be an arbitrary and grasping individual. He declared that Finn must pay him for the privilege of crossing the reservation. This the young man refused to do, and demanded with the written authority of the commissioner that the agent lay out a trail to be followed.

Finally, the officer agreed grudgingly, and ended the discussion with the caution that Finn keep to the designated route, and not allow his herd to mix with the Indian cattle on the way. Then, as Finn was prepared to ride away, this official stopped him and stated that two men from the Crow agency must accompany the drive across the reservation to watch that no Indian cattle were stolen. He also demanded that Finn pay wages to these men.

There seemed to be no way out for the young trail leader. He drew the four Shoshoni, Bishop Weshaw, Judge Tash-it-see, Ha-ve, and Wad-ze-naw, to one side and questioned them regarding the route which the agent had laid for him across the reservation. They answered that they had heard that it was the most mountainous trail in the country and that the provision wagon could not possibly follow it, if the reports were true.

Finn, without a word to the agent, mounted his horse and returned with the guides to his herd, which he found to be already on the reservation, and traveling along the route which had previously been designated by the Shoshoni.

He pushed on with the cattle unmolested until he had reached a bedding-ground four days' travel from the southern edge of the Crow land. There he was informed that several settlements lay ahead of him which would report his passing, so Finn rode to the agency and stalked into the office.

"My herd is on the reservation, and I want to get it off the quickest way possible," he informed the agent. "It will take me four days and here are the wages for your two men."

The agent blustered and swore, but there was nothing that he could do but select a half-breed Crow and a Mexican to watch the drive.

Every morning, Finn was careful to cull out all the Crow cattle that had become mixed with his herd, until they arrived at the river on the west side of Rocky Ford, the last camp on the reservation. When they were ready to push the cattle across the stream next morning, Finn rode to the two men from the agency.

"All right, you two, take your last look for Crow cattle, and there will be no further use for you here. You can go on home," Finn stated.

"We're ready," they returned. "Where's our pay?"

"I paid the agent. Get it from him," answered the trail boss.

"That wasn't the thing to do," one of them said, angrily. "The agent said nothing to us about your paying him our money. We won't ever get it."

"Well, that's your look-out," Finn answered. "If your

agent's a grafter, tell your commissioner about it. I'm on my way."

With that, he turned and began to cull the Crow cattle from the herd as the two agency men rode off with malignant scowls on their faces.

The cattle were in poor condition, and Finn had been obliged to exercise unusual care in handling them. They were a mixed herd of cows and calves, and had been able to travel but four or five miles a day. Now, as they proceeded on southward, the grass improved and they began to take on weight. There had been no cattle through that part of the country before, and after leaving the Crow limits, the feed was found to be splendid.

Jack Wilson proved to be an expert "broncho buster." On the trail, the horse corral was made by the usual method of tying a long rope from the wagon wheels to nearby trees, but the horses proved to be so wild that they would break their ropes in their efforts to escape, and frequently a half day was lost in rounding them up and saddling.

Wilson proved his value by getting them "corral broke," and in gentling them for the saddle. At the start of the drive there had been but five gentle horses for nine men, four of these being the Indian ponies, and none of the other men were expert riders. In a short time, Wilson had tamed more than two dozen wild horses into excellent saddle-ponies.

The Shoshoni scouted the way ahead. The Bannock were raiding in the country to the south, and several times the guides had crossed the trail of their raids.

When the herd arrived within ten miles of Clarke's Fork, Finn went ahead to look over the route for the next day's travel. As he rode along, he perceived a broad Indian trail before him leading off toward the mountains. The cattle were bedded down in the valley of a small stream behind him, amid a plentiful supply of feed and water. Under ordinary conditions, Finn would have felt confident that his small party could beat off an attack.

But he had serious doubts as to the effectiveness of the Shoshoni. They were related to the Bannock, and were in fact quite friendly with them. Their willingness to fight against their Indian relations was a matter for conjecture.

Finn rode back to his camp, and ordered the men to graze the cattle slowly through the valley until he had scouted the trail ahead. Next morning he called his Shoshoni scouts to his side.

"Today," he said in the vernacular, "I want you to help me to find the best road to Clarke's Fork. We will all ride together."

Bishop Weshaw looked at the white man gravely.

"Why you not tell us that you saw the Bannock trail?" he asked.

"I see no Bannock trail," Finn answered, looking around him in apparent surprise.

"You did yesterday," returned the Shoshoni. "This morning we rode out and saw your horse's tracks to where you saw the Bannock trail. You turned around and came back. Why did you do this?"

"I didn't want to get mixed up with the Bannock," returned Finn.

"Then, why didn't you tell us you had seen their trail?" persisted the old warrior.

Finn knew that he was caught, and stood silent, pondering his answer.

Bishop Weshaw watched him sorrowfully, and then spoke further.

"You were afraid that if you fought the Bannock we would not stand by you. We are ashamed. You are our friend who is close to our heart. We have known you for many years. We have come this long way to help you, whatever happens. Whether it be Bannock, Sioux, or white men that you fight, we will be beside you."

Finn was heartily ashamed. All that he could do in the face of such absolute loyalty was to shake hands silently and firmly. He was only then beginning to perceive the friendships that he had won through his years of government service with these people.

They proceeded on to the ford at Clarke's Fork. There, as they approached, they came upon a number of thickets where deep undergrowth and willows snuggled in the bend of the river. Here a large village of the Bannock had been erected, and it had evidently been attacked and destroyed.

The thickets had been blown to bits by cannon shots, and the dead bodies of squaws and papooses lay with the remains of Bannock warriors amid the wreckage. The fight had taken place the day before.

From the evidence, the Shoshoni guides were able to deduce the entire battle. A detachment of soldiers had caught up with the raiding Bannock, and after a brief engagement had driven them back to their village. There, the Indians had put up a desperate fight, and had killed several soldiers and had wounded a number of others before a cannon had been brought into action.

The resulting bombardment had blown the village and its surrounding willows into fragments. The Bannock had thereupon gathered the dead and wounded braves whom it had been possible to carry, had waded across the ford under cover of the brush, and had slipped away between the undergrowth and the high banks, to escape to the mountains.

The path along which the Bannock had fled, was still slippery with blood, proving that they had transported many corpses and wounded warriors.

This unrecorded battle broke the spirit of the raiders. They fled to the higher mountains with barely sufficient horses to carry the remnants of their belongings, and without tepees or provisions. Later in the fall, Finn was to accompany several expeditions which ran down the remainder of these raiders, to recover most of the fine horses which had been stolen from the Raymond Brothers' ranch on Red creek in Montana.

The cattle herd proceeded on southward toward Fort Washakie, with Finn scouting the way ahead every day. He found that while the Shoshoni knew the country in a general way, they identified it by their memory for incidents which had taken place at certain points rather than by the geographical locations.

They could remember that they had camped at various places in past years; that here a buffalo hunt had taken place; that there a skirmish had been fought with other Indians. But as far as remembering the exact course of streams or the topography of the country ahead, they proved to be entirely untrustworthy.

Every evening, they reported that on the following day the trail would become so impassible that the wagon would have to be taken to pieces, and be transported across the rough portion piece by piece. At no time did such a proceeding become necessary.

As an illustration, after crossing Clarke's Fork, and after completing a day's drive along Pat O'Hara creek, the Shoshoni informed Finn that he could take the wagon no farther.

Next morning, the young trail boss took two Shoshoni with him to scout ahead. They reached a small stream which flowed into Pat O'Hara creek.

"What stream is this?" asked Finn.

"Brown Water creek," they answered.

"Did you ever follow it to its head?"

"No, but we have chased buffalo all over this country."

"But, did you ever go straight up this creek, to travel over the mountains?" questioned Finn.

"No, because that would be foolishness," was the reply. "We couldn't get over. It is a high mountain. It is so high that it is called Givina-Cari-To-Yo-Be, which in the Indian tongue means Mountain-where-the-Birds-Stay."

The white man's name for that peak was Heart mountain.

Finn followed the creek to the summit of the divide and found it to be a fine trail for the herd. On the other side they came to another stream.

"What is the name of that?" Finn questioned.

The guides answered that it was Shawn-Hop-Oga, meaning Cottonwood creek. They followed it down until Finn could see that the herd would have no difficulty in reaching the Stinking Water.

Next day, when the herd proceeded over the trail, there was found to be a single sidling place about fifty yards long where the road had to be dug out with shovels, but from there on, the wagon had no trouble in going through.

Crossing Stinking Water where later the Cody bridge crossed from the depot to the city, Finn drove his cattle to a bedding ground on the bench where the Cody monument was to be erected in later years.

Next day, the herd followed up Sage creek to a bedding ground, then over the divide on a trail which the Shoshoni again declared to be impassable.

POST OFFICE AT FORT FETTERMAN

Near the summit of this high ridge, Finn and the guides were riding in advance of the cattle when they saw twenty Bannock riding ahead of them unaware of their approach. The four Shoshoni slipped behind a ledge of sandstone while the trail boss watched the raiders.

"Let us go back to the cattle," said Bishop Weshaw.

"No, I must find a route for the wagon through this way," Finn answered.

"But those Bannock are fighting men," the Shoshoni remonstrated. "They are too many for us to fight."

Finn decided to appeal to their true natures.

"If we return to camp, and tell them that we saw Indians, and that we were afraid to go on, and if they ask us if those Indians were men or squaws, what will we tell them?"

The old warrior blinked his eyes a moment, then he gritted his teeth.

"Damn 'em," he snarled in English. "We go on."

Before Finn could stop him, Bishop Weshaw rode from his place of concealment and started for the Bannock. They, on seeing him, evidently believed him to be a member of the scouting party of soldiers which was pursuing them, for they gave a screech and dashed away, never stopping until they were far up the side of the mountain among the denser timber.

Crossing the divide which ranged between the Greybull and Gooseberry creeks, the slope was found to be steep, but by allowing the two yokes of strong oxen to take their time they reached the top. From that point onward, the trail became narrow and sharply inclined, especially in one spot where it led around the point of a hill.

Leaving the wagon in the center of a flat, grassy

meadow, Finn reconnoitred to find an easier way for the wagon to travel down the mountainside. Hearing a call for help, he raced back to discover that the driver had allowed the oxen to turn completely around, cramping the wheels under the front, and overturning the wagon in the middle of the flat park.

Nothing had been broken, fortunately, and after all had been put in order, Finn started out again to find a way down for the cumbersome load. The herd had already gone ahead on the trail.

There was no better way to descend than down the steep mountainside which had a pitch at this point of about forty-five degrees. Two of the men then cut down a large pine tree, and tied it behind the wagon for a drag. The oxen were unhitched, and all hands worked at the wheels, letting the vehicle slip down the perilous incline inch by inch until it reached the bottom of the mountain.

From that time on, the trail proved to be excellent, and good traveling time was made. The cattle had improved wonderfully on the way, and when they arrived on Owl creek they were fat and in prime condition.

Finn's contract demanded that the cattle be delivered no later than October first. He had encountered so many difficulties that he did not arrive at Owl creek, which was seventy-five miles from the agency, until the fifth of October.

He selected a site for a cabin and a corral, put the men to work, got his supper, and started for the agency on horseback, as night was falling.

He reached his destination at 8:30 on the following morning, and was ordered to bring the 500 head of cattle which the contract called for, to the government pasture at the agency. He returned and drove 550 prime cattle from Owl creek, the extra fifty head being taken along to replace any which might be condemned by the inspector.

Lieutenant Thomas was deputized by the agent to inspect the herd. He had an excellent knowledge of the cattle business, and Finn was a little worried about his opinion.

As luck would have it, the worst-looking cow of the lot was the first to separate herself from the herd, to parade past the officer and to be tallied. She had horns similar to those of a goat, and was a mean-looking creature.

The lieutenant looked her over carefully.

"I guess I'll have to condemn that one," the officer declared.

"All right," answered Finn, "I have forty-nine more for you to condemn."

The tallying continued. The lieutenant watched closely as each cow went by, making notations in a little, black book until all had passed him.

"Well, what do you think of them?" asked Finn when the last cow had been driven to the pasture.

"That first cow was the only rough one of the lot," the inspector answered, smiling with evident pleasure. "I'm not going to condemn one critter out of a bunch like this. I'll accept the whole herd. They're as fine a bunch of cattle as I ever saw."

So ended Finn's first great cattle drive, not so huge in numbers as were those of later years, but great in the sense that it was the trail-breaker, and because the difficulties which were encountered were so ably swept aside.

Finn continued his ranch on Owl creek, and so became its first settler, and in the following year, 1879,

Charles Bruit also moved his cattle to that grassy valley.

J. D. Woodruff moved in, with Benjamin Anderson, and in 1880 a party settled at Embar. In 1882, the two brothers, Colonel Torrey and Captain Torrey moved their stock to the same creek, and that district soon became a well-settled area.

The Gift of Chief Washakie

The Gift of Chief Washakie

And so the story of the great transition ends. From a vast and unfenced frontier, the plains began their promise of unending wealth. The Indians, from a wandering, war-torn host of hunters, found their happier destiny in farming and stock-raising.

Finn began to plow the land about his ranch, and to raise the grain for his stock, and garden stuff for his little family. And, as the native sod was turned, and as it produced an abundant yield, so did the entire west develop from the primitive to the modern.

There was still one tender incident which occurred to Finn Burnett before the days of the old frontier had settled finally to rest.

Chief Washakie slowly trotted in to Finn's ranch one morning, followed by ten of his head chieftains. All were dressed in garments which displayed a curious mingling of the civilized and the native, but the feathers which flopped behind their coal-black hair with every jogging step of the ponies displayed their tenacious clinging to primitive ideas.

Mrs. Burnett busied herself in the kitchen through the morning, and at noon the chiefs sat down with the Burnett family to a huge dinner. Little was said until the last mouthful had been devoured. Then Finn pushed back his chair and glanced around at his eleven guests, all of whom were watching him with friendly eyes.

"Well, Norkuk," Finn addressed one of them, "where are you all going this early in the season?"

"Here," was the answer.

"Just to see us, and get your dinner?" asked Finn, incredulously.

"No."

"Something you want me to do?"

"Yes."

"All right. What is it?"

The chiefs looked at Chief Washakie, silently waiting for the leader to proceed. The old patriarch studied the pattern of the tablecloth before him for a moment, then began.

"We want to know why you have left us? Why have you left the reservation?"

"Why, I am not employed there now, Chief Washakie," answered Finn. "I have no business at the agency any more."

"We want you to come back," bluntly stated the old chief.

"But I am not in the government service," Finn explained.

"We know that," answered Washakie, brushing his hand aside as though thrusting away something of no importance. "But we have decided to give you and your wife and your children land, so that you will come back and live with us."

Finn and his family sat dumfounded. Here sat the great chieftain and the leaders of the Shoshoni tribe at his table. They had ridden seventy-five miles to ask that he return to live with them always.

"You stayed there in the first days," went on the chief. "You risked your life, kept our crops growing, watched over our cattle, and fought that our enemies would not run them off. We want to give you some of our land on our reservation, and have you back with us."

THE GIFT OF CHIEF WASHAKIE 365

From beneath his blanket, Chief Washakie drew forth a paper which he handed to Finn, with a gesture of dignified appeal. The young man opened it to discover that it was a legal form, properly executed and sealed, which stated that the Shoshoni tribe thereby presented Finn Burnett with a large, specified acreage on both sides of Trout creek, west of the agency. Below the description of this grant were written the signs of Chief Washakie and the other chieftains.

"I'm afraid this would be too close to the agency, anyway, Chief Washakie," remarked Finn as he studied the paper. "I have cattle and horses which would eat off the grass and cause a lot of trouble to the agency herd."

"Where would you like to have land, then?" asked Washakie.

"Well, west of the Lander road there is a fine tract. If you gave me any land, I should like some of that," answered Finn.

"All right," returned the chief as he signaled the others to rise. "Come with us and show us where it is."

The young ranchman saddled his horse and rode with them across North Fork to the east line of the land which he had suggested. To show them the size of the ranch which he had in mind, Finn then rode his horse around a square containing about 700 acres which could be irrigated.

Washakie shook his head impatiently.

"What do you want to take such a little piece for?" he growled. "We want to give you a ranch, and each of your children a ranch, and your wife a ranch. We have a great, large country, more than we will ever need. We want you to have this."

Finn's eyes sparkled with moisture at this proof of

earnest friendliness. To refuse would have been an insult to the chief.

"All right, go ahead and show me what you want me to have," he said.

So, the Shoshoni rode ahead, until they had gone two miles and a half, and from that side of a parallelogram, laid out the ranch, the deed to which they later signed before the agent of the reservation.

And thus ended the wild, Indian days of the last frontier. Soon were to come the drives of Texas cattle to the grassy plains between the Yellowstone river and the valley of the Platte. Already, on the horizon, were the approaching hosts of lovable, hard-riding cowboys who were eager to add their chapter of reckless and desperate courage to the history of the plains.

Surrounded by his family, with his future assured by an excellent ranch, amid simple, honest friends, Finn Burnett settled down to a life of love and peace and sweet contentment.

Index

Index